Pleasantries From the Skyward Side of Daydreaming

An Existentialist Memoir

Tucker D. Farris

Plum Publishing Co. Ltd

Published by Plum Publishing Co. Ltd.

Pitkin County, Colorado

ISBN: 979-8-9883801-2-2

Library of Congress Control Number: 2024950476

First Paperback Edition

Cover Art: "Bloodstork" by Kim Diaz Holm (https://donungeherrholm.com/)

In Loving Memory of

Sammy Houston

Thank you for the memories, the absurdity and the magic of a childhood well spent

Zoe Lu

Thank you for the solidarity, the safety, the laughs and the warmth

Wick Moses

Thank you for the gift of music, the power of radio, and the wit and wisdom to reach all the cats and kitties of Radioland

You are all missed daily and dearly.

TUCKER D. FARRIS

This Book Bears the Following Dedications:

To the space between spaces, the time between moments, those satellite outstations of the mind, the mystery of being, and the life lived between then and now.

And,

To all those voices that have been beside me in the composition of this madness.

You have been my pleasantries from the skyward side...

With Infinite Love and Gratitude,

TF

Contents

Foreword

By Iver Arnegard

I was teaching Creative Writing at Colorado State University when I first had the opportunity to work with Tucker Farris. In my classroom, he was a quiet, sensitive soul with an impressive intellect and equally impressive capacity for ideas, language, and writing. When he spoke, his classmates listened.

Ten years later we're not only still in contact, but close friends—something I can't say about nearly any other former student of mine. Over the years, I've followed Tucker's professional progress as he's gone on to graduate work and beyond—studying and teaching around the world. When we talk on the phone, I'm always impressed by his knowledge of Geopolitics, which comes not only from his formal and informal studies but the real-life experiences he's had living in different parts of the world. Though Tucker will assert, and I'll agree, that travel is over-rated and not equally accessible for everyone. As he says, "There is as much grandiosity in a solo meal in your local cafe with a book than there is at the top of K2."

As long as I've known Tucker, his writing has always been precise, seamlessly weaving poetic narratives of his upbringing in the mountains of Colorado with his own musings, influenced by his broad knowledge of Philosophy and Sociology, yet uniquely his own. Beyond that he's always understood that it is the job of a writer to not only tell or show—to influence or provoke new thoughts—but also to entertain. To keep the tension taut so that the reader wants to turn the page again and again. And also to make the reader smile and, sometimes, laugh out loud. It is rare to find a writer like Tucker who can bring not only the dramatic—often even melancholy or dark—along with humor and levity.

Pleasantries From The Skyward Side Of Daydreaming is no exception. It has all of the Farris-esque qualities I've grown to love. In a sophisticated, poetic, yet accessible way, Tucker explains the threads of life (like attachment, love, and identity) that weave together to form the self. Throughout these pages, you will learn not only philosophy but psychology, sociology, and more without, perhaps, realizing it because this is no textbookish slog. On the contrary, it's a smooth, poetic delight to read.

Tucker journeys us through introspection, reflection, and self-examination. He writes not only about existential crises we all can relate to but also crises more specific to his generation and his upbringing, like school shootings, the heightened fear of global warming, and the proliferation of WMDs. An upbringing of drastic change when cell phones began to do "more than make calls and blackberries ceased to be a fruit."

Tucker uses all kinds of anecdotes from his youth just outside Small Town, America, to his stories of love and loss. His writing transports his reader to the times and spaces needed to see the world through his perspective. The "...curiously addictive smell that comes from your dad starting a 1968 Kenworth log truck at 6:00 AM. The blue pale smoke lingers in the cold air almost as if it itself is frozen in time. The smell is not the toxic stench of the diesel engine, nor is it the pungent scent of burned sulfur from the diesel fuel. Rather, it is the encapsulation of a break in the rhythm of the universe."

When Tucker recently contacted me to tell me he'd finished his latest book and ask if I'd write the forward for him, I was flooded with emotion.

"Of course I'll write your forward," I said. "It'll be an honor. I'm flattered."

I felt, at first, proud, exhilarated, and euphoric. It's probably the best a professor can ever hope for—to not only see a former student master the craft you teach but to succeed in the profession and then ask you to be a part of their latest project.

But the exhilaration, pride, and euphoria I felt was quickly followed by doubt and fear. Could I write anything that would do Tucker's work justice? If a teacher of higher education is honest with themselves, there are rare occasions when one of their students challenges them as much, if not more, than they challenge that student.

In over twenty years of teaching, there have been a handful of times when I've had to admit that a certain student is, well, smarter than me. At least in some or multiple ways. Tucker Farris is one of those former students—and now one of those friends—that sets off the "Imposter Syndrome" for me. It makes me ask myself: Am I capable of this endeavor, this teaching thing? Or should this student be teaching my classes instead while I look for other work?

As a professor of mine once told my class decades ago: "Only two percent of you will succeed in this line of work. Master the craft. Teach. Publish. Whatever. It's just that competitive." A hard thing to hear, for sure. But true.

Well, Tucker is in that two percent. Over the past twenty years, I've had hundreds of students—at this point, well over a thousand—and Tucker is one of a handful, or less, of the all-time best. I just hope my words here, for as limited as we all know language can sometimes be, communicate my sincerity, clarity, and my love of Tucker's writing, poetics, philosophy, and musings.

So settle in, turn the page, and enjoy.

Author's Note

Dear Reader,

I am unsure of what precisely to write in this section, but intuition tells me that including it is somehow critically important. I'll begin with the more earthly pleasantries. I hope you are doing as well as can be as you sit to read these words. I hope your coffee or tea is hot but not too hot to drink. That "Goldilocks" zone that allows for a good sip of enjoyment without scalding. I hope you are comfortable while you are reading. I know that is always the challenge for me. Somehow, like many of us 'readers' by the time I turned 30, I found reading to be more of a physically demanding task alongside the challenge to *focus* long enough to do the task. I blame the advent of smartphones and the burdens of academia for my lack of real readership. Alas, to business.

The composition of this text was, in a word, madness. Madness to the purest degree. It is a motley mess of insanity laid out here as some coherent exposition on the nature of my social soul as it stands as I now exist in my third decade of being. Much of this text was initially composed out of order; like all good things in life, they come when you are neither planning nor expecting. A large portion of these chapters appeared as standalone public and free essays. I have since romanticized this process and will most likely now say that they were serialized prior to collation for publication. The reality is, like any honest writer, I have no idea what I am doing. There are words that fit moments in time, reflections reflected in those words, and somehow, they come together over a few years to be something of a collection.

This is not to disparage your readership but rather to contextualize it. Life as a 'young adult' is anything but easy in the best of times, and the times we've shared since the waning days of the 20th century have been anything but the best of times. Each of us has, in our time, experienced loss, trauma, tragedy, and that ever-present battle with our inner darknesses. That is what this book is truly about, I think. That darkness we have shared but never disclosed openly, the feeling of being but not really being, of existing just on the edge of existence, of being our own event horizons in a galaxy of pure darkness. I write to process what I experience, especially in the darkest of moments. Deaths, loss, dreams turning to nightmares, all of it. We now find ourselves having lost ourselves here at the crest of a future that would, on a good day, be classified as 'bleak.' I do not claim here nor in this text to offer the solutions, the freedoms, or the salvation from our impending days of reconciliation in the face of the darkness. All I can do is share my thoughts on my own, and it is my hope that somewhere in these pages, you may find something that resonates with you somehow.

This book came into existence first as a need to sit with myself after I turned 27 and take a long and very critical look at where my life had brought me to that point. I made a decision when I turned 27, and that decision was something that would have terrified me at the start of my postgraduate studies. I decided that I would no longer allow the forces of the darkness around me to dictate how I approached their pressures. This presented itself as two significant arenas, both of which defined my life from the end of my undergraduate until I made that fateful decision to leave my adoptive second nation of Canada to return to my wildwoods of safety and serenity in the Rocky Mountains to lose myself to find myself. The first was formal academia. I will admit, my dear reader, that I *loved* the academic lifestyle. Being surrounded by books, shoes that made the *right* sound on tile floors, 'working' for a few hours a day teaching and all of the endless office chats, colloquiums and talks. I *loved* taking a sunny lunch on the porch of the faculty club over a volume of Lenin, and I loved the reality of working with an extensive collection of knowledgeable and curious people. I loved the idea of being an academic, of the tweed, the pipe tobacco, and the endless nonsensical world we inhabit. I did not reject academia, but I opted to stop allowing it to be the dragon that it is. I jokingly began introducing myself as a "recovering academic" recently and the identity has stuck. I think it needs a rebirth somewhere in its institutional reality. The idea of the theory-minded academic, solitarily locking themselves in the dark and writing for the sake of writing is quite sadly not a profession we can genuinely claim anymore, and so in my recovery, I aim to do so. I still teach, I still do research, I still use citations and all of that, but I have found a rhythm in my academia that does not require all of the pure pain of the more traditional route. This is not a common experience in the craft. I feel infinitely lucky that the two institutions I teach for have accepted my eccentricities with open arms and administrative compassion. I, too, am thankful that I still have some wherewithal to write. Academia, the idea of it, is not a toxic thing. Philosophy, theory, and sociology are all things that still bring me so much intellectual joy, and the sharing of my words is no small part of that. What kills that soul is all of the socially constructed weirdness we place around our fields now. Publication in theory or philosophy is radically challenging to the detriment of the discourse, and social science has fallen heels first into a quantitative fetishism that would please even the most ardently emotionless scientist. I cannot do sociology as it pertains to my sociological heart in the field's present state. I lack the pedigree of a good philosopher, and I could never cut it as a psychologist. So, this is where I exist in the skyward side of daydreaming. Where to look up is to never look down, and to step forward is to fall backward.

Sociology, social philosophy, social theory, all of these things on my CV are *human* endeavours. They require human failures to come to fruition. Academia is not a place that is friendly to humanity, even in the so-called humanities. So, I needed to break free. I needed to evoke Fleetwood Mac, lay down in the tall grass, and do my stuff. This book is partially that. A return to the roots of the fields that so profoundly inspire me. They are not quantitative, reliable, generalizable or even real in some places. But neither is life. I have told hundreds of students now that there is no universal social experience that we can quantify or guarantee collective experience save for two. Birth and death. I am not an expert in the former, having found myself unable to remember my own and, unfortunately, not having been present for any important ones. The latter is something I may theorize, prepare for, and meditate on. Still, by the time that social experience comes to my door, sooner or later, I will unfortunately not be physically able to relate its reality to you. If the ability to do so exists, I'll exist as a ghost somewhere to try and communicate my findings. To my academic readers, I will say that I do not disdain your craft or your pursuits, but they are not for me in the same ways. Do good work to the best of your ability, and to Hell with "New Materialism." Those who truly know, *know*.

The second arena I escaped at 27 was a psychologically abusive relationship that had poisoned every core of my being for many years. In that time, I, in my brilliantly arrogant academic ways, tried to theorize my way out of what was very clearly a dangerous psychological space to exist in. Confirmation bias is a horror show when we make up hypotheses about our own relational existences. It warped me into a recluse of my own humanity, where for the three or so years I spent as an academic in Canada, I slept in my office because my home wasn't home; I came to know the nighttime sounds and sights of that campus more intimately than any living human in my periphery at the time. It broke me. In this book, you'll find my reconciliation with that trauma. You won't find strategies to overcome trauma, as I know I still have not done so in some respects. Instead, you'll get honesty. The honesty of the pen late at night. Nothing is more honest than that.

I do not know what to tell you to expect in this experimental thing I've shared on these pages. I can say there is a *point* to all of this. When I discover what it truly is, I'll elaborate further.

Until then, take care while reading this to hopefully find something to resonate somewhere inside. Remember, too, that in the face of all of our shared darknesses, the immortal words of Pajama Sam: *"There's no need to hide when it's dark outside..."*

Be safe out there,

TF

Introduction

In addition to the author's note, I suppose a more formal introduction may be required. This text bridges several genres and modalities of social research to present a somewhat coherent, if deeply eccentric, central thesis that is in response to two critical questions: Why are memoirs only something we write at the end of life rather than as milestones throughout? And why does the world feel so blisteringly nonreal once we make that critical crossing into the world of adulthood on the latter side of 25?

Rather than wax poetic or get lost again in my thoughts as I did in the Author's Note, I will instead present a synopsis or abstract of this mad thing by simply breaking down each part.

Prelude & We Were the Wonderkids

The prelude to this text represents the insipient thoughts that began this project, although not the first words composed in its construction. After a handful of the chapters had been completed, this section was my attempt to collate some semblance of an idea thread to follow. I cannot wholly claim that such a goal has been achieved, but the attempt remains. We Were the Wonderkids is an essay that consumed me for a fair portion of the COVID-19 pandemic. At the same time, I was adrift as a 'foreigner' in British Columbia, where in the insanity of the early days of that era of my life, coupled with the horrifically painful fact that my partner at the time was breaking quarantine rules to hook up with other people and a long struggle to find my stride in academia left me needing to examine what had led me to that point intensely. It is subtitled a 'eulogy for the 90s kids' and may read as one. My cohort of interrelated children of the late 20th century have some very profoundly damning shared experiences in this life that I believe deserve some reflection. It is reproduced here in this text as a setting stage for the meditations therein, as it functionally served as my first actual departure from traditional academic epistemological methodologies and, therefore, was the emo-tinted genesis of this memoir.

Part 1: Apocrypha

Much like the biblical Apocrypha, this section contains works interrelated to the central thesis of this book but without a cogent reality within which they exist. The first two chapters of this section represent the original starting point for an essay I had planned to compose with the same name as this book before realizing it needed to be a book rather than an essay. These are philosophical chapters on the nature of the self and being. They possess far less memoiristic eccentricity than the rest of the book and may seem to some to be the most 'grounded.' The latter two represent a significant step forward in the experimental philosophical method of this text that combines creative nonfiction prose with occasional academic inquiry. From this point, creative nonfiction further runs a unique path between real-life memoir elements and compositions relating to the world of dreams. I have yet to name this methodology, and I suspect I will do so at some point as it is not quite auto-ethnography, nor is it close to existentialist fiction. Time will tell how this unfolds. The first part of this book is a further dressing of the stage of our inquiry, the attempt to establish a fragility of self, a critique of nostalgia, and a posing of the question: "What even is life anymore?" It stands as a nearly orphaned precursor to the following sections. It exists therein as something of an invitation to the reader of this text to abandon expectations and establish new ones.

Part 2: A Strange and Savage Lament of the Heart and Hearth

This part and its two chapters are the heart and soul of this book, respectively. Two essays combined initially into one that tells a story of where life has pushed me to stand in the present moment. The Long Nights and The Valleysong. The Long Nights are reflective of trauma, abuse, survival, the arrogance of myself as an academic, and somewhere buried deep the love story of a hopelessly romantic gay sociologist (me) in his hopeful floundering through both a doctorate program and a failed relationship. It is innocent and terrible and painful and somehow charming I think. The Valleysong is the story of a broken (but still gay) sociologist returning from the dreamland of British Columbia to his homeland after making the realization that, yes, indeed, the dream had become a nightmare. These two chapters are close to my heart, and the fact that they exist in the public sphere, first digitally and now here in print, terrifies me to some profound degree. Be gentle with my heart, as it is in your hands now.

Part 3: I Write.

Ultimately, the love we take is equal to the love we make. Within this part, the final three chapters explore more eccentric topics. This represents the 'present' me, or rather where I ended up after the insanity of the past.

An essay takes the reader on the quest to discuss the nature of art and was a cathartic expulsion of toxicity that I was forced to write after enduring some truly hellish treatment at an 'artist's residency' earlier this year. Another essay takes you on the road of my return to teaching locally and the follies and hiccups of teaching writing. This section contains no veiled mask of my disdain for the process and for specific typologies of certain teachers. It represents the growth I have made in my academic and pedagogical rebirth. There is a chapter detailing a correspondence of an entirely dreamt space. The meanings of this meditation are mysteries to be unravelled. Finally, the last formal chapter explores death. The following epilogue does what epilogues do, and the appendix is explained in the final chapter. References are references, and the honour roll is a borrowed literary device from my early childhood mentor, Hunter Thompson, to thank those who contributed to the overall construction of this work. Part of my spirit wanted to make a dishonour roll to go along with it. Still, I haven't the funding to protect myself from litigious and sensitive-minded potential occupants of such a list, so it exists theoretically. To evoke the youth, *if you know, you know,* and those who are in the know, know full well.

Bon Chance.

-30-

Prelude

"The trouble with being inspired to perform the impossible was that the inspiration gave you no clues to the practical means."

-Ken Follett

There is a high degree of curiosity in this contemporary state of being. When we truly take a moment to reflect on the eccentricity of modern life, I cannot help in my instance to land upon a particular hill of despondency at best and nihilism on the darkest days. That is not to say that all that exists is solely a sense of despair, but rather that the experience of despair in the present is such that it presents in an almost deviant manner, lurking beneath the surface on such a level that even Freud in his most cocaine-fueled tirades could only dream of.

Kierkegaard posited the notion that despair, true despair, is the fragmentation of the core of the self. In short, it is a loss of self, a loss of one's self in the vast and misty milieus of the days beyond us and in front of us in immediacy. There is a temporality to the self, and from within that temporality, a space from which we may find that the self is not inherently even grounded in the most grounding elements of who we believe ourselves to be. The fragmentation of self sounds on a surface level to be something 'easy' to grasp. Not that anyone could define the act of losing one's self, but that we all might collectively empathize with that experience. That is to say, we have all, in some regard, experienced a degree of despair within our experience of life. To compound this empathic collectivity further, we happen to be deeply social in terms of how we come to recognize and process our reality itself. Therefore, this symbiosis between the self, the social, and empathy allows us to identify the boundaries by which our despair is defined while also fluctuating between the detriment or the privilege of having our reality dictated by that recognition. In short, the boundaries that comprise the individual sense of identity and reality are in a constant state of flux and things that we rely upon to 'make sense' of who, what, when, why and how we come to be. I will present here the notion that this state of flux contributes to a select curiosity of the modern age: a constant fragmentation of self and, by translation, a continual despair.

Quite grandiosely, I propose that life in the 21st century, life as a young adult trying to make sense of the world, is not solely despairing in its barriers, but that it is constructed socially as a present and persistent state of total despairing at the very core of our beings. This then breeds a raw existentialism within all of us, a passively active nihilism that colours the world grey while simultaneously building within us a smouldering of loss, of misdirection. It is, in effect, a magnet held to the southern pole of our internal compass, throwing all bearings and directions into their obverse, warping the world, the idea of life, and the very understanding of existence to alternatively horrific melancholia. It is not so much a mirror but a murky pond lying dormant in a long-forgotten woodland. There is a reflection of the world above, but the adage 'as above, so below' has since faded into a memory that is every day more distant to our present perception of the world above and beneath us.

I will not stand as some have on the principle that life is an illusion or that reality is some projection of imagined or fabricated social mores that allow us to live in the imaginary world of social magic. There is mystery, but there is no illusion of the magician in our experiences. There is no compulsory construction on the subject of fooling us into a particular perception. In my understanding, the sad reality is that the illusion, that life existing as a false reflection would be the brighter option in the present state of things. And, not to present as too much of a realist, I will say that what we call the illusion of reality is not an illusion. Illusions are constructed based on modifying our perceptions for our amusement or chicanery. No. What we are seeing now is not an illusion. There is no well-intentioned magician projection sleight of hand to modify our senses to suspend a belief in reality for a moment of brevity. Instead, what life has evolved or mutated into as of late is a conjuration. It is a malignant manifestation of competitive social magic, designed institutionally above to build and mask a proper horror of the self: a continually reproductive despair.

What Does it Feel Like to Lose Your Self?

It is my firm understanding that regardless of one's prowess for introspection, training in psychology, or intuitive internal connectivity, one can still take notice of the loss of self. We can feel the fragmentation as it occurs. We can watch helplessly as one piece after another stall out into the murky voids beyond the scope of the physical body. As much as we can speak to the universality of this ability, we cannot nor should we apply a reductive notion to how it may come to feel to watch as the core foundational elements of yourself fly off at the sound of speed into unknown depths.

One such presentation I will offer is the only one I can speak on in-depth with expertise: my own. I invite you, dear reader, to follow me on the subsequent archaeology of self as we search for and find the fragmentations of myself that have contributed to my state of existentialism. Not the commodified *existential dread* but the real grappling dilemma of coming to question the nature of my existence and a shout into the voids to question its purpose. I cannot come to know these answers. Still, by virtue of the imaginative element of humanity and the social nature of the fabric of reality, I invite you to join in this collective psychosis as we endeavour to socially create meaning out of meaninglessness. As we plumb the depths of this collective despair, we might do so in a way that lands us on an accidentally warmly optimistic path towards individual salvation of the despair via a transmogrification of the loss of self. Take a deep breath, refill your water skin, and ensure your boots are tied, comrades. We are venturing into the overgrown wilds of our own individually internal mystic forests of myth and legend in search of the pieces that create *us*. Like Gilgamesh and Enkidu, we shall task on through highlands and lowlands, over mountains and valleys, and cross streams and rivers to find the cedar woods that hold within our demons and our chance at greatness. Let us live our mythology together in these pages.

From the Forest Floor

To begin, I must address a valid concern about my earlier position. I cannot consciously propose a universal truth for all of human experience. To do so would betray the ethics of my craft and creations to this point. Instead, I will clarify the universal experience of this collectively dystopic sense of self-loss perpetuating a world of despairing realities. The question here lies in the nature of loss itself. To very reductively contradict my universalist approach, I will assert the simple philosophical point that to experience a loss; there is a need to both *know* what you have lost and to also *know* that you have subsequently lost whatever it is that you no longer have. That is to say, there is a knowledge bound to the sense of loss inherently. We have to have a conscious awareness of who we are, we have to know our selves, in order to lose our selves. Additionally, we have to know that we have lost our selves. Simple, but elegantly complex. This is not to say there is a superiority in knowing yourself or in knowing you have lost yourself. Instead, there is simply a differing means of existence. For those not in the throes of this post-modernist existential loss, there is bliss, I believe. There is a way to exist socially and psychologically removed from the horror, the true horror of loss of self. That is almost to say that ignorance, to some degree, is a blissful existence. We cannot establish a hierarchy or competition on who is most despairing nor on who is least despairing. Instead, it is critical in our quest to recognize that those of us experiencing this loss, this grief of self, this desperation in the face of total annihilation do so because of our attunement to the nature of our concept of self in a social world. We do not need to be philosophers or social scientists to recognize this fragmentation, nor will any psychologist, physician or shaman be the one to lead us to this realization. This knowledge is a knowledge that is sacrosanct to the individual. It is infinitely malleable and divergent in any and all regards. It is not a sunset guaranteed every day, but rather the emotions thousands upon thousands of people experience while watching the same sunset. It is not the measurable and understandable ripples in a pond but rather the diversity of those throwing stones from the shore. We are collectively lost together, but that loss individually manifests in hundreds of variations across every avenue of lived experience. In this knowledge, we only find awareness of the loss of self. I would so bravely venture even that one cannot honestly know one's self without also having experienced its loss. That is to say, knowing who we indeed are in itself is a loss of self, insulated and isolated away from the prying eyes of the more significant social, communal state of being, and we incongruently cohabitate on some far-out historical spectrum. We are lost, but we are not lost alone, but in the very same breath, each of our losses are themselves lonely. The human experience is to be an insular individual among thousands of others. Compounding this, our variety of experience, our individual historicity and the walk we have all taken through their unique winds and bends represents the crux of this archaeological work: we cannot hope to know where to begin to look. What we are reduced to then is a question of knowledge. Knowledge ideally can be communicated linguistically, experientially, and symbolically, yet the knowledge of self is such that it can only be done so by the individual themselves. One cannot experience the self of another, nor can we learn the nature of our moment-to-moment existence from another person's words or symbolic gestures. From birth to beyond the veil of death, we are singularly alone and afloat in a massive sea of countless other alone people.

However, this isolation is not in and of itself our despair—quite the contrary. To step beyond the contemporary commodification of the term introvert, I posit that it is within our nature to be isolated in our experience. That is a fact of existence that is neither positive nor negative but ontologically reflective nonetheless. That is to say that my experience and yours are not and will never be the same. We are alone in our observations of our reality, even if we come to experience some aspects with one another. Even the most intimate of shared experiences come to us in isolation. We cannot in any capacity even assume nor assert that we can interact within the scope of another's perception of their experiential reality. We belong in one another's stories but can never read them thoroughly. We may experience a redacted novella of others' experience, but it is neither in our cards nor our capacity to be anything other than a character in their experience. Existentially, this may lead us to an overwhelming sense of nihilism. Do we not matter in the stories of others? Are others unable to perceive my story? Neither is a fear confirmed. Instead, we may take solace that we have such a capacity to exist in multiple realities in a given moment. We may not be the singular character in any other reality, but this does not limit the degree to which our presence may influence the directionality of that story. We can exist for better or worse within one another's stories to even extreme degrees of entanglement wherein the divorce of the individual from one another in their stories can be complex and muddy as often as it might be cleanly simple.

How, then, do we acquire the knowledges that lend to the experience of loss of self? How do we unlock the secrets that lead us on the walk of despair? Where in our experience do some of us gain the insight to know ourselves enough to lose ourselves? And what does life come to resemble for those of us with this introspective horror? This is the object of our quest, and I do fear that within the broader scope of this quest, we may together stumble upon a sense, perhaps a glimpse into the stages of what might be considered a foundational understanding of the purpose of our lives. And that, far from being a self-help cliché is the true potential horror of not only having these knowledges but daring to question their nature as we may begin to do so here.

From Walled Uruk, our Journey Begins...

As I cannot speak to the lived experience of any other individual, I must then offer myself and my experiential mythos to the quest as both canvas and destination. We must then begin our pilgrimage and surgical intervention into the discovery and exploration herein. Within the scope of the journey to the discovery of the loss of self and the subsequent experiential impacts therein, from my introspection, I supplant three direct areas of exigent social being from which this analysis may come to fruition. These serve as the three keys to unlocking the door of this neo-despair. They are not "causes," nor are they components of the fragmentation of the self, but rather, they are lenses through which the self is filtered and through which we may come to recognize both its existence and its fragmentation. They are unique in that they build themselves in complete prohibition of the need for the social while being fundamentally dependent upon the existence of the social as socially real and regularly interacted within, even if that social represents solely the interactional landscape found deep within one's conceptualization of self. That is to say, these are isolated and solitary states of being, hidden deeply within the complex individual psychology of the individual, but they are not wholly 'personal' insofar as they may be lenses of the self, but social experience, even that which lends clarity to the existence of the self must itself gain a sense of clarity and existence from the social manifestation that lends to their creation and continuation. Effectively, each represents a cyclical socially isolating pattern of being that feeds the threads of reality and internal self-knowledge in a continually unfolding, infinitely complex round of symbiotic self-sufficiency. They are unique from other elements of social being in that they cross one critical divide between the heart, the soul, and the social. They are those threads that not only tie within themselves a sense of introspective meaning but also draw and subsequently compose deeply symbolic social ties beyond the individual. Within the exploration of each, it is essential to signify caution not to lose sight of this interwoven thread of existence. The essence of both the self in the social and the latter fragmentation of self represents an essential movement through the social historically and temporally. The fragmentation of self, *as reflected* in these foundational frameworks of being, is necessary to understand the social self and one's individual placement in their temporality. As a result, they stand as anchors in our individual timelines of being that allow us not only to come to know ourselves but also represent and recognize movements in our life course throughout the book of our experienced personal histories. All of this is to say that it is in the exploration not of despair itself but of crucial factors in human experience that we may look to find the investigation of these functional elements. We cannot define our despair but learn it experientially by examining our metaphysical being. From that investigation, we may form an existentialism of the individual self in the face of its forcible fragmentation. These foundational pillars of the self are attachment, love, and identity. From these abstractions of experience, from these social states of being that have universally unique and infinitely complex elements of individual difference, we may hopefully find the elementary understanding of the fragmentation of self in the sense of applicable transcendence from the limitations of simply knowing it. We must comprehend the elemental factors of the fundamental degradation of the self in the social before we may even hope to present a theoretical or philosophical representation of the world beyond that of the mind and interminable self. That the self is infinite in existence, variability and presentation given the very moment of exploration, ours must then be an archaeology of fluidity, one that may flex and adapt to the rapid change in the moment-to-moment states of being one may come to experience in any given instant of their personal history and experience. It is all this to say that whatever we may find in our excavation of self that is applicable only insofar as it can be a temporary understanding in a given moment; we cannot presume, nor should we be so naïve to present a notion of self that is static and therefore these foundational pillars cannot be viewed in any singular instance and instead must exist without temporality in a fluidic space of continual and perpetual existence that predates birth and extends beyond the veil of death.

We Were the Wonderkids: A Eulogy for the 90s kids

"Wake up kids, We've got the dreamers disease. Age 14, and we got you down on your knees. So polite, you're busy still saying please. Frenemies who, when you're down ain't your friend."

-New Radicals "You Get What You Give"

A disclaimer: The following passage may, upon first reading sound akin to a fiery sermon at the podium of some puritanical congregation in the 1700s. I assure you entirely, that the words here do not intend to embody these sentiments, nor do they hope to display some kinship or reverence of such folks as Jonathan Edwards. Rather, they are a conscious reflection and a product of a week without much sleep, too much coffee and that tattered, beleaguered rage that fills us in our late-night compositions.

One of the loudest refrains I hear most often repeated in conversations with other people both inside and outside my academic field is the seemingly obvious chorus of 'human beings are social creatures' or some other variation. In further conversations with those who have ventured down the path of psychology, or who at the very least are aware of Abraham Maslow present the notion that care, love and attachment are key components of his famous pyramid which is capped with the holy goal of self-actualization. Further, those who operate in my similar eccentric academic haunts find Deci and Ryan's self-determination theory and again offer the refrain that social relatedness, the feeling of genuine connection to others- is a key component of being a self-determined being.

For me personally, I have not actively engaged in classifying human beings as 'social animals' for quite some time. Rather I present the notion that we are individuals living in a social world. Invariably, we will connect with others, and rarely those connections will be 'special' to us. Toharbour so classify us as social animals reduces our lived experience to an instinctual, biological and pre-determined drive, deep within the folds of our genetics that pushes us to seek out any connection at all costs. It is my view that such a base-level approximation of the complexities of human connection limits our ability to actively and introspectively turn our eyes upon our own social connections to gauge the degree to which they are actually authentic as opposed to being fleeting instances born in our desperate need to reach out in the dark and find something/one beside us. This is not to say that I harbor negative feelings or opinions of those that classify human beings as social creatures, but I do harbour a particular shade of deep bitterness for the concept itself. My point is simply: we can be so much more than social creatures. We can be some of the only sentient beings on this planet to experience deeply profound emotional bonds with others of our species. We have the unique capacity to exist together in a state of affective synergy that compliments, challenges, improves and ultimately fulfils our lives. We have the capacity to live beyond the boundaries of our genetic codes, yet time and again I see my fellow Millennials and the younger Gen Z kids time and again opting to settle. To settle for a dismally disingenuous, inauthentic existence with respect to the social connections we actively try to cultivate. Collectively we fall short in the ultimate pursuit of true happiness and fulfillment that can be found within these rare connections. Our nearly universal settling is, to me a major source of constant despair as I see it flowing around me. To me, it appears to be an abandonment of our true human nature of growing past the simplicity of biology to explore, experience and revel in the complex social pleasures of our existence. This active and conscious abandonment of the wonders of human existence is one steeped in our contemporary culture social realities, and friends, those realities are darker than anything I can imagine. This tendency to shake off these sacredly complex qualities in favor of the easily consumed minutia of our current social landscape is not one that is entirely the fault of those who fall into the trap. Rather it is a deeply culturally constructed reality that is a product of a host of negative social phenomena. It is a deadly cocktail of toxic masculinity, heteronormativity, patriarchal expectations, consumerist late-stage capitalism, our digital addiction, and the fact that our generation for the most part finds itself feeling lost to redundancy in the scope of human history. This is not a personal failing of any one individual, but rather it is an inter-generational trauma shared collectively by each of us. As with trauma, we all react to the horrors it presents in unique ways, and it touches us all quite differently. Some of us fall prey to these demons more so than others, and there are carefully constructed systemic currents of privilege that lend to this fact.

I am a child of the 1990s, or rather, I was born into that era of crystalline optimism. I only experienced the latter half of the decade, and at that, only as a small child. However, there exists a certain degree of shared idiosyncrasy in the lives of children born around my time. We were born into a world that mellowed out after the cocaine fueled venture capitalism of the 1980s. In a world where the home computer was becoming more and more common, where the economy was somewhat stable, where Desert Storm and the first Gulf War were nothing to us kids whatsoever. We grew up in a world with Arthur on PBS, Star Wars on VHS and the new top 40 style of 2000s pop music. We were enamored with Nickelodeon and Cartoon Network. We watched a fully populated jet liner vaporize into the side of a building. We heard the muffled voices in the other room say "justice will be done" and "weapons of mass destruction" while we played with our LEGO sets on the living room carpet, only knowing that these things sounded scary if abstract and far away. Soon after we learned about a country called Afghanistan where everyone there hated us (Americans) because we had 'freedom'. We then, through the conversations of adults around us heard the name Saddam Hussain and with it the conjured imagery of pure evil. We grew up in a world of cognitive dissonance. Around us, our parents were happy. They told us we could grow up to be anything in the world. The world, as it was, was an entirely different thing. There was an intangible fear outside the realms of our homes. Us kids could feel it in the air. There was fear, trouble brewing, and for some reason every adult seemed to be really, really patriotic. Then as we got older we started to realize something was wrong. We started to learn the words to put meaning to the dread we were already feeling somewhere deep inside. When we started to ask our parents why we had to take our shoes off and put our stuffed kitty cat on the x-ray machine at the airport, we started to come to terms with the idea that maybe, just maybe, life wasn't as good as we were being told. We came to our teenage years to find parents that were trying their best to encourage us, while also still living in this world of uncertainty, and still existing in the glorious 1980s prosperity mindset. We don't blame them. It was the times, and the world they had the bravery to bring a child into.

In our pre-teen years, we also began to learn a new lexicon of terror: "Global Warming." We were told that due to the over-reliance on fossil fuels of the human race, CO2 emissions were building up faster than the planet could compensate, and it was raising the temperature of the earth to dangerous levels. Some of us watched an Inconvenient Truth. And then, at the wise old age of 13 were told that if radical change didn't happen, our world would be uninhabitable by the time we were our grandparents' age. By the time voices were dropping and bodies were changing, the children of this era had experienced a live televised mass murder, countless reports of school shootings, police officers in our schools, two unending wars of retribution, the threat of global mass destruction, being told people on the other side of the planet hated us and wanted to kill us (we later learned the word 'xenophobia' to describe this facet of life), and the fact that in the future we would all die a horrific death related to climate change either by drowning in the rising sea, or at the hands of feral pirates after our water. The truly sociopathic reality of this upbringing is that every single word of it was spoon fed to us alongside the 'sugar' of blind optimism for the future. The internet and world wide web transformed every single aspect of life, economic opportunity was everywhere, people could socialize in new and more 'fun' ways, cell phones did more than make calls and blackberries ceased to be a fruit. That optimism spread online. Suddenly we lived in the future only Gene Roddenberry could have predicted. Our parents could connect to the entire world for the first time and to them, that was heaven sent proof that we were in the golden age of American civilization. We got mail, we asked Jeeves, we sent emoticons through MSN and AOL chat. We learned what online gaming was through Runescape. We had digital friends, digital lives. We could know anything, watch anything, listen to anything. It was utopia incarnate. Maybe all of it was true, maybe things were going to be ok. Maybe our Pleasant Valley Sunday would last on into the dawn.

And then something catastrophic happened.

We grew up.

To me, reflecting on this era now, I am not sure anyone ever expected us to grow up. It seems almost that the late 1990s and early 2000s were just a sanguine dreamscape where the thought of escaping it was never really propagated. Time didn't pass then for us, but we were held there, frozen in a world built on Reagan and disco. The ideal utopia of the 1981 dreamer. Entertainment was everywhere, computers weren't calculators anymore, but they were places you could play games, talk to people, see videos, they effectively brought the public library to your living room in a cow print box marked 'Gateway.' And this dear friends, was the beginning of the long decline into our collective melancholia. Our nonstop indifference to any and all concepts that bind us to the very fabric of this reality. This careful melding of an over-reliance on easily acquirable digital entertainment and interaction, and the indifferent optimism of the early 2000s, against the inky black abyss of perpetual war, televised horrors, and the impending sense of our own premature deaths pushed us past the point of no return. It is that environment that fashioned the shells that barely hold us together today. It is the world that bred our nonstop nostalgic reminiscence of the times of our youth. All of these factors, the death, the fear, the implicit abandonment, the hope, all of it led us to be burnt out existentially nihilistic nicotine fiends by 23. It pushed us into a world where we simultaneously had no autonomy or freedom to choose who to be, and way too much of it. We were adrift in an endless sea but kept on course with naval mines all around. The perimeters were loosely defined, but deadly to cross. We were forced to play sports for trophies that said 'participant' on them. We watched our parents scream from the sidelines as we wasted Saturday mornings on the soccer field, the hockey rink, or the basketball court. We were told we could be anything and then told exactly who to be. Our clothes matched the mannequins at the

Old Navy, our identities matched the ill-fitted expectations of parents that tried as hard as they could to heed Dr. Spock's advice, while simultaneously moulding us into miniature placeholders for the lives they couldn't have lived two decades prior. Our mothers had preschool meetings, they knew the resource officers in our schools, they learned fun activities for us to do from Highlights Magazine, and then ran out of time to finish them before Oprah came on. Our PlayStation chimed to distract us from all of this darkness, but not once did we ever consider our lives to be dark or disparate.

Instead we look back fondly on the world of our formative years. We ignore the horrors and focus on the good. We remember Pokémon with nostalgic bliss while forgetting the news reports that said it was Japanese revenge for WW2 and was designed to kill American kids with epilepsy. Our TV heroes were a 26-year-old sea sponge that works for a capitalist psychopath for minimum wage, a kid whose parents were so abusive that the divine powers of the universe granted him magical godparents to protect him from his traumatic life, and on the other end of the spectrum, we 'knew' TV teenagers with cell phones, cool computer gadgets and parents who loved them. Do we reflect on how odd these heroes were? Not at all. Instead, now in our mid-late 20s, we rewatch them with bittersweet half-smiles on Netflix after the third joint of the night while we sit on our second-hand sofa. We played fun games on our big family desktops. Some of us ran around the magical land of Runescape and learned what it meant to be fully connected to the world online. Others wandered the frozen islands of Club Penguin and picked up our first spouses in the crowded coffee shop, nightclub or secret agent HQ. As we scoured this new online world, out of our parent's way we couldn't help but overhear Chris Hanson on the TV in the kitchen telling our parents to make sure we didn't talk to anyone online lest we become another statistic in the annals of the FBI child victimization reports.

This is the song of our youth. Fun, nostalgia, independence, hope and a sense of carefree existence uninhibited by anything beyond our walls, tempered by the true face of terror at every single turn. It is a strange fire to be forged in: one of blissful if unconscious terror.

As 2010 drew closer life changed again. No longer were we listing our crushes and best friends as our top friends on Myspace, listening to Green Day via LimeWire and scouring the internet for the best homepage layouts. This gave way to the Facebook friend list arms race which was in full swing by 2009. We gradually acquired iPod Touches, iPhones, and other smart devices and it is in this time that the final nail in our coffins was gingerly driven in. And these are coffins we are seeing far more readily and far sooner than those of the older generations. We seem almost destined to not grow old.

In my sociological reflections on this era of my life, and the lives of many people my age, I come to this point, that somewhere in mid-late 2009 where the death of authenticity occurred for those of us (un)lucky enough to be born before Y2K. It was around the time when the fad of Myspace died off and suddenly we were hearing about Facebook in the halls at school from one another, or at the dinner table as Brian Williams' 5:00 story was recapped over Stouffer's lasagna. Some of us joined without a thought, others had to straddle the uncanny divide of parents that raised you on the doctrine that the internet was the central hive of predatory psychopaths waiting to abduct you through your Napster account or whatever. But eventually we made the jump and went through the 'people you may know' list upon creating our accounts and gleefully added every single name you'd ever heard in your life and far, far more that you hadn't. Suddenly a new world exploded out into our social existence. One where we could interact with friends outside of school on weekends without the need to set up a pre-scheduled meeting. We could IM each other without needing to go to another site. We saw what concerts the cool kids went to, we saw the extreme lengths some of our friends went to in order to blow their minds out from Friday to Sunday. Suddenly the private lives of events that happened beyond our social circles were at our fingertips and the world was rapidly changing as a result. The veils of privacy lifted up off of us in an instant and we were all at once looking into each other's windows.

With a deafening crash our social media addiction began. We learned at breakneck speed that if a boy posts pictures or videos of whatever fucked up debauchery he engaged with over the weekend, the almighty popularity validation needle shifted into maximum overdrive in his favor. If girls posted a collection of beach pics that doubled as soft-core porn, suddenly they 'mattered' more to the boys in their classes and the social fabric of that dark corner of socialization we call young adulthood. We got validation. Instantly. It hit our fucking brains like a solar wind and went straight into that sad, lonely and desperate kid that lives inside all of us who's just dying every day to feel the feeling of being liked by someone else. It both answered the call of our modern society to be popular, liked and to be at the center of a vast swath of meaningless acquaintances we called friends, while it at the same time made us feel alone, hollow, and so hellishly desperate for the next hit of that sweet, sweet validation.

In the span of a year we were permanently rewired from the inside out. In the blink of an eye our youthful sense of self and identity died. It was replaced by this shell of a human existence that in every single moment of every single day craves, really craves the meaningless but meaningful hits of our social media validation. We went from kids growing up in a weird time that was a collision of optimism and terror to being emotionless grey beings that existed in a timeline of nothing that flitted between posts, likes and notifications. We lost the ability to feel before we could even buy the cigarettes we were smoking in the parking lot. We evolved a culture of secrecy around the little rectangles in our pockets. They weren't just for playing Pocket God or Crush the Castle anymore. They weren't for our Mayday Parade playlists. We got snapchat and learned that we suddenly had the ability to digitize and democratize sex. In another blink we had completely destroyed any chance we had on being able to develop any semblance of an ability to form lasting relationships. We commodified our bodies in a heartbeat because there is nothing more validating than the person masturbating on the other end of the snap telling you that "you're so hot." At 11:17PM on a Thursday night before you see each other in English class the next day.

Our parents tried their best to help us grow up in a sheltered world (with enough terror to keep it lively). They missed the fact that we grew up in secret. And we didn't do it well. Because oddly enough, if you leave a bunch of undeveloped pubescent kids to their own devices (pun intended), what did you think would happen? We lost any and all ability to feel fulfilled in our lives. We learned that what felt good was the instant gratification of 14 likes on a Facebook post, the late night liaisons over 'Snap,' and the sudden rush of pure fucking ecstasy when the likes started rolling in on the Vine of us getting absolutely trashed at so-and-so's house party in the gated community that weekend.

In all of this growing up, we lost our concept of self. We lost the ability to look inside and feel true to who we are. Our capacity to feel long term, engaged fulfillment was all but obliterated by this unfortunate case of digital maturity. I can only shudder at the younger kids who didn't have to make the transition-who were born with a phone in their hands and by the time they were 13 were having the same explicit conversations with one another that we discovered at 17.

Facebook was the beginning of our digital maturity. It was our conception, our genesis, but it was simply the first of many steps to our downfall, to the death of authentic experience, true human connection, and any hope of self-determination. What truly, truly destroyed us here was the evolution of human sexuality that grew out of this dystopic reality. We rarely discuss this in non-academic circles, but sex has become something wholly different than what it was 30 years ago. I don't just mean that the kids are kinkier, but that the very nature of human coupling and human connection has made a tidal shift to the strange and terrible. Tinder, an app I often 'trash' both professionally and privately is a perfect case study for this shift. It is not, by any means the only contender for the title 'murderer of human sexuality' but it certainly is the loudest one. To be reductive, Tinder is an application secreted away in most people's mobile phones that exists for the sole purpose of connecting two people for a sexual encounter. Tinder operates on shallow value judgments summed up in limited character biographies and 3-5 pictures. We basically post an ad selling ourselves, and potential buyers swipe through and if their attention is piqued, they 'swipe right'. Swiping right is a complex social interaction, that, when boiled down to its bare minimum constituting factors means either: "I would like to put my penis inside you" or "I would like your penis inside me". Of course there are non-heteronormative liaisons orchestrated through this monstrosity as well, and as such the preceding statements are adaptable to fit the pragmatics of the specific context of reference.

The tragedy of this proliferation is that it removed any semblance of sociality to our experiences first learning what sexuality is. There was no longer a courting procedure. There was a jump from 'that picture is sexy' to three and a half minutes of missionary while mom and dad saw "World Trade Center" with Nick Cage (A Fitting Irony). I am not such an old souled romantic that I would say Tinder removed 'romance' from our lives, as I don't particularly sociologically believe such a thing exists at any rate. But rather Tinder excises the intimacy and authenticity from the experience of sexuality. It reduces it from a complex web of social interactions to a transaction wherein boxes are ticked and nerves are stimulated.

What particularly horrifies me though, beyond the loss of authenticity in free love is what happens when Tinder connections make the jump to 'relationships'. It is in this hellscape of social life that we see the optimal observation conditions for the total degradation of human coupling, the culmination of this strange and terrible upbringing that is in some way, shape or form universal for everyone reading this under the age of 30. In the quiet context of the millennial tinder relationship we may see that any and all hallmarks of authentic human connection are absent entirely. To some extent, based on observation these pairings are not made of genuine connection, but rather the sharing of a handful of traumas and experiences. The chief of both being the preliminary tinder hookup. When I say shared trauma, I am referring to the conditions of our maturation. The collective trauma of living in this half optimistic, half hellfire world as kids. We never learned a sense of stability and that has lent itself to ongoing traumas that reach into the inky unknowns of adulthood. We can't yet ascribe words to these feelings (or at least the majority of us can't) and so what happens is we end up feeling a void within our 'souls' that must be filled. That void is the point of convergence for our nihilism and jaded sense of nothingness. It's a void that comes from being raised by the internet in a historical period of uncertainty masquerading as certain, guaranteed success and happiness. This void is our longing for authenticity. This is the calling within our embodied spirits of being that draw us to want to feel like we mean something to someone, anyone at all. Tinder is the drug that fills that void for us. And when two addicts come together to share in a hit, it never ends well for either.

What contemporary young adult coupling has evolved into is two people coming together for the sake of convenience, and with the false assumption that because they have had sex and met through an app that they are soulmates. These relationships are built on that very idea, that since we had sex a few times we're now dating. The thread of inauthenticity in these pairings is that neither person really truly knows the other. There is no need to build trust as a path to sex and intimacy because the intimacy and sex are already pre-built into the coupling. Tinder gives us the false sense of trust, openness and connection because it commodifies the very basic core concepts of these realities into a very simple algorithmic exchange of a day's worth of chats before six months of confusion and fakery. The relationships that are born out of this digital world are ones that are built not on trust and transparency, but on anonymity and a generally shared lack of interest or understanding of the word 'commitment'. What we see is two emotionally damaged people, meeting on an app while horny out of their minds, they set up a 'date,' have 11 minutes of sex and then have an emotional reaction to it. That emotional reaction, which in days long gone was understood to be a flood of oxytocin and endorphins released by orgasm have now been re-defined in the minds of desperate 20 year olds to mean 'true love'. The sad thing, aside from all of this, is that 'true love' comes to these people every six months in the form of new tinder dates. Because these pairings are not conducive to longevity. Their entire design is to be fleeting, immediately gratifying and ultimately replaceable universal.

What we learned from this reality, with respect to personality is how to be who we need to be depending on whose bed we're shagging. We've become chameleons, adaptable to the nth degree in order to be who we need to be to get what we want. Yes, this is nothing new, but the staggering universalism of it combined with the digital reality of commodifying real life has transformed us into a collective of individuals that cannot inherently present our authentic selves even in our most naked and vulnerable moments. This is beyond the social psychological phenomenon of code switching. This transcends our dramaturgical motivation to align ourselves with the expectations of our audience. This is a deeper transmogrification of our interior sense of being and self. We change to such a degree that our personalities are no longer salient, our core sense of self no longer has anchors to tether it to some sense of self-actualization. We are, in effect, beings losing our concept of self. We have replaced it with the unending trek for validation, rather than the nobler pursuit of fulfilling human experiences. Every aspect of our lives, from the minute to the grandiose have been reordered by this new reality we inhabit to such an extent that I confess that I've lost hope that our generations will prevail in any meaningful way. I see this almost as our collective death. An ending, a cessation of the core focal criterions of humanity. When we can no longer wake in the morning without wondering what validation we've received in the night, when we can no longer see how we may develop meaningful relationships that are not built on meaningless sex from our phones, I cannot see a hopeful outcome. My capacity for optimism died at the hand of the almighty notification bar.

"At the innermost core of all loneliness is a deep and powerful yearning for union with one's lost self."

-Brendan Behan

Now we're 25. We're no longer the little kids let loose in a doomsday machine. We real grownups now. And we're fucked up. We aren't the beacons of eternal hope and prosperity that our 80s kids parents dreamed of. We're a mess. We are shells of human beings. We are cold and hollow broken casts of something that maybe one day resembled a smiling child. We became creatures of the night with nicotine addictions and a clinical depression diagnosis. We learned to binge watch and never stopped. Our lives have become distressingly lonely.

The absolute sad fact of this loneliness however, is that we are lonely both alone and with people. We cannot find the inherent fulfillment in being comfortable with our own conceptualization of ourselves, and so, we are forced to seek that meaning elsewhere and in other people. What we have become is a generation starved of the ability to feel alright even in the most basic aspects of knowing who we are inside. We are locked into a reality where we cannot feel like someone unless we are constantly seeking that next hit of validation. And there is no hope of this slowing down any time soon. We have grown up in such a way that any validation calms the storm of dissonance inside us. And we would much rather have that quick shot of feeling like someone than sit down for a year and try to figure out who we really and truly are.

This unhealthy obsession with feeling good for indiscriminately small amounts of time at the expense of literally all of the other aspects of being true to ourselves is the saddest and most damaging thing I have ever seen people actively doing. At times too, it fills me with such a rage that I can't function, I feel my body temperature rise, my heart rate skyrockets and I find myself behind a keyboard at some awful hour trying desperately hard to make sense out of this world that I see spinning out of control every single damn day.

We are collectively so broken and lonely that we shed off all aspects of meaningful social connection to instead form the most fleeting and meaningless bonds we can. Our broken minds gravitate to the new social media world that opened up for us after we graduated from sending nudes on snapchat. We landed in the hookup app era of our social decline. We're glued to them. They attract those of us who are so broken emotionally and psychologically that we cannot form even the slightest symbolically meaningful bond with anyone else let alone with ourselves. We coast from toxic relationship to toxic relationship, punctuating each with an arbitrarily painful breakup. We fall in love at first swipe, and then realize over 2-6 months that holy shit, this person is a walking mass of red flags. We breakup, we unmatch and we're both back out in the sea of destitution yet again. Where ultimately our only path to salvation is swiping right again and trying it all over because this time, this time I'll get it right.

We cannot realize this simple fact: everyone else is just as fucked up as we are, and none of us have the tools to actually do anything to fix ourselves or one another. Maybe, for a brief moment at the onset of your third breakup in as many years you meditate for just a second on what went wrong and maybe, if you have some semblance of humanity left, you recognize that maybe, just maybe relying on the other 20-year-old basket case from the sex app on your phone for mental health support was a bad idea. We quickly forget this though because we can't bear our own company for more than eleven days and are then right out there again putting on the same persona, the same production for the next 20-year-old walking red flag. We pretend to have come to some great realization about relationships, we regurgitate the meaningless texts and quotes we've seen on Tumblr and Instagram to anyone who will listen. We become our own relationship therapist. We talk about trust, transparency, commonality, and so on, only to abandon our own advice the moment we see someone that kindles sexual attraction. We're not primal beasts with sex drives, we're broken children who can't feel anything beyond an orgasm anymore. We never learned how to really live in this world and so we are constantly moving from one toxic reality to the next with no sense of purpose, stability, peace or fulfillment. We are broken.

We have become so divorced from what it is that life actually has to offer, how beneficial it is to form strong bonds, how deeply critical to our physical survival it is to come to terms with the person we truly are. We are looking for meaning in people with no meaning, with random strangers we decided to fuck based on four pictures and a three sentence biography before we even meet them in person. We are nothing now but affectively blank hermits thriving off of validation and the ever present anxiety of not being validated.

I speak heavily of validation as the bane of this modern existence and I feel I must somewhat explain my case here. Validation, as I've noted in other writings is the fleeting sugar rush of feeling like someone else thinks we're decent. It typically is very very short lived. It's the rush of dopamine from hearing 'good job' or 'oh my god it's so big' or from matching with that one 'really hot girl' and then sending screenshots of your conversation to all of your equally immature friends from high school.

Is this a conservative essay demanding we return to 'traditional values'? No. This is a resignation letter. This is a reflection on the fact that there is no way to backpedal, to reclaim love and humanity for us. We are on a path destined for destruction. A runaway train with no way of slowing down and we are too enthralled with the entertainment carriage to see where the tracks are leading. I do not have the narcissistic predilection to assume I can singlehandedly return us to a world of cloud gazing, love letters and authentic life. I am not even sure I can even practice what I preach anymore. It is exhausting to be a 26-year-old person who prefers the authentic to the immaterially validating. Our generational trauma has sincerely put us in a place where we cannot hope to live or love in such ways. This is what haunts me. What drives me to a state of pure and unending pessimism is the fact that I've watched everyone I know descend into this hellish reality and I can't help but wonder when my time will come too.

In closing, I cannot say what the solution to this is. I cannot say when if ever we will grow up past this. It is not simply a phase, nor is it a hallmark of immaturity. It is a bloody battleground the morning after our childhoods were murdered in front of us. It is the loss of innocence, of happiness, of the ability to be anything closely resembling a person who knows themselves even a little bit. All we do is have fun, because that is the only thing keeping us from ending our lives, it is the only thing keeping us holding on and that is the saddest reality of all. That we are so broken that we destroy each other emotionally with our addictions to sex, likes, and retweets is the true legacy of this generation. It is not our fault, but it is in every respect too. We let this happen. We were not put in the position to refuse it, but we never even tried. We do not have the capacity to be self-reflective, nor do we have the ability to understand how our actions impact those around us. Words are hollow and "I love you" has been reduced in commonality to 'do you want fries with that.' We are lost, broken and damned to a future of bleak existence if we even make it to 30.

TF

Part 1

Apocrypha

Chapter 1

Attachment: A Toxicity of Longing and a Blurring of the Lines Between Reality and Fantasy

"Attachment is the great fabricator of illusions; reality can be obtained only by someone who is detached."

-Simone Weil

There is an edge to be balanced in a contemporary examination of attachment. There is a calling, an almost unconscious binding that leads the western investigator of self to slip into a commodified and poorly understood Buddhist tirade, wherein one is only the unethical purchase of mass-produced prayer flags away from a full on loss of integrity of investigatory grounding. That is not to negate the incredibly rich examination of attachment in some philosophical schools of Buddhist thought, but rather to spark a degree of intellectual contempt for the propensity of the western millennial to carelessly adopt the plumage of an ancient and inspirational spiritually philosophical tradition without the care required to do so ethically to the sanctity of the ideology. This is all to say that I will not dive into an Instagram worthy expose of the dangers of attachment and the contaminations it may bring upon one's *karma* as I am neither well-read enough in the philosophical tradition of Buddhism, nor do I intend to commodify that historicity for my own investigation. There are writers more adept than I and their work predates mine by centuries as a result. And so I present my own investigation into the nature of attachment.

We cannot simply define attachment, nor can we list modern attachments as a means of defining it. Attachment is not a definable state of being insofar as the manifestations of attachment come to become symbolically real in an infinite folding of possibilities and probabilities. We cannot point to one attachment and say that it is what brings despair, nor can we accumulate attachments to the measureable point of determination of the loss of the self, or its fragmentation. Rather, we may, through a careful examination of the attachments that resonate within us, come to see the despair only insofar as it grants us a preliminary boundary of the self as it manifests in the social. As mentioned, we cannot experience attachment without the social, but our experience of attachment is definitively isolatory.

To argue also that attachment is inherently toxic is a position I cannot take. I cannot stand to reduce the existence of important elements of attachment to a state of pure toxicity, and via that correlation advocate for a total condemnation nor moratorium on the state of being attached at all. Rather, we must decide however sparingly to dissect the nature of attachment insofar as it relates to where one considers their existence in a grander temporality of being. Attachment presents not as anything inherently toxic to the state of being in the social, but rather, it operates as a vector from which we might form social bonds that contribute to an overall toxicity of self. That is to say that attachment represents itself in the social life of the individual, not as the *cause* of despair, but as a probability factor in its composition.

To more closely examine the nature of attachment, we may recognize that on a surface level of metaphysical introspection, attachment is the subjective substance associated with what we may call in a Symbolic Interactionist sense: the symbolic exchange of socially significant interactions. It is not so much an emotion, nor an affective state, but it is a social-metaphysical means of existing wherein the individual as conduit, producer, product and subject of active agentic social interaction may find themselves laying threadworks of their social being via which significant social symbols they draw and foster an attachment with. To put it simply, attachment is the vehicle by which we come to recognize the social as something socially real. It is a groundwork upon which the social consumption and recognition of reality is built. From the persuasions of attachment we find ourselves able to form an association of the social significant and as a direct result, we facilitate the incorporation of our own social symbolic alphabet. From these glyphs of attachment we come to recognize and compose our own socially significant symbolic communication of meaning both within the internal spheres of our minds and beings and without into the world of the other. Attachment then presents itself not as a feeling, but rather an internalized methodological strategy of meaning-making from which the individual actor may come to know and understand the world beyond and within them. It is in effect the rattle and hum of the socially symbolic language that facilitates every single momentary point of interactional social reality.

What this means is not that attachment is unimportant or lost upon the needs of the individual actor to consider or come to know the self, but rather it is a divining rod in the capacity to both know ourselves and to recognize the fragmentation of our very core idea of self. Attachment is a current, not an island. It is a fluidic spatial flow of interchanging social interaction that contributes a deeply intimate means of communicating and understanding the social. It is the vehicle by which the objectively real transcends its composite factors and becomes something cherished, nostalgic, feared or loved. It is the underflowing ribbon of order that comes out of the perpetuation of reality to hold us dear to things we experience as we flow on through our dawns. It is what transcends a hug from a collection of physical stimuli to a moment remembered for eternity. It transmutes the words on the page from simple communication to profound interlocking melodies of hope, of love, of connection. Attachment, while serving as a potential fountain of despair and toxicity, serves equally in the inverse, constructing within us a rich comprehension of our worlds that breeds a deep and intimate social bond that stands out and above the typical consideration of an objective social.

We can consider the attachment in the context of its most powerful and potentially ruinous manifestation: longing. While attachment itself is metaphysically neutral, longing presents a curious combination of complex sufferings that inherently hold our hearts in a particular perpetual darkness with an extreme toxicity. Longing is *not* attachment, but rather it is the absence of attachments with a comorbidity of unfulfilled desire. Desire being the wish, the hope, the dream for a fulfilling of a perceived need or want of the ego. Longing in this regard is a foundational element of both the attachments we establish in our social formation of self, but also it is a manifestation of the potentiality for those attachments to breed a resentment and destruction of the self from within. It is in effect a dissonance of the ego and the social, a classic mythological dilemma of the battle between that which is desired and that which is real and realistic. It is in this fixation on desire that we either intentionally or unintentionally construct our own deconstruction. It is a curious pain, a cyclical process of abject horror for the sole reason that longing, desire, and the dream that connects them sometimes comes true. It has always been my nature to question the dreams that come true, to investigate the sources of light in the world around me. Perhaps that is my own existential horror manifested, but I have always felt a serious suspicion of longing being requited. It stands as a curious reality to have perceived a lacking attachment, to have imagined an ideal outcome that fulfills that lacking, and then to fixate, to long, to *hope* for that longing to be supplanted, and then to finally arrive at the point at which it is fulfilled. It is not a common reality in my experience, and as such it presents as this uncanny valley of direct combat to the naturalistic components of longing itself. It *removes* the longing for longing. And in doing so we have to question the emergent attachments that come from the fulfilled longing, as well as those from the unrequited desire. In both cases, there is a divergence from the normative perception of reality. In both cases, the social actor falls to the world of the imagined ideal, the best case scenario as a means of fabricating the solutions to the proclamations of their ego. It is in these instances where we must take the most care, to question with any and all fortitude the nature of the realities presenting themselves as fulfillment to us. We must hold within us a suspicion of the longing revealed as with each dream that comes true, the precipice from which we may fall back into nightmares grows.

The Inception of Desire

There is a need for a divestment from contemporary popular understandings of the idea of desire, both in a sociological sense and in an existential sense. Desire, at its core, does not refer to the classical theological definition specifically pertaining to the desire for sexual intimacy (discussed later). Rather desire is the simply manifestation of one recognizing something in their reality that is lacking, and then fixating on that lacking element as a *need*. Desire, is not a luxury, nor is it a passing fancy of basic wants. Rather, a social desire represents a directly tied thread between the individual's own mind and their concept of self and the outside world, in that you may reflect most starkly upon yourself via an outward comparison, and it is in this curious interactional landscape that you find both yourself and what you are missing. Missing even, in this case does not simply imply the absence of something, but the active recognition of its absence in a capacity that it compounds a negativity of spirit of the individual. It is not simply seeing something not present, rather it is recognizing the component of the self, the social and your reality that does not exist and feeling a curious emptiness from that piece being nonexistent or existent just beyond your grasp. To desire is to *know* what you are missing. It is a knowledge, not an emotion, it is a social truth of the individual to come to recognize what it is that you require (or think that you require) for your social experience of reality. It is a drought of symbolic meaning, wherein the individual feels an existence devoid of whatever elemental factors that would lend to their sense of a more complete state of being. This is where desire begins. In knowing. Knowledge, ontological and epistemological of the individual state of life is the root cause of the framing of one's boundaries and scope of existence in the pursuit of defining the things that are *in absentia* in their states of being.

This is not to be confused with a more fundamental basis for physical survival. The desire for water in the desert is not the same as the socially constructed desire for intimacy, or the rumination on one's isolation. There is a divergence between the base requirements for the sustenance of life, and the desires of the social. It is inherently within itself a mark of privilege to compose the symbolic desires of the social. Not to say that it is limited to specific social strata, but to imply that one may not reflect with terrific depth on the need for companionship or fulfillment in a pursuit of passions when they are faced with systemic obstacles to their very survival. That is, it is difficult to care about what makes you happy when the system is designed to not only place those things so far away from you, but to also actively target you with mortal precision. Nor is it the implication that those marginalized by the experiential being of a targeted group cannot experience the desire of the social, but it is clear that the marginalized experience informs a very different experiential reconciliation with desire. Where desire transcends the socially symbolic luxuries of the privileged strata and instead the object of desires can manifest as liberation, as freedom, as reconciliation, as the ability to exist without a continual existential threat on your very being as perpetuated by a systemic force of ill-will.

This is the sin of the evolution of contemporary society, in a gross modification and commodification of the individual, do we see a neoliberal trend towards the systemically sociopathic withholding of that which lends to a symbolic desire for the individual actor. On this spectrum, the curiosity of our late-stage capitalist neoliberalism is that it does a fantastic job of constructing a social that dangles the objects of our desire just beyond our frame of being. It holds up the illusion of the life that is most fulfilling and buries it under a wellspring of unseen and sometimes un-perceivable obstacles. It is a top-down imperialism of the self and the social. This is not to say that the fomenting of desire is perpetuated by some external cabal of systemic oppressors, but rather it is inherently tied within the systems that govern our very ways by which we come to know our social. These constructions are so subtly in-built into the society in some cases that individuals cannot recognize when the system has led them to longing. And that is because, in the most concerning of all manifestations of this imperialism, the things we desire are fundamentally tied to our attempts to live true to ourselves. It is not the sociopolitical abstractions we desire, but it is the intimate interpersonal and internal symbolic social glyphs that we crave. These glyphs are not the inherent needs for a socioeconomic liberation, but rather are the very foundational core elements that contribute to a sense of development of self that represents a total oneness of intergration of the social and the internal individual world to one that allows for not happiness, not joy, but a *knowledge* of the self. It is the knowledge of who we are that we are ultimately exploited away from. We are then conditioned to reconcile the knowledge of self in otherworldly social endeavors that land us in a state of feeling unfulfilled. This is effectively the lost nature of our species being, via Marx.

It is not my goal here to write a manifesto for the liberation of the individual social actor in the face of neoliberalism. I do not believe I have either the capacity nor the ability to do so. However, what I do intend here is the examination of that which draws us to desire. The questioning of our social that we endure that lands us in a space of questioning the very fabric that weaves together our reality. Rather than focus on the examination of the social from a purely sociological framework, I propose this, rather than a scientific treatise on the horrors of the neoliberal century, I propose we return to a state of internal wonder together. We harken our being back to the time when we laid out under the stars and truly felt a sense of wonder. Let us instead turn our gaze to those moments that are infinitely fleeting in our own personal histories where not only did we feel at once both deeply interconnected with the world, but also deeply isolated within it, but also we came to know more about ourselves. These moments, those tiny infinitesimally small moments of pure introspection that left their physiological marks upon us. Cast your mind to the moment you first felt butterflies in your stomach, the first time you remember blushing so hard your face burned with such an intensity that you could feel it in the air around you. Think to the time you first cried, not out of despair, nor as an infant, but the first time you were *moved* to tears. When did a song cause you to weep? When did a painting hold your gaze for your own private eternity? When did seeing the person you love laugh, watching your child walk, or feeling the warmth of your dog cuddling beside you after a hard day jolt you from your autonomic movement through time and make you stop and say: "wow, this is life?" it is this moment we seek to explore. The moment upon which we come to recognize that we are not only experiencing, but that we are living. We seek the moments of dissociation from the monotony of reality to the point that we recognize the uniqueness of our being to such a degree that it jolts us into an uncomfortable reckoning of our place in the scope of the realities beyond our being.

That is our attachment. It is these moments that call us into the reality of the worlds around and within us and create and cement those moments in our states of being in the social. It is in these miniscule events wherein our entire states of functional being are overcome, not with emotion, but with the momentary lapse of consciousness that speaks to a loss of total and complete agentic individuality, wherein we regress to a natural state of existence, where there is nothing but us and the world and intimately so, we are tied ever so tightly to that experiential understanding of the world. We are removed from history, from the passage of time, from the laws of the universe, while almost immediately being so irreconcilably bound to each of these natural states. We *become* living history in that moment, we transcend temporality and exist across all planes of the past, present and future to live our own cherished apotheosis of the self. It is in these moments via that transcendental state of pure awareness and *a priori* ontological recognition that we form attachments. It is in these threads of atemporality, of existing outside of the historical and biographical spectrum of our lives that we find ourselves, truly. We see inward with a clarity unmatched in the entire scope of human experience to in that instant come to form a purely correct assessment of who we are in the deepest folds of our inner worlds. It is an exploration of the divine interior of that which bends the realities around us to produce joy, love, and a glowing validation in the pits of our stomachs. It is, in a word, the most sacred form of pure pleasure we may experience to actively recognize in the moment the fact that it is core to the foundational elements of who we have been, who we are, and who we shall further endeavor to be. It is these pure moments, free from the impurities of the modern existence wherein that spark within us fires. This spark, this heat within us that radiates through every fiber of our being is not an affective state, it is not a feeling, it is our humanity. That is, the attachments we come to compose in our world, the feelings of knowing the social, of appreciating the symbolic nature of the construction of self in these iterations of being, they represent the core elements of our own unique human nature. And it is in the variability, the infinite potentiality of what may constitute these moments of attachment forming clarity that represents the astounding depth of the human experience, the degree we share collectively to experience reality differently is the center of what it means to exist as we do in the time that we do. It is our humanity that is fostered by the persuasion of the individual to form attachment, and it is its own sacred beauty that we cannot control, predict, nor replicate these intensive bouts of self-awareness. It is a testament to the infinite complexity of the lived state of consciousness that we have such a capacity for variation in the moments that reach from the milieu surrounding us to touch our hearts and foster such a keen sense of true self-knowledge.

To even attempt to placate a sense of understanding as to what may constitute a moment such as this, to what functions actively as an attachment composition would be ill-advised given the variety of human experience. As such, I offer this personal recollection not as authoritative knowledge, but as a singular example in an expansive global sea of infinite moments. I task the reader to do the same in their own historicity, to examine where within your path of life you found a sense of absolute and total recognition of your *self* as an active entity separate from the pressures and preludes of the universal flow around you.

Prelude to the Valleysong: A Memory

Dawn breaks across the valley floor. The mid-October climate foreshadows the impending winter. The temperature hovers above freezing, but below the pleasantly bearable early morning warmth of the summer months. Autumn is in the process of emerging from its hibernation. From the hill my childhood home stands on I am sheltered from the sunrise by the opposing side of the valley. As the rays reach out and touch the opposite side, the warmth is lost on my domain. There is a blue quality to the air, an illumination that is not yet sunlight, but that is stronger than the receding twilight. The sun blasting across the east has begun to illuminate the striking face of the mountain that stands silent vigil over the valley to the south. I am not in my bed as I should be. I am outside. There is no school today, so I have total autonomy over where the day takes me. This was the beginning of my lifelong love affair and cautious experimentation with nocturnal existence. I am 14. There is a particular scent hanging in the air as I migrate from the porch of our house out into the wilderness. It is not the sweet smell of morning dew. I have spent my fair share of time in the morning dew and never was able to detect its scent. No. The smell in the air is something warmly nostalgic to me even to this day. It is the curiously addictive smell that comes from your dad starting a 1968 Kenworth log truck at 6:00AM. The blue pale smoke lingers in the cold air almost as if it itself is frozen in time. The smell is not the toxic stench of the diesel engine, nor is it the pungent scent of burn sulfur from the diesel fuel. Rather, it is the encapsulation of a break in the rhythm of the universe. It is a fragmentation of the natural peace and quiet of night as the machine of humanity breaks its respite. However, this is not a violent break. It is a slow mutual agreement. It is not a shock to the ecosystem, as the mountain lions, deer, squirrels and birds carefully await the long tall figure of my father to make the daily walk from the house to the truck up the narrow drive way. The crunching of the dirt, or the squelching of the mud under his boots serves as a quiet reminder for the creatures of the wilds to begin their days. The low rumble of the engine as it kicks over to run, the two or three soft breaks of smoke out of the exhaust stacks come across the frozen air. In a handful of times observing this experience as children, my brother and I were always fascinated by the ability of the truck to create perfect rings of the pale blue sweet smelling smoke rise over the valley expanding to impossible diameters before fading away.

But I am not watching this ritual today. It has passed already and all that remains are the fresh tire tracks in the mud, and the hint of the smell in the air. I can see my breath in front of me. As the sun has not yet fully risen I recognize that there is a moment I can seize here. I can ascend to a vantage point, nestle myself down and watch the sunrise splash across the canvas of the dominating silhouette of the mountain on the horizon. I decide that the place to view this event is not on some treetop, nor in some secluded special spot in the wilds. Instead, I decide to climb the old firetruck parked in our driveway and nestle myself among the cloth hoses of the hose bed. It is 'comfortable' but most importantly, it faces the mountain. It lays out an entire vista of the natural landscape of my youth ahead of me. But I do not go alone. I have a thought. An impulsive one, but one that has lasting impressions to this day. Before venturing off I look into the wide warm brown eyes of my golden retriever named Bailey. I ask her if she would like to come with me to watch the sunrise. Our other dog, who is considerably older has the almost tangible reaction of gratitude at my question, thanking me for taking the excitable young retriever away from her so she can try to get more sleep. It is too early and too cold for her to indulge the nonsense of her teenage charge. Bailey however, is more than happy to accompany me. I haven't a need for a leash for her as she somehow knows what we are doing without a communicating word between us. She too, I think somehow, recognizes the gravity of the situation-the 14-year-old boy who not only is up way too early, who has been up for far too long, and who probably has too many thoughts on his mind in that moment to warrant a solo ascent of the firetruck's summit. She walks in step with me to my right. There is a determination in her where instead of her usual desire to charge ahead and explore, she is with me. Beside me in this life moment. In reflection back on that moment as I write this I recognize retroactively that I believe Bailey might have been the most influential philosopher I have ever had the privilege to meet or interact with. We reach the base of our ascent and I recognize I have made a potential miscalculation in my plan. Dogs are curiously not as astute at clambering around heavy equipment as human children who have grown up doing it are. So the question presents itself: how do I hoist this dog along with me. I decide on the 'under the arm' approach and she already seems to have known this was the idea. She stands stalk still and ready. I hook my arm under her chest and bring her up to mine. Close and secure. We then begin our climb, which in reality is nothing more than two meters of vertical gains. As we reach the summit I place her down on the folded hose and again meet those eyes. She knows, I know. I lie down in the tangle of just-soft-enough hose, careful to not sit or recline on the hard metal couplers. Instinctively, she knows to wait for me to get situated. I am unsure how she knows. This hyperactive wild retriever is not nor never was one for 'rules' or etiquette. But the moment I am situated in my prime viewing seat, she gingerly positions herself to expertly curl up both on my lap and on my chest. I am instantly blanketed by the long warm fur of this great dog and she situates her head in such a way that a quick look up and to the left lets her see my face and place some strategic licks under my chin now and again, but her natural orientation is such that she is viewing the sunrise, just as I am. We fused together in that moment, her keeping me warm, but also grounded, aware, and alive it felt like. It was a primal moment. A transcendence back to pre-history when at the onset of winter an ancient ancestor would have cuddled in with their canine companion for the warmth and safety that entailed. She expressed a grounding too, something unknowably mysterious, a sense of pure purpose, as if all of the atoms in the universe comprising everything in that moment had been waiting for millions of years for that one moment where the two of us huddled together to watch the sun come up. I do not pretend to understand the knowledge of dogs. I think they far outpace our understanding of any and all elements of life, the universe and everything. The sun crept across the peaks and draws of the glorious mountain guardian of the valley. Slowly, the silence of the morning began to be punctuated. There were the last remaining small songbirds calling one of their final morning serenades. An owl behind us in the wilds let out the last hoot of its vigil. A flock of geese above began their migration, bombarding the valley with the loud hammering of their calls. And Bailey and I sat in total stillness and observed the richness of life around us. Our unique sensory evolutions complimenting one another's perception of the event. Where she saw a distorted and almost colorless changing in contrasts and saturation across the mountain ahead, I saw a brilliant explosion of golden warmth clashing with the blackness of the thick subalpine forest. I watched the pink of the new day break across the snowdrifts in the avalanche chutes. I saw the summit spark to life with the solar fire of yet another day in its long life. Bailey, conversely did not just hear birds as I did. She no doubt experienced a rich understanding of the life around us on a primal level of canine expertise. Where I simply heard the caw of the raven across the valley, she knew precisely where it was when it called, and where it was now. Where I smelled the feint evidence of the blue diesel smoke and the cold air, she 'saw' a rich readout of the past few hours on the wind. As I watched her nostrils flare with the breeze I knew that by some miracle of evolutionary brialliance this little golden retriever was actively effectively seeing back in time, understanding where and when things had been in places. We could together theorize the humdrum of the pre-dawn communities of wild creatures, but she somehow *knew* these things and that was reflected in the subtle narrowing of her brown eyes in the emerging light of the day. She had a scared knowledge to her about the goings on around us. She was keenly aware and incorporated into the social norms, realities, routines and experiences of her domain, of this wildland place we called home. Our wordless exchange proved this to me on a foundational level. Effectively, this was a moment of pure and perfect contentment for both of us. Watching a sunrise cuddled with your dog in the brisk Colorado morning air is something I would recommend to any and all seeking an existential enlightenment. It was a moment of pure bliss. One that stands unique in my history as one of my most cherished experiential memories for several reasons: It taught me first that even as life gained complexity as I grew up, as I experienced the hardships that follow anyone through development and life, that there were things removed from that that directly contradicted the darkness and that curiously, the thing that truly stood to stem the flow of the darkness that morning was not some overture of a human construction, nor was it anything particularly unique, what it was, was my approach to that moment. The deliberation to undertake this journey, the serendipity to invite my four legged companion along, and the pure social solidarity that grew between us in those moments. What came was an hour long silent conversation of pure equality between the two of us, pure validation of experience and expert recognition of the life and times of one another in the moment. Most importantly though, I learned in that experience that I did not need any human interaction to feel this level of peace and safety in the swirling horror show of modern life. In the following years, I would learn more from the lessons Bailey taught me that morning, specifically that I did not even need her to have them again.

But this memory is *not* my example of the social magic of attachment as it lends to being a lens for us to understand the nature of self. Rather, the true attachment here, the movement to tears, the symphonic crescendo of history and experience lies further into the future of this recollection. This experience is the root of the attachment. As attachment is not something that simply forms in a singular moment in all cases. In many, it follows us through life, with a continual replication, with many instances of opportunities to further strengthen the fabrics of our social bonds.

Rather the thread of attachment that truly manifested from this day sings a different song all together.

The moment the importance of that morning came into clear and undeniable consideration in my mind was the day Bailey died. When our 11 years of partnership in the strange and terrible road of life came to an end. She died in the best way a dog could: snuggled in her bed, wrapped in blankets, near the warmth of the fireplace on a snowy morning. Our other dog was with her in the end, as was my dad who stayed with her into the night and as he went to bed, somehow she decided that that was the moment to slip into the great wide open. Her death was as transformational if not more so than any moment in my life up until that moment. The immediately striking reality of it was crushing to me. Not because of death itself as death and I have a unique relationship, but in distance. I was over 2000km away from her when her life ended, warm in my own bed in another country, with my own dog quietly snoozing in his bed next to mine. The distance between you and those you love becomes infinitely tangible in moments like this. Not only was I miles away, but I was existing in a new frontier of isolation. An isolation that itself bred both creativity and the worst abject despair I have since endured. But what could I do in that moment? I woke up to the news. Hugged my dog close and told him that his 'grandma' had passed away.

However, the simple news of her passing does not represent the attachment threads either. Rather, the moments that fostered this attachment, that were facilitated by the symbolic exchange of meaning had come months prior.

A cornerstone in the life of a young academic is the navigation of the travel between school and what was once home. There is a sense of belonging and grounding in the windows and walls of the family homestead for some, for others the striking out into the great unknowns of the wilds of the world is a liberating experience. In my case, this reality is split almost evenly in two, where one foot remains firmly planted in the soil of my youth, and another is in the complete disconnect that is academia. First I moved five hours from home. Then two days by car. Then to another country. The feelings surrounding home have fluctuated strongly throughout my life. Unlike a handful of friends I knew growing up, I never felt the same drive or calling to totally abandon my home. Granted, I exist in a strange reality in that I am both from a small town, and from nowhere itself. I grew up almost completely isolated from the happenings of the small town life although only existing 3 or so miles from town. There is still a theme of social disconnect there and I feel that did not breed within me the resentment needed to facilitate a flight to new horizons. Leaving home the first time was devastating, leaving home the second time was overwhelming, and finally by the third I thought that I was finally flying to where my heart wanted to be only to realize slowly after nearly 4 years away that home is not a place but it is a state of existence itself. My state of existence abroad fluctuated between the rare instances of pure joy, the perpetual state of mild contentment and the overwhelming experience of abject despair in a situation that deconstructed the very nature of self, of hope, and of home for me.

Aside from such memoirs however, we must come to a particularly poignant cornerstone in my investigation of this attachment thread as outlined above. What you have read to this point is the premise, the context, the social landscape wherein interactions had built the scaffolding for a true socially metaphysical attachment in my own existential understanding of life and the concepts of my inner self in how I came to know that person. You have also read the end of this story and now in a sense I must provide the final arc preceding the ending. As mentioned, I have a particular relationship with the social experience of death. I equate it to a sort of murky familiarity, a passing of the ships in the night, so to speak. I think about death quite frequently. I write about death, I live with the knowledge of it, I imagine my own and that of people close to me quite often. Somehow this emerged as a way of making a living and so I now teach about death to twenty year olds who have not thought about it nearly as much as I have. And this places me in some very awkward places. In one moment I am giving a lecture to an eager class of wonderful students on death. In the next, I am receiving emails from colleagues about deaths they've personally experienced in their lives. In the next, I am sitting alone with my grandmother beside the wood stove frankly discussing her views on death and specifically the plans she has for it. It is odd in the latter case to be told both "I am not telling anyone else this" and to be a 28 year old sitting across from one of the most important people in your life as they candidly reflect on the approach of death after a long life. It is harrowing, but not something that eats at me. Death is a friend of mine, I have said in classrooms. I still feel the same way-that death is someone, something, some state of being that I somehow have come to know, to recognize and to welcome albeit with a sense of ontological apprehension. I reflect on my mortality, but it is not a thought process I enjoy, nor is being a source of discursive outlet for the people in my life on the topic of death. It is not distressing, but it places a certain shadowed veil on one to be the expert on death. I feel at times a confluence between many different streams of social existence from all manner of people.

A snapshot of this occurred one spring morning in Victoria, BC wherein I stepped away from the environs of my office to steal away to the smoking bench a short walk away. As I did so, between checking emails and endlessly scrolling through social media, a woman who was working for the university as a painter came by and asked if she could join me. 'Of course' I said. I find that some of the most intriguing conversations on the nature of life and death have come over the curled smoke of the literal embodiment of diminishing mortality. We struck up a conversation and she asked if I was a student. Since starting my 'career' teaching about death, I have opted to say that I teach rather than I study. She asked what I teach and I casually replied "death". Now typically when I say this to people I am immediately entrusted with either their own personal worries about their health, or that of ones close to them, or their philosophical ruminations on the subject. Often though, I am the recipient of very stark stories of heartbreak. As we chatted and I drank my coffee, she told me a story of how when she was a child (ten years old I believe) that she was on a road trip through the US with her family. They had a flat tire on the family car and she being the oldest stepped out onto the side of the highway with her father to help change the tire. She paused here to tell me about her dad, he was a warm man she said, he loved us kids a lot and he really liked the Beach Boys. I remarked warmly that my dad also introduced me to them as a kid and since then I grew up from Surfin' Safari to Pet Sounds. I could tell though that something was coming and she asked if she could borrow a cigarette from my case (a request that should always be granted mind you), and as she leant over my lighter she leaned back on the bench and told me the horrific account of how as a ten year old girl, beside the car containing her mother and numerous siblings, she stood next to her father as he changed the tire and in exacting detail described to me hearing the rumble of the engine of the car tearing down the deserted roadway, and how in a split second, not a meter away from her, she watched as a drunk driver drove headfirst into her father as he stood up to turn around at 70 miles per hour. She was shaking when she said this and nearly crying and through the choke in her throat all she could manage was "he just...he was just gone". Ten years old. I did not know what to say other than that despite the horror, despite the loss, that I'm sure that wherever he was her dad would be proud of her and she laughed at that. She told me about the trauma that followed, about how her mother never remarried, about how her brother has never been the same, about how she still dreams about it once a week 50 years later. My heart broke for her and then she said something I was not expecting. I took off my sunglasses to meet her gaze with my actual eyes and she said thank you. She said it twice more. She said it helped somehow to just talk about it with someone like me. Mind you, I said next to nothing during this exchange. She said she had to get back to work and we stood up together and all she said to me as a parting note was 'I do hope I see you here again, I like you." And she faded off to her work and I to mine. I never learned her name, and I never saw her again. I was, in some element a catharsis for a terrible attachment that she had been carrying for most of her life. A tangible loss, a physical and horrific reminder of the loss she experienced in the most traumatic way possible. And 11 minutes in the brisk morning air was enough to lighten that to a degree. It speaks to the power of the social interaction, to how via the exchange of these symbolic experiences, we can foster true moments of pure humanity wherein two strangers connect on the basis of the soul itself in a moment of solidarity in the horror of the chaos of life. This is my relationship to death and it comes to me like this more often than I am able to count. It is odd to be the person people open up to so voluntarily.

Where this relationship with death fits into my conceptualization of self and the further fragmenting of self that represents the thesis of this work is in how I approached my relationship with dear Bailey as both her age and my distance from home increased exponentially. You see, this dog and I certainly had a special bond one that was built on a mutual trust and companionship and love. But I knew via this special bond with death that I would outlive her. I knew that by the limitations of linguistics that I could never truly convey this to her, nor could I communicate truly my appreciation for her. But I was going to try. So I started a tradition I kept very secret and very close to my heart. Every time I left home to return to school, be that at the end of the summer or winter holidays, I would, on the last night, sit down with her in her bed. As the years went by, her breathing would evolve to become much more ragged, and the energy of the once hyperactive golden was reduced to the regality of an aged and mature canine matriarch. Gone were her days of full force sprinting straight up hills to fetch toys, and towards the end she preferred a quiet and secluded snooze in the sunlight at the end of the porch. I would lie down with her in these secret midnight meetings. With everyone else in the house asleep I would nuzzle my face against her impossibly soft floppy ears and I would whisper to her my goodbye. I would tell her the night before every return to the nonsensical mundanity of academia that should she die while I am gone, that I did not leave her, that I did not forget her and that I loved her. I would say thank you over and over again for everything she did for me. For the hours she listened to me talk about the troubles I faced in my life. For listening to my petty dating life woes, to my complaining about various stresses, and to my endless ramblings as I did my writing. I thanked her for helping me make majorly important decisions in my life by being a silent moderator of my anxieties. I thanked her for taking care of me the day my mother loaded one of my sisters in her car and abandoned our family sending it into a chaotic fragmentation that lasted years. I thanked her for her hugs, for drying my tears and I thanked her for that morning all those years ago. I told her goodbye and that she was the best dog in the world. I repeated that speech to her for three years. Every single time before I left. And each time, I would come home three months later to her smiling face with her grey eyebrows now over the brown eyes. Until one winter, that smile wasn't there anymore. And it was in that interaction, in that cessation of all future interactions as punctuated by my mumbling my goodbyes in her ears, that I found myself fully and entirely aware of my attachment with her. And not the toxicity of it, as my approach was not inherently toxic, but rather in the deep profundity of the meaning of that attachment that had grown over 11 years. It was not cemented in me until it ended. This is the nature of true attachments, and those of importance for this investigation, that with the truest of attachments, of those social threads that are fostered over emotional exchange of these deeply meaningful symbols of social interaction, we cannot come to recognize with any epistemological authority their importance or permanence until met with their stark impermanence. To echo Canadian philosopher Joni Mitchell: *"You don't Know What You've Got 'Till its Gone."*

This, aside from the autobiographical presentation represents the critical point of focus on the discussion of attachment in the broader context of the exploration of how we come to know ourselves. That being that attachments are not fully appreciated nor understood until their conclusion and it is this challenge that presents us with the need to revisit the earlier discussions of attachments in this piece. The understood attachment at its conclusion is radically different from the self-defined attachment during its course. And as a result we may notice an emergent discursive truth emerge from this: that just as there are self-defined attachments operating at an end of the social spectrum of meaning that is drastically different than those reconciled in their endings, there too are divergent presentations and manifestations of desire along the same spectral lines. That is, there are desires born of loss, and there are desires that manifest as a definitive personal discourse in the moment of social existence. One is dependent upon the conclusion of attachment or interactional relationships, and the other manifests in an insidious capacity in the intermediary stages between beginnings and endings. Without venturing into a territory too reductive, we might come to classify these divergent spectrums of desire on the basis of where they manifest from and from there, we may offer what some philosophers may refer to as 'irresponsible value judgments on the nature of said desires'.

At the onset of this discussion we may present a desire that is founded within an attachment that ends. I would posit that this type of desire, that which is existent in the absence of that which previously was present represents a more inherently classical notion of reconciling desire with the self. This is due to the fact that it is founded upon the idea that what has been meaningful of that attachment has already made an indelibly mark upon the individual and their presentation and understanding of self. That is to say that desire that emerges from the loss of an attachment is one that is a representation of the self-recognizing the boundaries of where the extent of the socially symbolic interactions it once relied upon for self-definition have vanished in the haze. It is in this negation of a positive situational social reality that lends to the clarity needed to recognize the impact of such attachments on the sense of self one may perceive.

The clarity in recognition of loss provides ample opportune modalities for social and self development, but what it may also lead to is a confluence of despairing over the deficiency of the loss of that singular attachment and within that despairing we are led onto the dangerous path of the desiring of the lost. In cases of the loss being permanent, or where the reclaiming of the loss exists so far outside the realm of possibility that the individual finds themselves lost in the mist of having to *imagine* what it would be like to have that connection back. We develop a longing from this desire. A longing for familiarity. A longing for the pressing understanding of what we once came to recognize as a constant normative state of being. It is in this longing that we may find such elementary affective states as grief, as depression, as a perpetual longing not solely for the attachment we have lost, but a longing for a history we have progressed beyond in the temporal spread of our lives.

It is a standing testament to our true nature not as simple living beings, but as creatures that exist within the unique and exigent state of understanding and socially constructing the idea of time and temporal being. That is, we exist in a varying degree of moments in time at any given point in our existence. The existence of our experience of loss of attachment, of longing and the desire for the re-experience of that attachment, stands as a solid argument for the ability of the individual actor to *"exist in memoriam"* or to live in our memory as a fluid and continual state of being and existing that is tied to experience, attachment, and symbolic exchange of the history of our lives. To say that our experiences make us is an understatement, rather there is some semblance of an individual existing in perpetuity in our living and continually re-experienced memory. That is, our history is with us, it forms a complex and foundational element not only of the composition of our concept of self, but in nearly every current and thread of our contemporaneously lived experiences. Past interaction, affect, symbols, and attachemnts are with us to a constant and compositional sense in every single moment we thread forward into the future. Conversely, the future itself represents a lived abstraction, an amalgm of unknowable potentialities that we both hinge our moment to moment being on and come to interpret that *in memoriam* element of our existence in new lights. The future too presents such a uniquely human experience that transcends the instinctual understandings of a pure survival instinct: we have the ability (or the cures) to *predict* the future. To interact with something abstract *in absentia* in such a way that it allows us to shape our everyday states of being, or our continual understandings and perceptions of our realities in a way that is predicated on a prediction of that which is neither real nor occurring. We have this uniquely intimate relationship with the future wherein it holds both a spectrum of hope and angst that interplay within and without one another, often in the throes of the insomniac's magical hour of three in the morning. The curious hint of this futuristic existentialism we are capable of existing in is that we can, via our preservation of our historicity explain or ascribe these symbolic glyphs of our past to threads of moments that continue on through the present into the future. We can ascribe, socially, a sense of nostalgic reality to the minimal or the maximal elementals comorbidities of our waking social lives. We can see the echoes of the past in the symbols we ascribe to the social objects of our surroundings in the future. This is social magic. To see reflections of our past attachments, and the unfolding of our own unique histories in corporeality that we come to construct as we progress through our existence in time is nothing short of one of the most intrinsically wondrous capacities of the human spirit. That is, we may reconstruct or continue to search for the same social meaning in new and old symbols alike and graft upon them these echoes of where and when we once existed. In a sense, we can, in the event of a loss of attachment in the subsequent mourning of that attachment modulate our desires for the past states of reality into new and intrinsically social instruments of nostalgic impression.

There is a knife's edge of care we must tread in this regard. It is both a beautiful magic and a dangerous sorcery to imbue that which exists with the symbolic meaning of that which has long past, and it is ever more so dangerous to so fundamentally inscribe a sense of meaning on the abstraction of the future in the processing of this new alchemy of the social. We must take care to not transcend nor sacrifice the blossoming of new attachments, of a new social language in the languishing on the past. Nor can we be so careless to ascribe a previous attachment and the composite socialities of that attachment to newly emergent ones. As we may be able to see remnants of our lost pasts in the moments of our present, and we may even ascribe a deep sense of attachment and meaning to these new scripts of the social, we must take care that we do not become lost in them. That is we cannot enter into new connections, new loves, new relationships if we are still projecting out the attachments in our grief of their loss onto new social endeavors. We must have the courage to trudge on through the dawns of the abstract clouded visage of the future insofar as we do not lose out on all of the developmental new attachments that can and will modify the state of understanding of the self as we come to recognize it in its contemporaneously presented projection. We must then, from this recognize the placement of our care of self in the aftermath of loss. We have to recognize on some level that there is a component of that which have now come to *know* as socially real meaning from these attachments in who we presently are and will continue to be, but also that we have an unchecked ability, a power, a capacity for socially miraculously transmutation to, in a word, never let go. This is not to say that we must relinquish the memory of lost attachments, nor does it mean that we cannot exist interactionally with these losses. Rather, it is a standing testament to the simple procedure of taking care when doing so. We have a curious ability in tandem with ours to create the past in the present and manifest it into the future: we have the ability to reconcile the loss of the past, to exist within it, and to experience it over again, but all while also incorporating its teachings, meanings and lasting impressions into a growth of self rather than a backsliding stagnation. It is in this space at the end of a loss that we have to face our longing.

We find ourselves at the end of a partnership, at the passing of a loved one, at the transition between social and temporal spaces, and we are hurt by these losses. There was attachment there, in the space, the people, the relationships and upon its end either that be something drawn out and tragic, or sudden and horrific, we know in the end that it was attachment to say the least. It is what we do then with the knowledge of our loss and the existence of past attachment that stands as a crucial point of discernment for the individual social actor. Do we incorporate that attachment into the inner folds of the self and grow beyond that which we have lost, or do we *desire* for it to have remained, for it to continue on again? In that critical moment, choosing one over the other is not a conscious decision. One does not sit alone and decide one afternoon that they will "healthily" reconcile their loss into their social knowledge of themselves and endeavor to incorporate the knowledges of their loss and the attachments that precipitated it into their future being. The reason one does not do this is because I can firmly attest that I do not believe anyone is this rational or sociologically metaphysical in the immediate aftermath of a loss of this social magnitude. On a grander insight, I do not think that often we are as aware of these foundational processes of self as one might imagine given the nature of this text. These things, quite frankly, are manifestations of a clandestine element of our states of being. They do not represent active internal dialogue, but shadows at the corners of our realities that speak to us in codes and dead languages from across the darkness of our rooms as we drift to sleep. There are hints of these thoughts somewhere in our actions, in our processing of loss, but there often is not a term we can confidently ascribe to that feeling. "Closure" comes close, but closure is a construction predicated on the awareness of that which one has lost and the importance of that loss to the social soul of the individual and that knowledge does not ideally manifest itself in a convenient *eureka!* moment in the middle of the day. It would be far simpler and much less emotionally taxing to exist in this world without that delay, and with the advent of instant self-awareness.

I feel at times that when I see content in my social experience that focuses on *"mindfulness"* that this is what the 'motivational' content creators are trying to manufacture for their audience. This wonderful dream of pure introspection that removes somehow all the pretense of that which clouds our knowing of ourselves: the social. While I have yet to hear a "mindfulness" creator explicitly explain this in such a fashion, it is my suspicion that this is the assumption they are proposing. That somehow through the will of the individual's mind they may simply suspend the social milieus of their experienced reality and through 'focusing' engage in a reflectively perfect metacognitive experience. Perhaps some are capable of this, but I must again echo earlier sentiments to offer that one cannot simply will one's self, their actual self, into a space of asocial isolation. We exist, in our isolation within a social isolation itself. There is not a pure introspection, nor a pure knowledge of self that exists without the social in some capacity. And so to remove or attempt to remove these threads of interactional internalized social history from our processing of the world in its past, present and future, for the ultimate goal of internal peace in times of challenge, we are then advocating somehow for the negation or reassigning of the social that precipitated loss and the affective void of despaired longing from playing its true roles in our evolution of self and our presentation of the next modality of our experienced social reality. It is in this persuasion that we find the danger that again crops up in these moments of loss or conclusion: bypassing the darkness.

Now, I am not aiming to totally shred the mindfulness circles' ideas, as I am not fully entrenched enough in that persuasion to offer as much of an informed condemnation as I am an ill-informed one. But it is critical in the moment of loss to recognize a monumentally important step in the processing of loss of attachment: existing in the darkness. Or, to echo Donna Haraway, we must stay with the trouble. We have to exist in the inky voids of despair that follow a loss of socially significant attachment. We must allow ourselves the time and experience of the pure horrors of loss in order to reclaim them into the folds of our ideas of who we are. We cannot then try to placate the loss by mapping the lost attachment on to the new attachment. This is the true path to a total and complete fragmentation of attachment and a foundational element of the Kierkegaardian despair we are so desperately seeking to explain in this text. We are doomed to repeat doomed history if we do not allow it to destroy us in the sense that we are so aware of the loss that we do not see the ability to reconstruct it beyond a casual reminder of the glow of the past.

This is to say that if we become lost in the fruitless pursuit of reconstructing the past in present symbolisms, we are doomed to experience both the lacking despair of never being able to recapture the experiential joys we are seeking, and the dangerous careening into an addictive cycle of repetition where we stop pursuing new and therefore enlightening social attachments and instead we descend into the world of hopeless recreation. We resign to the dreams of the past at the mortal sacrifice of the self and the social in the present and the future. We can respect and interact with that self of ours that exists in memoriam within our historicity, but we cannot allow a faded obsession of replication become the driving point of our continued existence. The past, in its sickly sweet memories can become the most lethal drug to the self. It is in this regard that we arrive at yet another horrific element of our investigation into the variance of attachment and the manifestation of longing as a result: the mortality of self.

Chapter 2

The Killing of the Self by the Venom of Nostalgia

"I'd trade all my tomorrows for one single yesterday."

-Kris Kristofferson

On The Mortality of Self

We are mortals. This is not a new nor controversial topic. Although it is one we are not particularly predisposed to dwell on, it stands as it is as one of only two adamantly universal socially universal experiences or knowledges humans can share collectively. That is, we are both mortal and born. The fundamental ends of the timeline of life are all that we are guaranteed in this existence, both socially and physically. To the social scientist, this is the only universal law of social experience that we have to claim. We exist in pre-natal nonexistence, and then we are born, we live, and then we die. The inherent ontology here is one that we are capable of examining critically in our own individual realities. That notion that we have the knowledge within us that we will someday sooner or later die. And that is as horrific as it is liberating. This text is not dedicated to the mortality of the individual. There are other times and other places for such meditations. Where the focus of this text lies in something far more clandestine in the continuance of life and the living of lived experience: the mortality of the self. That is to say that the self, the complex web of experience, history, identity, love, attachment, interaction and symbols, is, in fact, a fragile and tangibly mortal component of the individual. The implication herein is that the self itself has not only a sense of conscious life to it but also the inherent ability and destiny to die its own death. What is truly terrifying is that folded into the mysteries of what we collectively come to call this 'self' is that the self can experience its death prior to the physical death of the individual themselves. We can watch our internal understanding of the world, of reality, and our implicit individuality vanish into the haze of death while we remain conscious. We can live for decades without the self, and what emerges therein is a truly dark reality to imagine.

The body without the self, a socially constructed purgatory, endless days of bleak loss of individuality and eventual resignation to the currents of the social beyond us to such a degree that no longer do we live to experience nor do we form attachments, nor do we step through life with a sense of internal wonder at the continual changes experiences through the interpretive lens of the self. It is this mortality of self, the fragility of all of these metaphysical things that exist *somewhere* in our psychosocial body is so susceptible to an illness of the self. This is Kierkegaard's *Sickness Unto Death*, in a sense. Although the despair explored in this text and set forth within his is not a *death* of self so much as it is a fragmentation, a *loss* of self. And it is in this regard that we must discern the epistemological difference between loss and death. Loss, as previously defined, requires a definitive element that is impossibly attainable in a death: knowledge of the possession of that which was lost and the loss of that subject in itself. That is, we cannot know what is lost without first knowing it, and even if we come to know the subject of our losses in the moment of that loss, there is an epistemological consideration to be held therein where there is some degree of social knowledge of that loss. Death is conversely the permanent cessation of a state of being, whether that is the physiological state of being alive or the state of being in the social. Death represents a unique conundrum for the individual subject of it within itself wherein the question can be asked: does the subject know that it is dead? Is there a tangible knowledge, an experiential ontology of a subject's cessation of existence? This is one of the greatest metaphysical mysteries of the human condition wherein all evidence physically and socially points to a resounding 'no,' but an expansive history of human mythology speaks to the contrary. I am neither theologian nor physician, so my best submission to answer this query is the existentialist take, which is that I will "let you know when I die if I know or not, after the fact." Or, more familiarly, as proposed by my own grandmother on the subject of what should be done with her body after her passing: "We *want* to be cremated, but honestly, we're not going to care at that point." The resounding ontological consensus is that, no, the subject is unaware of their death as they themselves are the ones experiencing the loss of being as a functional reality of their death. As such, we can transfer this notion to the discussion of the mortality of the self in two disturbing veins: the self knows, on some level, that it has a mortal coil that it can shed, and the self will not know when it has died.

One may assume I am equivocating and therefore essentializing the death of self with the death of body, and this is not the intention here. That is to say that there is a capacity for the self to reach the end of its mortal existence far before the physical expiration of the body. The two may exist and occur independently from one another. Just as the body may continue beyond the death of self, arguably, with a symbolic interactionist exploration, we may suppose that the self has the capacity to exist beyond the mortality of the body if only existing in absentia of agency and autonomic activity. That is to say that in some (more often than not) cases of individual death of the body, there is a transmigration of the self into the social milieu of the body wherein the memory of individual passing remains alive within the symbolic exchange of interactions between and within the self and the social. To put it very bluntly, the memory of the dead lives on in those who remain among the living after having known and interacted with the dead. By that, and the incorporative factors of interactive meaning, the interactions of the dead fold within the history and experience of the living and again influence and communicate through abstraction Infinium. The same can be said for the body of the individual post-death of the self. There is a continuation of a thematic reconstruction of illusory social interaction that carries varying degrees of abstracted interactive potential.

But beyond the survival of the self and the body after the death of either, we must instead focus on the death of the self in the case of the individual body surviving. This tangential exploration is situated in the middle of the section on attachment (and attachment via loss specifically) insofar as it is in the loss of such attachments that we see the longing for that which has been lost lead to a total and fatal corruption of the self. This endless pursuit to replace that social attachment that we have lost drives within us a near-total self-destruction. It transcends the despairing of the fragmentation of self and presses on to the bleaker: its total and complete death. Nostalgia is the poison of the self. It is the thick, sickly sweet hemlock cocktail that we willingly and hopelessly consume in the plight of our loss of attachment. As it takes hold, much as it did with the body of Socrates, we outwardly appear serene, slipping into a daze, then a slumber. It is a peaceful and elegant execution. We are seen to melt into quiet acceptance of our fate, as all mortals should. But what is seen externally is a far cry from what is felt internally. From our fatal nectar we are shocked into the sensation of pure fire as it ravages us from the inside out. We are paralyzed from the potion. Unable to move, to scream, to even process the agony of our demise. It is a pure white-hot, burning pain that radiates from the center of our bones outwardly through every fibre of our being. We scream in our minds, with thoughts flashing in total mania, with panic seeping in and around from every corner. To the world beyond, we are peacefully sleeping. To those dying, we are in an eternal suffering. A suffering transcendent beyond any other physically describable sensation. What is most surprising in this moment, is how deafening a scream internal can be.

This is the death of self personified. It is a quiet horror, a comprehensive pain of the body, the self, the mind, and the social soul. It is a cascading of every singular moment of past, present, and future existence into a focal point of abstract destruction. It is the event horizon of desolation of the self. This is a slow process. Even in the event of the sudden death of the self, there is a deliberate quality to it wherein the perception of time slows to a crawl, and what can occur in mere moments to the rest of the social environment can take eternities in the inner eye of the subject. It is a process we feel every moment of in a visceral display of a haunting surrealist nature. One cannot describe the death of self in a visual sense in the same way one cannot explain the warmth felt in one's heart at the viewing of a pure sunset over a mountain lake. There is nothing in written form nor linguistic communication that can fully convey the utter destruction of this crucially terrible moment. There is pain. Physical pain at the death of self. It manifests in entirely different ways depending on the subject and nature of the death. Some can feel a hollowness in the depths of their abdomen. Others a pressing illness and nausea. To say that there are always tears is too universalist, but there is somewhere in this experience a shed tear to be seen or felt either internally or externally. It is this moment in the temporality of self where the present passes into a monochromatic facsimile of real life, where the past crumbles to the sands of history and where the future blurs into nonexistence. It is an embodiment of atemporality. A loss of that which grounds us in the cyclically linear flow of social time. It suspends causality, supersedes logical self-perception, and lands us in a state of existence that is solely reduced to simply that existence. There is no longer a social occupation of time, historicity or personal biography. There is simply the occupation, both social and material, in the space of reality from moment to moment. You are 'there', and that is all.

This may read like a prophetic hallucination or the description of some science fiction adjacent punishment on some imagined intergalactic world. But this is real. This comprehensive death of the self is something that does very much exist in our experience of self and the social and of the construction and maintenance of our realities. I have seen it. My own internal bearing of self and my own social have come very close on numerous occasions to this death. They have sipped the first bitter drop of this hemlock and somehow, almost autonomously, have survived. Or, at the very least, resisted the inevitable. I would posit that many of us have come close to this edge of the death of self. It is in these moments that we mischaracterize our experience as 'despair'. That is to say, that we misidentify the death or near death of the self as the classical despair, but the distinction made here is that death of self is not a fragmentation, it is a cessation. In the case of despairing, one may still have some semblance of self, but it is fraying apart into a loss. In death, there is no chance of the self simply being regathered together and reconstituted into exactly that which has existed before. With despair, one may reconstitute the self through a transcendence and reconciliation of the self at the endpoint of a transformative journey of self rediscovery. One cannot so easily perform a necromancy of the self. It is then that the death of self lies beyond despair. It is in this space beyond the dissolution of self, in the death of the self, that we can observe the true potential horror of the nature of attachment, and we may do this by reconstructing a post-mortem of the deceased self.

A resignation to the strange tidings of the shattered dream

As I have said, I have not yet felt the death of my internal sense of self. Not in totality, at least. I do believe there is a difference between the death of self in total and the death of self in sequence. And I can certainly attest that *parts* of myself have died in the passing years. They have been intrinsically linked to deeply important interactional attachments, and within these attachments, I have experienced the required poisoning of the self that has driven it very close to the totality of death. The death of self requires three components: a lost attachment, hope, and imagination. Inherently tied to the death of self is the variably horrific human ability to transcend the trappings of reality via the creative imagination and our frustrating psychological skill at constructing an idea, a fantasy, a notion that itself does not have any basis or evidentiary existence in actuality with the cruelty of being *better* than reality itself. That is to say that I have made the very human mistake of having dreamt. To have hoped. To have imagined. And from those unencumbered ventures into the great blue beyond, I have formed attachments. And I have lost those attachments. In the grief of that loss, I have fallen into the world of imagining them, of recreating them via fantastical thinking, of modifying and augmenting my perception of reality to fit these fantasies. I have attached nostalgia to the horrors of the past and now peer through a grimy mirror at particularly dark moments with a fool's hope that it is not the end, and I have additionally modified my memory of these attachments to allow for a retrograde misinterpretation.

That is, I have fabricated, somewhere within myself, a recognition both of loss and also a total negation of the acceptance of that loss. This is beyond the 'bargaining' nonsense. This is a nostalgic psychosis. It is, at its core, the foundational pitfall of the human spirit. Even those grounded in realism, in pessimism, in the strange and terrible depravity of our being have the inconvenient capacity to toxically revisit our dreams and hopes and perpetuate them into infinity in the pursuit of that singular human desire: to not be alone. In essence, there are two categories of dreams we may have. We have dreams that are dependent upon our actions to come true. Aspirations, career goals, personal triumphs, these are the things we have some semblance of an ability to "manifest". Failure, catastrophic failure, can exist here, of course. But this failure I feel is less positioned to poison the self. It can set us back, force us to rework our plans or modify our dreams. The insidious nature of the dream is that which is dependent upon others. That is, the dreams we hold near and dear to our hearts lie in some degree within the potentiality of the social beyond our bodies to manifest within our existence. We do have the capacity to make our dreams come true when they are ours. But when they include the autonomy and agency of anyone else, the potentiality of futurity in this regard is mapped so strangely into a complex system of what-ifs, potentialities, nuance, and so many countless elementary components of the tradecraft of the social that blends a random emotional, infinitely varied, and irrational external world into a state of senselessness of the self. It is the greatest danger of the human spirit to trust in the socials beyond our selves but it is also our greatest source of excitement, joy, fulfillment, and solidarity. This is not to condemn the social nor the need of the individual to engage and interpret it; rather, it is to say that when it is joyful, when it is 'right', when the astronomical potentialities align in the favor of the individual, then this is the truest and most pure form of safety we have in the uncompromising darkness that is our existence. If there is one lesson to be taken from this disjointed text, it is this: life is darkness, and the dreams we make come true with others are the most cosmically sustaining light in that dark.

I have fallen into these dreams. And, in their failure, in my failure, in the terrible interference of affect and hope and imagination and nostalgia, they have transcended the simple nightmare to become perpetual waking melancholia. We can wake up from nightmares, and in some sense, we are safer waking than sleeping where nightmares are concerned. I remember a great deal of my early childhood nightmares. As a kid starting at around the age of three or four, I began to create an imaginary theatre of my dreams. I imagined it to be a starkly white room. There were stairs for some reason, and I never ascended them. There was a screen embedded in the base of the wall that the stairs ascended. With this screen, I could 'scroll' through 'thumbnails' of my dreams with a specifically memorable moment from them represented in the carousel. Oddly, this framing of my dreams existed before streaming services or YouTube. I somehow had this imagery internally. Curiously, my nightmares also appeared in the selections offered. I do not know why this is, but this psychological theatre has helped me to retain those images even to this day. There is an image of my father standing in the kitchen of our home from that time in my life. But he is not himself, and the kitchen is warped. One of my true fears as a child and one that lingers today has been the idea of the vampire. This I believe is caused by my grandmother, telling me about vampires when I was a small child. In this selective dream sequence from my imagination, my father is a vampire in our kitchen. The dream involved a horrific sense of being unable to leave the room while this undead being that was *not* my father pierced my neck and killed me. This nightmare was not a reflection of him being abusive or neglecting or anything in that vein. Rather, it was a manifestation of a safety failing. It was my source of validation, safety, love, guidance and warmth, devolving into a warped facsimile of itself and performing the opposite of each of those warm roles. The theme was the loss of stability and safety of the things we trust the most to be collapsing around us. Death, particularly my own death, was a strong theme in my childhood nightmares. Often with inexplicable reflections of future events hidden in them somewhere. I remember after Columbine, I dreamt of being in the parking lot of our grocery store with my mother and seeing a man with a gun, hearing a shot and then feeling my head become enveloped in a deep cold. I dreamt of being on a river surrounded by terrifying things. Guns, explosions, human horrors. And the true pain there was that my brother, who was with me, was allowed to go home, but I had to stay. A final horror came when I was older. Around the age of 16 or so, I dreamt of a very long and drawn-out drama set in the jungles of the American war in Vietnam. There were two brothers inexplicably named Credence and Clearwater occupying the relationship dynamics of George and Lenny from *Of Mice and Men*, respectively. I remember following this pair through the horrors of that time and place, surrounded by death and suffering. Watching Credence, the older brother takes special care to watch out for and protect his younger brother Clearwater, who is scared and more immature. The dream lasted for what felt like hours and it ended with Clearwater watching Credence fall to a hail of bullets. I woke up crying from this and proceeded to lie in bed until the sun rose, moved to raw emotion from watching these horrors.

Why do I share this? To highlight the reality of nightmares. I feel we have a certain taboo over the sharing of our bad dreams. It is somehow intimate, and even now, in writing this, I feel a degree of self-consciousness to think that anyone might someday read these reflections. But why? What is the source of this angst? Why is there a socially constructed feeling of apprehension for me to share that which has scared me in my sleep since childhood? Does it diminish me? Does it reflect some implicit and insidious manifestation of toxic masculinity? We can't be sharing our nightmares lest it make us less manly. I tend to avoid such binary norms as best I can, but maybe there is something there. Maybe there is a hesitation to protect myself from anyone knowing my intimate fears and how they even more intimately presented themselves to me in my mind alone in the wrap of sleep. I don't think we share our dreams enough. The good ones maybe are shared more, but I challenge the reader to reflect on their nightmares, especially if they remember any from childhood. And wonder to whom you might have shared them. Nightmares are a crucial element of our unconscious as they show us emergent things in our lives we need to think of. Mine reinforced a desire to appreciate my family and my not having to experience these horrors firsthand, where the bullets can actually kill. I have learned a great deal about myself from these nightmares, and their persistent reminder of my own mortality has itself been both unsettling and very beneficial to my approach to understanding my mortality. That is, I was grappling with horrific first-person experiences of death in my dreams since the tender age of 4. Somehow, that brought some comfort to my reconciliation with the idea of my own death. I have said in my most vulnerable moments with close people in my life that I do not want to die. I actively avoid it the best I can. But, I am at peace with the fact that such a thing exists. Even now, as a meta-confession to you, the reader, as I sat writing this earlier this evening, I felt a dull lingering pain in my left chest under my arm. My thought as the thirty-minute mark of this phantom pain continued to throb was: "I must make sure to leave this essay open on my computer so whoever finds me can read it". And fear not, this is not the acceptance of death by one intimately preparing to inflict it on themselves, nor is it nihilism towards life incarnate, but it is a peaceful acceptance of death and its place in the natural temporality of my being. This is my strange relationship with death, as I alluded to before. We seem to have known each other intimately for most of my life. I do not necessarily think this kind of relationship, nor that these nightmares are unique. Simply we do not talk about them enough. In my life, I have only ever heard about nightmares from people intimately close to my heart. And have, until now, barely ever shared them beyond the scope of my very small social circles. If there is advice here, it would be to talk about your nightmares but don't analyze them. And do not tell anyone who still thinks psychoanalysis is an acceptable school of clinical practice. Be safe with your nightmares and their distribution, but do not allow them to be lifelong secrets. Maybe, in some mythological sense, the notion of sharing them allows us to meet the grave free of them so that we may sleep in peace beyond the veil of death.

These are the nightmares of sleep. What of the nightmares of the waking? While my unconscious dreams were profoundly terrifying and continue to still be when and if they return, those of waking existence are far, far more painful to every instance of my being. I cannot wake up from the nightmares of reality. In my life, these have manifested in ways that I think can be mapped and understood to other elements of human experiences. Namely, of these nightmares, the ones I have dared myself to dream that have shattered my core more times than I can recall, are those existing at the focal point of a desire for attachment. At the risk of confessing hopeless romanticism, the dreams that have fundamentally pushed my concept of self so close to the edge of its death are the ones wherein I foolishly threw myself into the idea that an attachment was not only what I wanted, but I allowed them to become entangled in my own concept of self.

That is, I built dreams both with and upon other people. I fell into a dreamlike state of innocence in these attachments. Daring myself to feel love, to feel vulnerable, to succumb to the passions of interactional joy that can emerge in the lines and lies of intimacy. I dangerously allowed myself to feel comforted by the words and actions of other people. Not my family, but people who I had come to love beyond that sphere. The modern relationship. Things I have written about previously, but true waking nightmares in their own rites. We are no longer seeking a partner in the world but a dream of one. We have an awareness somewhere within of what voids we need to be filled in our movement through space and time, and we so very dangerously hinge our being and affective states of existence on these attachments. This may now read as if it is a grieving of a lost relationship. It is. I will shamelessly admit that. This piece of philosophy has been emerging on painful nights wherein I fluctuate between my desk and the outside of my house in a state of pain, anger, grief and deep sadness for the sense of an ending. As I said above, I offer myself to you as the subject of our analysis. Had I set out to make this a book of academia, I would have called it an autoethnographic study. As it stands, however, I do not pretend this is a work of academia, and therefore it is not a study. It is an investigation of interpretive transference. I offer you my darkness so that you may contrast your own. This is ultimately not a self-study but a mirror for others to use my experience as a means of further contextualizing their own. There is a fear in this, but I feel it is justified in my overall pursuit to at least spark some kind of reflective idea.

I am not going to wax poetic about the relationship I lost. I am not going to divulge intimate details, nor am I going to backtrack through the hundreds of hours of pain, of the fights, of the darkest years of my life. On some level, and in conversation with a friend once it came to my realization that I somehow survived an abusive relationship. This is not how I would classify my experience, and that friend would tell me that I am rationalizing. It was dark. I was hurt many times. And I caused an equal amount of pain. It was not a power dynamic of abuse. It was simply two lost souls carrying too much trauma and dreaming dreams that were too divergent to work together. In a sense, I think we both survived an abusive relationship, and neither of us was the instigator on this front. We were not abusing one another, nor being abused by one another. We were victims of our traumas. Of our pasts. And of a future we wanted, but that was often overshadowed by the pains of the immediate present. Such is life with dreams of the social. They operate well in abstraction, but in the day-to-day, they can be infinite in their pain. The person I went through all of this with and I survived together. In that survival, we bonded. But the edge of the death of my self came as the cost of this survival. For nearly four years, I was buried. Buried under the idea of a dream I cherished and the horror of watching it burn in a thousand different ways depending on the day. I intertwined myself in the idea that we had a future together, that we had a common goal, and that the I love you's we told each other were real. I hoped, too. For four years. In direct contradiction to the advice of every single person in my life. I stayed in the dream. I was pressed into a world of dualities, and the responsibilities of this dream, and this attachment began to form sharp divergent identities for me. There was the person trying to be kind, uplifting and professional in my teaching, in my friendships, and in my familial relationships. And there was the person who did not know what to expect to see or experience upon crossing the threshold into my home at the end of the day. I reflected in those early days that there is nothing more crushing to be watching the home and the life you built crumble around you due to the actions of someone who tells you they love you. I spent many nights on the floor as a result of this. Sometimes in my bedroom. Many times on the cold industrial carpet of my office on campus. For nearly six months, I only ever returned home to shower, living essentially in perpetuity in my small office. My colleagues saw this as a hallmark of graduate school. Some of the people I thought I had as friends around the time expressed concern veiled in the same praise of the grad student identity. In reality, the four walls of that cramped room became a prison of my mind as much as my home did.

Yet, it is in these painful memories, in these horrific experiences, that I formed this attachment. I did not give up on this dream of mine. I did not lose hope in the potential for the spark of intimate loving solidarity to reemerge. I saw the threads of trauma that were pushing me to be treated as I was, and I saw those horrors reflected in brief moments of humanity where, in the cycle of abuse, we would break down together, cry, hug and fall asleep together only to be back to the pain in the morning. I told myself in that moment that I would change the cycle. I would not abandon this attachment. I would not give up on my dream. I would sacrifice my sanity, my safety, and my health for the fact that I saw in the person I loved more pain than what I was experiencing. For every sore back from the office floor, there were a thousand more folds of trauma in their reality. I am not writing this for the sympathy of having watched a relationship fail. Rather, I want to convey that there is nothing in my life that has been more painful than to watch the person you love the most in the world, the person who built dreams with you, the person upon whom you've hung a great deal of hope destroy themselves in real time. To this day, I do not reflect on this period of my life as having been traumatic to me on the basis of what was done *to* me, but rather what I witnessed. What I tried with every extension of my abilities to mitigate and to remedy, or at least, to ease the suffering. I watched in horror as the person my heart had beaten the strongest for fell into their own darkness. A true darkness. A loss of self. Despair. And this nearly killed my sense of self and identity. The manifestations of that trauma in my own life left me, at times, depersonalized to the point of exhaustion simply because of how much social labour it took to be a warm embrace for someone in the deepest pit of self-destruction. I will not bore the reader with all of the details, but what I can say is that I sacrificed my internal self for someone else. I nearly pushed my metaphysical self to death because I suspended it in lieu of empathy out of love. In the trenches of my traumatic experiences, being on the receiving end of lies, of shouting, of the worst things possible one could say to a partner, I suspended the idea of 'me' in this path and instead looked at caring or preserving this dream at all costs, with the cost being the idea of 'me'. The thing with dreams is that no matter what we put into them as far as effort before falling asleep, we do not have a guarantee that that is what will happen. Even more so when we place the dream in a space dependent on someone else. There is no degree of lucidity in these kinds of dreams. There is human innocence in the desire to be loved and to matter to someone as much as you love them and as much as they matter to you.

What pushed me to the precipice of self-death was reaching down into someone else's darkness and being the lifeline on many occasions. To be that close to despair but to be ultimately powerless in its resistance, to then, in turn, be the focal point of someone's struggles with their darkness, destroys you. At the end. I was the one who eventually said that I could not do this anymore. That my involvement in their darkness, my hope that it would get better, and my constant state of being the target of the rage and despair of that darkness had taken away my very humanity. Even though I 'ended it,' there is a lingering pain. I feel it constantly. To live with and love someone so deeply, to see them at their absolute rock bottom, to hold them in their darkest moments on the edge of oblivion, and then to be reduced to a subhuman whipping post all within an afternoon over years finally pressed me beyond my point of ability to function.

In the end, I retreated to where I was safe. I went home. I went to sit among the cedars and junipers of my home, to nest astride the stream and under the blue skies find out who I was all over again. For three months, I grappled with the idea that what I was during this dream was not a human being. I was not something I felt even worthy of recognizing as me. I threw myself into the swirling vortex of dissociative social horror for the ultimately selfish reason of loving someone and hoping, dreaming, wishing that somehow the love that exists between us would someday manifest again. I told myself in these months that although the love and the attachment was there and tangibly so in fleeting instances, that I could not force myself to survive it either psychologically, metaphysically, or physically for the time it would take to even have a chance at feeling 'normal'. I resigned myself painfully during this period to move past this chapter. To relegate it to historicity and to carry it with me as memory alone. I did not succeed, but I felt that I had come to the edge of losing myself and pulled back just enough to work on recognizing how I could move beyond this. And then it all came back. I didn't escape it. I was forced back into it. And this time, after having disconnected so much, after waking up from the dream partially, me now in the aftermath and among the same junipers this morning, I feel part of me is still lost in that horror. The pain has not left, and I have not been able to move on. I am both regressed and trapped in a cyclical state of pain. It is like a depression, but it is of the social. It is because of this attachment. It is from more than a decade of memory, of experience, of love, of collective pain, of intimacy, of horror, of pain, of the exchange of countless millions of intimate symbols of social interaction. This attachment. This bond. It is severed. I feel that now. But I also experience these terrible slips back into the dream-like state of wonder and hope that so actively poison me. The idea that somehow, someday, a phone call will come, and life will be how it should be in the context of what I had been so foolish to have hoped for. I hold out hope for the day that we spontaneously reunite with a tearful embrace and begin the chapter of our life together that we were 'supposed' to have. I somehow involuntarily torture myself with this daily. I see photos, I hear a song, I am reminded at every turn. I associate so much of my lens of reality through these years that divorcing myself from that which could have been and that which was has left me hopelessly and horrifically alone. I offer as another meta intrusion: at one point, I, for a very brief moment, seemed to have even forgotten what humans actually are. In the throes of a marathon writing session with the house empty save for my dogs, I saw a picture on my phone of people and, for the briefest of instances, was confused by the creatures I observed. Isolation, in the purest sense, has been both what has saved me from this darkness here and now and something perpetuating the hope of it. Now, rather than selecting a dream from a carousel as I did as a child, I now work until my body physically cannot anymore, where the caffeine is no longer enough to keep me upright and conscious. When I surrender to bed my last waking thought has been more often than not a wish to be back in the warmth, in the embrace, in the memories of the moments of pure joy. I wake up then the next afternoon after having passed out at 9 or 10 am, and the first thought is that it will never be that way. I poison myself then with rationality even though

I have already created the environment for that toxicity by falling prey to the desire in and of itself.

It is pathetic, in a sense, to be so broken that the simple imagined scenario of even a momentary relapse of love can cradle my mind to sleep through the bleakness of reality. It is maladaptive. But, it is *human.* It is somehow a natural feeling to wish for that which sings the songs of our hearts. To search with dedication for that which we know to be the resonant truth of that which will complete our sense of self, or at the very least enrich it infinitely. I liken my fantasies in the darkness of our shared abusive life together to the phase of a tortured body where the prisoner begins to imagine the pain stopping as a way to ignore the pain. The pleasant valley sunrise blocks out the interrogator's blows. This was my survival method then. By analyzing my hope and my faith that someday this pain would lead to pleasure of some kind. Some mutual love blossoming again. I found myself comforted in a sentiment echoed earlier in this text from Donna Haraway: *"Stay With the Trouble"*. And so I did. And now the dream is different. Because it is just in my mind. It no longer lies in reality. There is no chance of falling asleep together anymore. There is no reason to have the hope that someday it will all be better for us. And in this futility, which I still *know* to be factual, I still somehow fantastically deny it. I still build the dream. I still filter the nostalgia. I still replay the best moments in my mind to lull me to sleep and I imagine a million more potentialities that transcend any moment of joy we ever shared.

In this I am experiencing that which makes a true attachment: an ontology of loss. I know what I have lost. The awareness of its absence and the negation of any future potentiality is such that it is so crushingly final that I am able then to look back on every aspect of this horrific way of living with loving nostalgia. Nostalgia really is our poison. The association of a warm sense of dormant joy in memory is truly one of the worst things we are somehow able to imagine. I know what I have lost, and so out of the shattered pieces of the most important dream in my life to date, I constructed some kind of warped and insane warming sensation. I look at the pictures, I remember the sweetest moments, the memories, the intimate language of referential symbols that constitute a closeness beyond the average pairing. I reflect, even in the lowest moments of sadness, how, after the directly formal ending of our partnership or whatever it was, we could still slip back into it seamlessly. We could be invited to dinner and present a perfectly ideal relationship that embodied real love. I was told after this dinner that I was truly with a person who loved me a lot and that it was so obvious because of two factors: that my theoretical rantings weren't just listened to, that they were remembered and understood, and that the way I was looked at with loving admiration without me noticing while I talked and waxed poetic over Georgian wine. It is a strange pain to be told by someone outside of your intimacy, who isn't aware of the pain you're feeling, having watched it die, that the love between you and your partner is tangible. Tangible to the social idea of a partnership, maybe. But to me, the only feeling that was tangible was the knife in my heart. It was seeing the threads of the potential dream and knowing that the attachment that built it was dead beyond resurrection.

These are the moments in our loss of attachment that the boundaries of the self become so painfully observable. When we are met with either an explicit reminder of what that attachment once meant or when we are met with the most painful evidence that not only is it lost, but that it is irretrievably gone forever. Prior to this dinner party, where the cognitively dissonant insights into my relationship were presented to me, I listened to any last hope fall into nothing from the cold and unforgiving floor of the second bedroom of the home we tried to build together. At the risk of venturing even further into the dramatically despairing, I will offer this: no pain I have ever felt in my life compares to hearing the person you've loved so deeply having sex with some random person they've known for a month or so that they met via some depressing hookup app in the place that supposed to be your home together. Nothing compares. That is the death rattle of an intimate attachment. To be alone and cold and isolated and broken down the hall from a fleeting and ultimately meaningless one-night stand meant to simply satisfy some social trauma and latent sexual identity trauma. That place on the floor was not new to me at that moment. But the knowledge of what was lost as far as this entanglement, this intimate attachment that had defined me and my work, truly cemented the absolute pain in that moment. And then, somehow, I had to make casual small talk over the breakfast table while watching the saddest farce of fake intimacy play out in the midst of every fibre of that which aligned a meaning to my metaphysical knowledge and interpretation of myself melted into the haze of mundanity. As a cynical aside on the nature of the digital sexscapade, there is additionally no greater secondhand embarrassment to watch someone you know try as hard as they can to charm some other person, having been the subject of those charms yourself. Watching someone swoon over the bare minimum of providing supermarket pastries and under-extracted French press coffee after a night of over-hyped and underperformed sex is not the pinnacle of true love. It is the mask of romanticism in the digital world, but on a purely observational level, it is the most shallow and depressing thing to watch. I think, given the above neurotic accounts, that relationship advice is almost null and void within this book, but I would simply offer that if your go-to 'date' involves brie, white wine, chocolate-covered strawberries and a beach blanket, simply stop that at once. Save the $30.00 and create a memory that does not appear on Pinterest after having googled 'white millennial wedding ideas.' And I offer that barb as a white millennial myself. There's no taste in what is essentially a dollar store Valentine's card cover. That is not to entirely negate this, but if your mating routine is so predictable that you only ever buy a wheel of brie when you need to fuck someone, then there is something there that lacks a degree of socioepistemological finesse. And this is not a condemnation of one person nor is it a targeted dissection of a former partner. It is a veiled call to embrace the idea that dreams that truly matter are not prepacked in a cookie-cutter mold that allows for universal transferability. If your attachments are all similarly artificially manufactured, they are not going to grant the fulfillment you desire, and you'll be doomed to repeat a cyclical process of building a cheap relationship and then watching it fall apart in front of your eyes multiple times. Build one on serendipitous synchronicity-that allows it more of a natural flow.

Aside from the nature of the attachment, I find myself here in these reflective weeks dealing with that loss and subsequently trying every life support intervention to not allow this part of myself to die in these memories. I feel they are simultaneously occurring yesterday and a decade ago. The most depraved nature of this self-sustaining is the fact that even still I find myself falling into a cycle of hope, of somehow fooling myself into the halcyon glow of imagining that I have what it is my heart desires. Not that it ***will*** happen, but that it ***is*** happening. This is how I trick myself to sleep. I imagine that I am not here alone, but rather that I am still living in the memories of the moments of intimacy that are now lost to my own historicity.

This is the methodological death of the self, the core focal point of this section: that we provide our self with all of the tools it needs to suicidally implode upon itself via the nostalgic reminiscence of that which we have lost.

We hold on so desperately to the point that we manage to compose some kind of schizophrenic, obsessively fantastical re-telling of events gone by. This is not the standard reaction to the loss of an attachment, but it is a very tempting opiate of the spirit to continue to live as you had, to fully embrace that unfolded history of the self and to stand in grand resistance to the approach of the future and the recognition of the ending. That is to say, rather than a pure psychotic state, we exist solely in our historicity, with a total negation of that which may abstractly exist in the clouded future and in a modified and psychotic interpretation of the present. This is not to equivocate the state of living fully in your past as a mental health crisis, although it certainly may manifest as such, but rather to say that it is inherently a maladaptive departure from that which is plainly realistic in our immediate surroundings.

The death of self comes from the murder of the future. From the ignorant remoulding of the present and from the fixation on the past. It is then that each and every slip into our safe and warm historic fantastical constructions, every time we close our eyes at the end of the night wishing and hoping things had been different, every instance wherein we imagine the most ideal fantasy of what could have been right to the point that we feel the peace enough to sleep, we are in effect complicit in the death of the self.

It would be the logical idea then to say that we should simply not do this. This is easier said than done because anyone who has gone through the loss of such a symbolically powerful attachment can attest that simply moving on is not as easy as it may seem. I would alternatively theorize that those who have had such ease in 'moving on' in the face of a loss of an attachment have not experienced an attachment that has had as deeply of a social impact as they may believe it has. One cannot fall to the state of self death without having had a meaningful connection of the most intimate degree, and one that ends or experiences an end in their attachments who does not fall to this darkness to some degree, who does not find themselves existing in that which could have or should have been has not truly experienced that purity of attachment. This is not to negate the attachments of those who have escaped the experience of the darkness; it is simply to recognize that there is a degree to which individuals can be bound together through such a thick milieu of sociality that the loss of that attachment is catastrophic for the experiential understanding of what it means to be an individual alone in this social world. These losses are chemical indicators directly holding a mirror to our eyes, showing us not only what we have lost but what faults lie at the core of our being that had led to such a loss to occur. Guilt, internal condemnation and self-hatred are symbiotic to the death of self. We are crushed to a point that we see the reflections of the darkness in all human hearts upon our own, and we question, in these moments, why we even believed for a moment that we deserved to have that darkness lightened. Someone cynical may state that such a reflective state of introspection no longer exists, that the ego of the individual has grown to such unchecked heights that there is no capacity for that reflection. To this I would offer the simple foil that those lacking the reflection have not lost 'enough' to feel the abject destitution of self that is the fertile ground of that reflection. We cannot come to truly know ourselves without slipping into the darkest insanities we are able to experience. If we do not have a complete breakdown of the self and the social, if we, in our beds at night, do not undergo the vivisection of the self at the hands of the crushing darkness surrounding us, we have not yet experienced the loss I am referring to in these pages. Loss can hurt, but it takes a loss with such a high degree of compounding social symbolism to truly reduce the core of the individual to the razor's edge of self death. We have to push on through the river of death to the end to take the full plunge into the madness of the human spirit. We have to sacrifice the very nature of what sustains our being in the face of love of attachment. We have to bleed into these social pairings to shed not only tears but every illusion that hides our vulnerabilities. We have to be purely innocent in what we bear towards the attachments around us in order to be driven into a total dissociation of the self at their loss. It is a mortal wound to the soul, not a depression during a breakup. It is that which creeps into your mind uninvited and tortures the very elements of your being to the point where you have to make a choice: to let it kill your self or to live with it. To stay with the trouble. To greet the darkness as a familiar face wherein you might recognize who you really are. I believe we never come to truly know ourselves until we are confronted with the shadow of madness that lives within all of us. This is beyond behaviour, beyond emotion and affect. This is a primal reckoning with the very real fact that to exist is to form attachments, and to do so is to suffer. That is, life itself is a continual abating of the suffering of simply trying to survive to the next day, the next month, the next attachment. It is dangerous to fool yourself into thinking that you do not hold this darkness in your heart. You do. It is there. Each of us has within us a self-destruction sequence pre-programmed where, at the right social moment, we will enter into the spiral. Where nostalgia will crackle around what we used to be, darkness will nihilistically cloud out what we can hope to someday be, and the clouds of uncertainty blot out our understanding of the day-to-day existences to the point that it is all a bleak grey. That fall is built into all of us. To understand it, one may simply look to Conrad's Heart of Darkness, wherein we may find the sentiment that that which forces us into the insanity at the core of all of our hearts is the simply horrific process of the soul looking too far inward upon itself. That is, the self coming to see itself for what it is at a point of absolute destitution of the society. The loss of attachment, of grounding to the world beyond the fixated internal realities, is such that we cannot hope to come out unscathed, and at the very best of such an experience, in our own wilderness at the end of the river, there is not one that sees inside and does not lose some part of themselves. It is this loss of the self into the gaping void of its imminent demise that lends to a contributing factor in either the despair of the human experience or the death of self. This is that razor's edge. We can lose a part of ourselves irrevocably, or we can lose all of it. All or some, but no one escapes the horror without changing. To place this in the modern reconceptualization of Conrad's novel, our self has two potential outcomes from our time up the river: it either dies in its darkness as Kurtz does, or it begins the long and horrific trek back down the river permanently and ultimately changed like Captain Willard. We have that momentary questioning of how we may come to face the world, in the fire of the death of the self or in the long and winding dissociation bearing with us our traumas and moving on but not beyond. In each instance, be that the death of self, or the survival in some form of it, we are left with the immortal words nonetheless: *The Horror! The Horror!*

On the Far Side of Never: The Unrequited and Unfulfilled Attachment

"Like a poem poorly written

We are verses out of rhythm

Couplets out of rhyme

In syncopated time

And the dangling conversation

And the superficial sighs

Are the borders of our lives."

-The Dangling Conversation; Simon & Garfunkel (1966)

The above is but one of the two forms of the loss of attachment that leads us down the path of the dissociation and fragmentation of self. It is one that carries with it a somehow noble romanticism to it. A loss of an already existent attachment. It is poetic and has been a long-understood point of philosophical discussion from the discourses on the pain of it in the annals of the written word and every good breakup song recorded. Human misery at the loss of that which means most to us is not a difficult concept to understand nor chronicle. But, there lies a more insidious functional type of loss of attachment within our scope that finds itself occupying a more under-discussed niche in the relaying of human desperation. That is, it is the attachments we form without them actually ever existing. They are the desired fantastical connections we build para-socially in our own minds, from which we derive a real but non-corporeal meaning. It is the obsessive, depraved calling card of the lonely and tortured soul. But this is not the siren song of the incel nor the lonely and broken.

The capacity to form some para-socially constructed fantastical relationship is one we all possess. We all may fall prey to the cloak and dagger of imagined connections, and within this, all of us are vulnerable in our own unique ways to the dangers of daring to be happy. It is within these daydreams that morph into waking nightmares that we find the lowest presentation of the depravity of self. It is a decadent indulgence of pure and perfect utopian idealizing. And it is dangerous. It is one of the most dangerous drugs we can experiment upon ourselves with. And we do it often, to excess and to our grand destruction.

This is not in sole reference to partnerships or companionships; rather, it is reflective of a broader sense of social idealizing, that is, we have the capacity and the persuasion to radically imagine and live within the imagination of utopian futures of all social forms. That is to say that rather than simply constructing an ideal relationship, we have the unfortunate habit of constructing *any* social situation that is both immensely pleasurable to us and radically incongruous with our contemporary modality of existence. These escapes into the velvety embrace of the best, most amazingly beneficial future that we can imagine serve as a warming elevation of our immediate social consciousness into a world of pure bliss that is only limited by the bounds of our imaginatory brushes of our minds. There is a fine line in this kind of social imagination wherein we straddle the boundary between brilliance and delusion. This is not to say that all imagined scenarios are particularly toxic to our ideal understanding of the self, but rather that we have the capacity either to make wondrous breakthroughs in our social experience and the capacity to construct for ourselves a forest of mirrors that leads us into the beyond of fantastical thinking that transcends the thought experiment to the realm of psychosocial obsessive toxicity. There is a perversion of these innocent abilities to create in their transmutation into self-serving ego satiations that solely draw upon our reconciliation of that which we lack in our lives and that which we desire to fulfill those elements we find to be lacking. This is not the ability to set life goals, or to fixate on that which we want to improve in the pursuit of self-growth. Rather, these are the escapes into fantastical oblivion that we do not have an ability to actively manifest in our lives, instead these are the things that a realist may say that can never occur, or that have a near-zero chance of becoming 'actually' real.

This is akin to lying in bed in a stressful state of anxiety over the bills being due in the morning and fooling yourself into restless sleep by mentally picturing the entire experience of winning the lottery. It is a satisfaction of real life problems with the imaginary total solution that perfectly and exactly fixes our cause for anxiety. It is a pattern of social thinking wherein the individual processes their struggles without a pragmatism to their thoughts but an imagined complete resolution of their problems. We are very adept at satisfying ourselves with thoughts of everything being perfect, but our skills in approaching those problems can be lacking. This is compounded by the fact that many of the stresses and voids in our lives are beyond our scope as individuals. That is, we cannot simply wake up in the morning and 'fix' those systemic social vectors of oppression that keep us in anxiety in perpetuity. The proliferation of the notion that we can has been one of the most disparaging horrors of the rise of social media. The idea of 'the hustle' or 'hustle culture', which has grown to incurable cancer on the minds of those impressionable enough to fall victim to it, effectively holds within it the idea that if one simply follows a set behavioural routine, if they only do what everyone else successful does, then all of their problems will fade on into the dawn. If we simply just do what Elon Musk does, and wake up at 4 am and work hard then why ever would we need to stress about the water bill going unpaid? Curiously, these preachers of this doctrine gloss over how easy it might be to experience financial security if your parents owned emerald mines in apartheid South Africa. By all means it is 'easy' to be 'wealthy' if you fully exploit the system of colonialism. But for the individual locked into a class struggle with whatever other compounding social obstructions in their way, the idea of simply 'doing work' in the hustle sense is just not a feasible means of modifying their lives.

So what do we do in these dark moments? We steal away to the imagined utopia of what things *would* be like if we did not have all of the obstacles in our way that we do. These imagined fantasies are not inherently horrific, and if they can serve as a means of coping with mundanity or oppression, I am not within these pages going to take that away from anyone. However, the challenge emerges when these fantastical realities, these imagined utopias that serve to just satiate our egos become so prominent a coping mechanism that they augment our very experience of reality itself in ways that place us at odds with the gravity of our material reality.

To explore this, we may turn to the fabled parasocial relationship. This refers to the construction of a relationship between the subject and someone they do not know or do not have a relationship via a transmogrification of the social to the point where the subject *believes* they have a relationship with someone when they do not. This is compounded by the fantastical imagining of that connection, the idealizing of what could become real, and a manifestation of the individual reconciling what they do not have in their world in a given moment. Essentiality the parasocial coupling is a reflection of the deficiencies we experience in the day-to-day existences we suffer through. It is loneliness and the dark isolation of the social propagated to the extreme. Social media has accelerated this process but it is not a newly emergent phenomenon. In classes I have taught, I have had the pleasure of exploring this horror with students and the typical example we all collectively rely on, and one that permeates the literature with increasing density is the social media influenced parasocial relationship. That is, in brief, when an individual consumes social media content from an 'influencer' and suspends the social distance between them via interpreting the relatable personability of the influencer's online content with a direct sharing of intimacy in their private lives directly with the individual consumer. It is when someone transcends enjoying and consuming content and starts to interpret this consumer/producer relationship as a mutually assured connection. They insert themselves into a fantastical relationship with the subject of their desire and transfer their understanding of their relationship with this person into a shifted interpretation and engagement with reality. This is an emergent phenomenon in the sense that it is so prolific across users of social media, but the concept of fixating your infatuation with another person into an imagined reality is not in any capacity a new thing.

There are ample examples from history that we may look to in order to understand this process. From the obsessive nature of super fans of the Beatles during the height of Beatlemania to a more esoteric and academically impressive source. Dante Alighieri's masterpiece, *The Divine Comedy*, while being a monumental achievement of literature and a piece of art that had a profound impact on the interpretation of the gospels and apocryphal texts, also represents a monumentally epic poem that is a manifestation of his infatuation with Beatrice Portinari to the point of obsession. Beatrice, being both the focal point of Dante's obsessive attachment and a central figure in the latter two parts of the comedy, represents this manifestation in a liturgical form. It is a veiled parasocial dedication to his love, and within its cantos, which I shall not detail in the analysis here, we may see, in coupling The Divine Comedy with *Vita Nuova,* that there is a pervasive imagining of the ideal partnership, the manifestation of a total and complete coalescence of the social reality Dante so heavily dreamt of. It is in the tale of Dante and Beatrice, Poe and Lenore, or even Yoko and John. Artists have the capacity to mask their parasociality into works that touch the soul and speak to the longing journey of existence through the pain of sociality that lacks the companionship one craves. Dante's work, a horrific journey through the depths and rings of hell, finds salvation in the guidance of his Beatrice, who leads him through purgatory to paradise. Poe reflects on the loss of Lenore, his wife, in actuality, Virginia, and we see a parasociality of the deceased. A modification of the reality of the world one inhabits wherein the loss of the individual's focal point of love and attachment falls away, and they reconcile via the imagination and physicalization of the loss into a parasociality of the love lost. Finally, the two artists, John and Yoko, manifested a parasociality wherein Yoko projected her love and obsession over John to the point of it becoming real and grounded in the world she inhabited. Each case, each echo of coupling from history represents an elemental component of the parasocial relationship: Dante presents unrequited imagined reality, Poe the end of reality and its posthumous idealization, and John and Yoko is the rare case of infatuation incarnate in the real world.

What is the point of these brief historic vignettes? Not to prove any point but to illustrate a historical lineage of the human capacity for longing, for desire, for the dream to be intertwined socially, physically, and emotionally with the objects of our desire. A mutual assurance of this intimacy is one of the rare joys we can experience in this existential suffering called life. There are many ways we may find this joy, this attachment, but in the reality of it not being found, of us having within ourselves the flaws or inabilities or lack of agency to manifest them into reality, that is where our hearts fall to the darkness. We want what we do not have, and then we can fantastically manipulate our experience of reality to satiate this hunger. We map our desires into parasocial relationships, into fantasy, and even into real relationships that are not truly fulfilling as a means of masking our desperation through a projection of that fantasy onto what we do have. If we are alone, this becomes a manifestation of the purely fantastical; if we are attached to someone, but they are not what we truly desire, we augment that relationship with new fantasies. I have seen in my millennial social circles the latter happens often. Just as social media allows for the proliferation of parasociality, so too do dating and hookup apps allow for the proliferation of the symbolically hollow modern relationship.

That is, through a gamified, commercialized and emotionally shallow process of what is essentially a sexual lottery, these apps open for us the ability to step into relationships that meet social needs in the interim and those which we may come to modulate on the basis of what we want, not what we have. I have seen the devastation these types of pairings bring to the social soul and the self of individuals falling into them. I have seen people use these commercialized pairings as a means to mask, hide, to suppress their true desires as a means of fitting into the social expectations of their world, and then through the use of imaginative thinking and the manifestation of true desire, I have seen them destroy their attachments and take true damage to heart from the failed pairing. In these instances, we see a real-life exposition of the desperation of the self and the internal conflicts that come to compose one's existential pains. Someone who so desperately desires companionship to the point that they sacrifice their sociality, their integrity, and their identities to have it the quick way. They then map a false sense of empathy onto this relationship and transform it from something fleeting and cheap into a total obsession laden with fantastical constructions of grandiosity. We so carelessly describe these infatuations as 'honeymoon stages' wherein we become overly sweet and attached and obsessed. We sequester ourselves away from our typical social worlds, we modify our behaviors, interests and external presentations of self to some new modality that allows for the expression of relational perfection. Ask yourself, dear reader, how many Instagram couples have you seen emerge in your social spheres? How many people build this world together of pure blissful existence only to have it crumble a year into the partnership? Ask yourself this then: how many do you think we're using the relationship to fulfill some immediate desire and then realize that these desires were not being met? Is it simply the fact that people cannot form real connections if they start their partnership with sex from their phones? Or is it deeper?

I have watched three relationships form, combust, and fail along these lines. It is tragic to see, but ultimately it does not stir an ounce of sympathy in my heart. What I have seen is the tale so very common among my generational peers that it now breeds such a collective existential depression in me as I watch the world unfold into failed partnership after failed partnership. I have seen the traumas from this and have seen the traumas that lead to it becoming real. And in every instance there is this deception within it. A masking of true intentionality, of the true self, of the projection of some idealized utopian perfection of love and limerence that reflects abject absurdity in the face of that which constitutes a socially symbolic meaning of interactions. Each of these three relationships follows a person with deep-seated identity trauma, with confusion about their internal realities, but with an obsession for the social reality of being loved and loving someone. In each instance, they began on Tinder, of all places. They all became 'serious' within weeks of the first date. The first date is the aforementioned cheaply basic chocolate strawberry affairs. And within this first moment, it seems that there is not even a glimpse of social compatibility but simply the shared experience of an orgasm or two. From this, I have seen both partners in each of these three relationships become so holistically obsessed with one another while simultaneously presenting vastly incongruent and dishonest images of themselves. In one case, a person belies their desire to isolate their new partner away from any and all ties they formerly had. Conversely, the other partner has entered into the relationship to prove that they are heterosexual to their family. The next sees one person existing in a double life with their partner, being sweetly dedicated in person but having a secret Twitter account where they post daily about how bad their partner is at sex, how stupid they are, etc. The other partner then goes on to cheat on them the first chance they get. Finally, I observed an obsessive person seeking the idea of a long-term lifetime monogamous marriage at the age of twenty. I then watched their partner manipulate them into consenting against their will to a polyamorous relationship while simultaneously being destroyed by hypersexuality.

These are not isolated cases but rather reflections on the variable nest of red flags that emerge in modern relationships. They are things we do not see explicitly, and yet they are there. We respond to their observation with anger and projection, and we fold ourselves in to be terminally destroyed socially by each one. But we cannot get enough either. All of these relationships described were the reality of one person I know. And each of them began mere weeks after the previous one ended. And in each instance, this person was a different person in each of them. It is code switching to the extreme degree of existing as a chameleon of personality wherein one can modify and adapt their entire identity solely for the social acceptance of someone they have an already shallow connection with. In each case, what occurs is the reality that one cannot prolong a false presentation of self indefinitely. That is, the fantasy can no longer relate to reality and they find then that their true self is one that cannot sustain who they are pretending to be. And this may sound simply like a condemnation of modern dating, but it is deeper. This is the contemporary snapshot of our dangerous flirtation with fantasy. We fantasize that these relationships are perfect, strongly founded, and able to provide us with a sense of absolute social perfection. In reality, they are not relationships, but they are dreams we display to the world to numb the pain of existence and to calm the desperation in our isolation. In the post-relationship breakdown of each of these three instances, the same sentiment was echoed: "I just wanted to be loved, to be held, to feel safe..." The question emerges then: why did you not when you said you did? Because we lie to ourselves on a constant basis. We transfer the pain we feel into other vessels and fixate on these intimacies as a means of numbing ourselves to the knowledge of that which is truly destroying our social souls: the isolated nature of human existence.

Are these relationships exemplary of the capacity of the human to create that which they do not have? Are they akin to imagining the winning lottery money the night before the power is shut off? On the surface, they do not seem to be, but I would argue that they indeed are. The only difference is that *some* of the desires are being met somehow. I myself am guilty of this as well, of projecting what I want to be true about a relationship onto that relationship. It is not an uncommon human pattern of existence. But it is damnable in the potential pain it stands to create for us. Because an honest presentation of self is so hard for us to perform, there are breakdowns in these attachments that precede and succeed this fantastical thinking. We imagine things are one way in total ignorance of the actuality of their presentations. I imagined myself to be more important to my partner; they imagined me to be less important to them. We each did this out of a social desire to modify that which lends to us feeling content. I wanted to fulfill a void of loss in my social soul, they wanted to downplay the attachment we had because of their own voids. Together, we prospered in tangential asymptotic denials of reality to form something that left shattered wounds on both our souls. To live in denial of your true self and your true desires, to then fantastically invent counter-foils to those desires is a social pain; to live in denial of that which is lacking as a means of coping with a grander sense of emptiness is yet another social pain and both reflect the pain in my own partnership. To watch as these horrors unfolded, I was blind to them in their manifestation, but in retrospect, now I can see them. I refused to believe or see that the love, the attachment, thy symbolic partnership was less than existent. My partner refused to reconcile the strength of the bond that was there and instead chose to mask these desires by projecting them fantastically into other relationships. The power of psychosocial transference of fantastical utopian thinking is a dangerous thing. These things come to be through lies, through misinterpretations, and through painful withholdings on the part of both partners. And this is the crux of the fantasy, the denial, the avoidance, and the projection.

This is not simply a review of contemporary red flags in relationships, but rather it is speaking to the larger sociological question of what it means for the individual to be in such a position that their conceptualization of self fades away to leave nothing but despair. In the contemporary sphere, relationships, partnerships, and pairings each have a drastic impact on the individual's conception of self. And this is not an accident. There is an emergent commodification of these relationships, spurred on by the gamification of dating via hookup apps and the cheapening commercialization that occurs through the broadcast of our personal lives on social media. In effect, we are existing in a new wave of sexual revolution wherein the tenets of free love have transcended the reality of the capacity for the individual and have instead placed the intimately personal into the shallowly impersonal. It is of critical importance for the social scientist as well as the everyday individual to take notice of the means by which these emergent social realities are manipulating our understandings of relationships and the ways we form social bonds.

Essentially, the story of the modern relationship as it exists in the spheres of commercial and commodified reality is the story of the neoliberal imperialism of self to the most barebones intimate degrees. If we can conceptualize that modification of our lives that is most inherently dear to us, our intimate social pairings, romantic or otherwise, then we might be able to form a more complete understanding of where in the space of this late-stage capitalist hellscape we can and will exist within. This is not to say that a social obsession with couples is in any way emergent, but rather that the new forms by which it is presented and manifested as this obsession are things we must take note of in the presentation of self in the modern era. Social media and the explosion of apps that keep us commodified and connected are such that it becomes almost impossible to escape these realities in and of themselves. It transcends the heteronormative presentations of relationships in media and advertising from the last century and instead places them into the daily existential stream of digital consciousness of the individual actors comprising society. Historically, this has been a great advantage to heteronormative identities, but I would postulate that the emergent commodified relationship has, in some small ways, been beneficial to the authentic living of divergent sexualities' existences in the modern scope.

Where they become dangerous is in the abilities they foster for us to imagine this parasociality of existing in a relational connection when one does not exist. I fear too, that in the non-hetero pairings, this proliferates at an increased stage as well. We find that our abilities to seek out relationships hinges even more so on the need to theorize and interpret the society around us in ways that are fundamentally tied to our core beings and also require a sharp interpretive lens from which we may build and understand a working knowledge of that sea around us. The added layers of investigation here fall into the fables we often construct around that which we desire to lead us down paths of nonsensical personal theorizing to the point that we cannot fully reconcile the stability of being to such a degree that our perceptions of that which *might* be real become warped by what we hope to be real.

Effectively, the experience of the individual in the modern age is one of investigation, interpretation, theorizing, and miscalculations that represents effectively a web of mystery that we are somehow tasked to solve. There is a divergence in the solving of these mysteries as reflected in the marginally depressing reality that we are so positioned to create our own solutions that are not bound to the experience of reality. How, then, did we get here? I will posit one theory for a contributing factor as I have seen in my experience as a digital citizen in the rise of the age of social media: manifestation culture. I am not sure how internationally relevant this reflection may be, but in my American upbringing, I remember a distinctive moment when this new brand of suburban neo-mysticism hit the scene. 2006. A book emerged on the shelves and subsequent home nightstands of almost every suburban mom I knew in my experiential social circles. *The Secret*. From this, we saw the rise of the idea of *"The Law of Attraction,"* wherein effectively, the author presents 'strategies' for one to incorporate into their own lives as a means of attracting or manifesting all of those things that they desire. I saw this phenomenon sweep the lower-middle-class families that I knew via my own mother's obsession with the book and subsequent film. Suddenly we were making vision boards, being told to fixate on and manifest those trappings of childhood we were after, and being told that all that we could ever desire would be ours if only we put in the psycho-spiritual work needed to tell the universe to bring it to us. We were told to look for signs, white feathers were one of these 'signs' and from that encouraged to believe that every white feather was evidentiary of our every wish being fulfilled. There was a pseudo-spiritualism to this craze, where there was never a definitive exposition or expectation of Judeo-Christian values, but they did exist, I think, somewhere just below the surface.

Interestingly, these are not values I was wholly unfamiliar with growing up as I did in a family of accidental neo-hippies with distant and tangential ancestral ties to Eastern Europe and Romani culture. On both sides of my family, there are legends of great-grandmothers and their gifts of sight and practices as seers in their respective communities. Somehow, these displaced travellers came together generationally in America for me to experience the rise of The Secret in 2006. What a strange thing fate is. But there is a difference I think from the spells, rituals, secret collections of divination tools and tarot cards wrapped in altar shrouds and the commercialized manifestation of the Law of Attraction. If they were alive, I could go to one of my great-grandmothers and we could cast a spell together to 'attract' what it was I desired. But there is a beauty in this that is lacking from typical contemporary manifestation. Beyond familial solidarity and the preservation of oral history and traditions of oppressed and outcast social groups, there is a persuasion of the universe to flatly tell you a firm and steady "No" in response to your request. On the subject of manifesting a relationship, as I have seen so prominently lauded in Instagram anniversary posts, I could very easily burn a basket of laurel leaves while repeating an incantation, and then supposedly, my true lover would come and visit me within a day. I could carry in my pocket peeled lemon rind and sleep with it under my pillow to see if I would dream of my lover that night. These things are ancient practices of manifestation, and if one were to read into the storied practical magik of the Roma people, one would find that there is varied and specific lore for the manifestation of any and all manners of things and situations. However, there is not, in my experience, a fixation on the ego. There is nothing within these practices that represents a specialty of the individual in their universal experience.

"Love is Pain said the Reddit User to the Reddit User"

Pretty Bird Comes

Like a Ghost-

Just the Silent

Rustle of Her Wings

-Author Unknown, Found
Written on a Piece of
Mail in a Desk from the
Pitkin County Courthouse
in Aspen, Colorado Circa.
-1970

Chapter 3

G.D. The Air is Full of Rockets: Early Morning Atomic Age Meditations

"If the button is pushed, there's no runnin' away

There'll be no one to save with the world in a grave

Take a look around you boy, it's bound to scare you, boy"

-Barry McGuire, Eve of Destruction (1965)

"G.D. The Air is Full of Rockets"

"I had a very strange and unsettlingly philosophical dream"

"And weirdly, it was a strange polarization of one I had had as a child"

Texts to my Partner on Awakening; January 25th, 2023 12:34 PM

Phase One, Wherein the Passage of Time Begets the Weary Time Traveler:

A pattern of existence I have adopted recently with little to no rationale is the practice of the micro-nap or interrupted sleep. For some odd reason, over the past month, I have tricked myself into a dangerous game of setting alarms for 10, 15 or 20 minutes and daring my sleep-deprived body to only taste the nectar of slumber. There was, I think, at the onset the idea that I could somehow go 24-48 hours without sleep, supplement with a stretch of two twenty-minute escapes and then reclaim a semblance of productivity. In reality, this has all but destroyed my ability to sleep without anxiety, and now the concept of restful relaxation has all but faded. What has instead unfolded is a series of manic, horrific bouts of unconsciousness wherein I dread the alarm and hate myself even more for sleeping through it or resetting it. I have become something of a slave to the bed and the blanket, wherein I now lovingly refer to the space as my eternal prison. The only freedom comes from either total dedication to the cause of maintaining a semblance of productivity or the rare occasion wherein one's muse lies in repose of pure beauty within the folds of the prison to push you out into the writing chair to protect you from the eternal confines of sleep. Muses do truly keep the writer's soul somehow bonded to this world.

Alas, as of now, what has roused me from the prison of creature comfort into the chair at this hour is something far darker, far more existentially crushing, and more worrisome to my soul. A pattern of experiences through time and space, reflective of the human condition, comes to me in the darkness of my slumbering mind. It seems that as I have grown up, the behaviour still remains the same. Rather than wandering down the hall to my parent's room as a child roused by a nightmare, I now wander half-awake to my keyboard as an 'adult' violently awakened by the unsettling and bizarre forms our mind may project in the throes of a nightmare.

I have written elsewhere (to be released) of my dreams and their unique cyclical existence in my memory. To summarize, I have had, since a very young age, two unique components of my 'dream self'. Those have been a profundity of nightmares involving my personal existential demise (some of my earliest dreams are of my own death, and this has not changed into adulthood), and secondarily, there is a pervasive sense of memory surrounding my dreams. I have, since an early age, been able to recall dreams almost in their entirety through some kind of crystalline episodic memory and even as a child, I remember entertaining myself before falling asleep by "scrolling" through a "carousel" of past dreams to choose that evening's performance. Sometimes it worked, other times not.

But what draws me to the page tonight is not a fear of the dark that came from these nightmares of childhood. This was not my bedroom door materializing as a mass of spiders, nor was it a visit from an Eastern European vampire of my grandmother's tales. No. I find that the terror of dreams is their grounding in the real world. Without a pure Freudian deep-dive, I will say that a theme of many of my early nightmares, aside from my existential erasure from time itself, was the feeling of being trapped in a situation I knew was bad but that I could not, by either social or physical forces, escape.

This is where we lay our scene now.

"Slowly desparatly slowly the remains of passage debris

That encumbered the lower part of the doorway was

Removed. With trembling hands i made a tiny breach in the

Upper left hand corner and then widening the hole a little i inserted the candle and peered in. The hot air escaping from the chamber caused the flame to flicker but presently details of the room within emerged from the

Mist x can you see anything q"

-Howard Carter upon opening Tutankhamun's tomb as enshrined in the sculpture titled "Kryptos" that lies on the grounds of the Headquarters of the Central Intelligence Agency in Washington DC.

Part 1: The Student

I am 14 and I am dreaming.

I am in my 7th and 8th grade social studies/language arts classroom. Within these walls, I have been led on many a journey within my own mind. My teacher took us to many spaces on the edge of joy and horror in the literature he would read to us. The Illustrated Man, The Masque of Red Death, Harrison Bergeron, Carl Sandburg's Chicago Poems, Fahrenheit 451, Upton Sinclair's Jungle, The Night Thoreau Spent in Jail, The Ones Who Walk Away from Omelas, and All Summer in a Day to name a few. It seems a fitting setting. There were many times in my yellow-orange desk over my notebook that I fell into strange liminal spaces of reflexive thought in that class. He would read to us on occasion from our assigned books. Especially the shorter stories. I used to love that. He had a good voice and would always follow up with our reading with a discussion of the key points. I think, at times, he saw us as far older than 10, 11, 12 or 13. We approached the veil of death on many occasions in that class, where the idea, discussion and existence of the end of existence were always there in some capacity as a spectre following us in our journeys through science fiction and other contemporary American literature.

However, in this dreamscape, there is something slightly off about the room itself. While the space was never fully square or symmetrical, there was a dizzying unease in the physicality of the room. It felt askew in a way that was indescribable. As if the vertices of the walls were maybe off by two or three more degrees than they already were. There is too, the unmistakable vignette of the dreamscape in recollection. The colour-shifted filtration of light, the feeling that one exists just to the side of reality and is not firmly rooted on any plane one may recognize. This is the underlying horror of the nightmare. Not the vampire's fangs, nor the wall of spiders, but the sense that something is so off that anything horrific may be the realistic norm in this abyss. This is what throws us into the first sense of unease, the first sense of an unknowable fear. Like being alone on a dark and unfamiliar path. Dare I say, taking the road less travelled, but Frost thankfully never told us what it was on that less travelled path that made all the difference.

In the scope of the room, an unknown, unseen figure is teaching a class. I cannot know the person, nor can I see his face. He seemingly does not have one. He is a presence. A void within the void presents something I need to pay attention to. This itself represents another layer of uncertainty. Who is this figure? Where does he come from? What authority does he have to teach our class? Where is our regular teacher? My body feels heavier, almost as if some kind of gravitational well is holding me to the ground with more force than the usual 9.8 meters per second squared. I am locked into this analysis, whether it is comforting or horrific.

We are analyzing a poem. A new age, creatively formatted poem. The words of the poem are laid out in a spiral, and they begin at normal font size; as the spiral tightens, the words disappear into the page in ever-shrinking reductions in size. The poem is illegible. In my dreamscape I cannot read 99% of it. It is a mess of characters from many alphabets. There are Latin letters, Cyrillic, Greek, Armenian, runic, hieroglyphic, and Cuneiform characters, and some letters or shapes that are not part of any known language. I cannot recall nor even perceive their order. They are jumbled to the point that there is no recognizable pattern. The poem is untitled in my memory as the shapeless teacher never said who wrote it or what it was called.

He told us though what it was, and the unease crept even further into the corners of my perceptions. He said it was a poem based upon the last radio transmission of a single jet fighter pilot. He told us the story of the pilot. He was flying his jet across some landscape, and through the polarized visor of his helmet, he noticed to each flank a wall, a swarm, a fleet of rockets flying across the surface of the earth behind him. He calls into his wing commander. No answer. Static. That is what is represented in the jumbled text. Static. He switches his radio to civilian bands. Makes the official military call sign. Static. Nothing. No one. No answer. Static. The poem is a representation of a garbled transmission. Something then as a child I did not understand. But now it is my theory that what the spiral of the poem represents, what the static, the loss of signal represents is the overtaking of radio waves by the oncoming gamma ray storm of fire and death. There are simply faster particles in the way.

We may read one sentence fragment. Its meaning is unknowable while also frighteningly direct:

"G.D. The Air is Full of Rockets"

"G.D." is not an abbreviation. It is verbatim text. A full sentence? A remark? A name? Goddamn? God? We are told by the faceless voice that we do not know what G.D. is. The second sentence The Air is Full of Rockets is frankly clear. It plays several times throughout the recording, we are told. It is a lament or an epitaph. Or a call for help. The spiralling text of the poem reads both without emotion and with all of them. It is the final note of the apocalypse somehow immortalized on magnetic tape for us, the living to re-experience. To listen to.

The discomfort is palpable at this moment. I am locked into the seat, locked into the spiral. The voice continues the lecture. It is unrecognizable at times, buried between what I can only assume is higher-level analysis and jargon.

There is an air in my mind of not being able to escape either this class, the horror of this pilot's last thoughts, and the impending nuclear destruction. There is a sense of imminent danger in the room. That the flashpoint of the hydrogen bomb is only moments away and that I will die having not seen my dad's face since the night before and not being able to hug my mom, my siblings, or my dog ever again. I am alone. Sentenced to thermonuclear destruction in a room of people I do not care about with a voice that Will. Not. Stop. Almost like an arrhythmic summoner of the coming destruction.

The drone of the voice continues. The class progresses, and I cannot speak close my eyes or leave. He tells us that we do not know who the pilot was. We do not know his name. The only evidence of his existence is the recording of the anonymous poem and a rough sketch. I remember vividly now the sketch. It was crude. Pen on paper. Like a quick crime scene sketch of a suspect. He has a square face, buzz-cut dark sunglasses and stubble. I do not know him, but I look into the dark rectangles where his eyes would be, and I try not to. I can't feel empathy for the face. It feels distant and wrong somehow. A unique feeling of being 'off' all its own. It is generic and specific and it haunts me with its lack of detail. In the text of the poem, he is flat in his delivery. I do not know how he would sound in the recording. I think, though, that I do not want to hear it.

The voice continues. The analysis deepens. We start flipping through the poem. Every concentric circle now. There is no reduction in size. Twenty or so lines of nonsense text. The static. G.D. The Air is Full of Rockets. It's there in every single circle. The surrounding nonsense text is different but that message is there. More analysis. More words. And then it starts. Somehow, out of the wilds of the dreamscape, we start to hear the static.

I have had the ability since childhood to know when I am 'done' with a nightmare. There is a point I reach the capacity my mind has to handle the horror and I say to myself some variation of 'ok that's enough' and I wake up.

That is what happened at the static.

It was another day. I cannot remember if it was a school day or not, but I know in the cool blue pre-sunrise light in my bedroom that I was not ok. I was scared. Not of the demons or monsters but of the humanity outside the window. I cannot remember my exact thoughts verbatim, but I remember the dread. The unending sense that somehow I was powerless to the whims of the world and that somehow they were beyond the sunrise plotting the immediate destruction of everything.

I stayed in bed. I was 'mature' I didn't need reassurance from anyone. This became a rehearsed pattern. One that I think may share some threads of commonality across those of us that are either labeled as 'old souls' or 'mature for our age'. In other words: the kids who grew up too fast. I remember in those days, my brother and I had a cassette/CD player combo on our nightstand beside our bunk beds, and from the bottom bunk, my role was to curate the analog facilitation of our audiobooks we would listen to at night. We had a varied library of staples, but I also had music CDs. I do not know what I listened to that morning or if I did at all, but I remember in those sombre mornings of maturity, I would sometimes place a song titled "I Still Haven't Found What I'm Looking For" by U2 on repeat and lose myself in thought to the lyrical landscape. As I got older, this would change, but as I write now, I am called back to that haunting gospel. I remember the images I would construct in my head as I listened. Sometimes a mother, my own mother, searching a war-torn battleground for her lost child. Sometimes it was just the image of a house fire. But despite the heaviness of these images, I found hope in those lyrics and a sense of reassurance that regardless of what horrors we may face, there still exists beauty, hope, love, companionship and a sense of humanity in us. Fred Rogers told us in times of horror to always look for the helpers. Look for the people helping; there are always people helping. From an early age, I idolized my dad because he was a helper. He was a firefighter who would charge into burning buildings, mangled cars and other disasters to help people.

Tangentially I am reminded of a story from my childhood involving him helping. There was a fire call for a baby trapped in a bed under a collapsed wall. Somehow a car had driven through the wall of a ground-floor apartment and had knocked the wall down onto the bed. Asleep in the bed was an infant child. My dad arrived on the scene in his work clothes and his old Dodge pickup to see a sombre standstill of shock. The kind of pressure that exists when even the helpers know that there is no help to be offered. That hope has fled, and the angel of death is lingering in the crowd. But being the helper he is. He sprang into action, the deadly calm in the face of tragedy that I have so deeply idolized flashing into being. He grabbed the on-call officer and ordered him to back the GMC on-call officer's pick-up truck up to the car embedded in the wall. Without a thought or pause, my dad grabbed the heavy-duty chains from his work truck and rigged them to the car and said, "GO!" and the car was pulled out of the wall. As he recounted the story to me then and even now, he tears up, saying the last thing he saw was Allan, the paramedic on the scene running to the ambulance holding the baby in his arms and performing infant CPR. That was the last thing he saw at that scene. They had helped, but he didn't think the kid made it. Those are the hard days he would say. When you try but despite the help, it doesn't help.

Several months later at the Christmas dinner the fire department hosted, while my brother and I were nestled by that stereo listening to an audiobook, the chief got to announcing the lifesaver award. The first name called? Brian Farris. To his surprise, the help had helped. The kid lived. He gets emotional telling that story because of how against all the odds, a life didn't end that night. He learned that the child had been airlifted by helicopter from the nearest hospital to a much larger one and, through the efforts of many doctors and those old rusty chains in the pickup bed, that that kid lived.

Several years later, he came home from training or a meeting and told us that the kid had come by with his parents. The kid was now in middle school and was perfectly healthy. This and many other moments are punctuated by a phrase my dad has said to me many times, often in a shaky, teary-eyed recollection of these types of calls: "It just...it just wasn't his time yet."

Look for the helpers. Stay with the trouble. Embrace the Darkness.

I think that tangent represents a core component of how I have come to process the horrors of the world. The scary things that exist out there are beyond our control and beyond our ability to predict. I looked up to my dad's calm in a crisis, and not just the calm, but the drive to go above and beyond to help rather than to preserve one's self. When I think of nightmares, I think not of the monsters or the horrors of fantasy but of the horrors of real life. The things we cannot hope to ever imagine we will engage with. This dream was one such thing. It was scary because it was real. Or rather, close enough to real to be plausible.

In that dead calm after waking, I had questions that come back to me now. Of course, the identity of the pilot, the nature of the rockets, the static, the messages, the fate of humanity, and what that damn recording sounded like. But also deeper things. The faceless voice told us it was real. By that logic, it happened in the past. It had already happened. That is, some poor lonely pilot watched the sky blotted out by a cloud of rockets and called out endlessly into the spiralling void until the font disappeared. How. How could we know this was real? How did it exist? What did that mean for me in that schoolroom in the dream? Was it post-rockets? Why the feeling of immediacy of my danger? What did it mean? I confess, I cannot remember my findings of analysis if they ever even materialized. I just knew that at that moment, I was the only one awake in my house and out of the six of us, I was awake because I, at 14, had just, in a dream state, reconciled my vulnerability to a sky full of rockets, and had done so on the wings of the warning poetry of a singular pilot's spiralling descent. There is a weight in carrying that on through the dawn and into your day. While I cannot imagine it cradled too much stress into my daily being, the feeling of waking with my heart thumping and the sweat pooled on my pillow from such a situation was memorable throughout that day, as were the images of the spirals, the sketch of the pilot and that lingering refrain: G.D. The Air is Full of Rockets.

For many years after that experience, I had a host of other dreams involving nuclear annihilation. I cannot for sure state why this was, but some were clearer than others. Usually, after seeing a movie that focused on the subject, my nightly thoughts wandered there more often. The Terminator films terrified teenage me on a philosophical level. The plausibility of it all (time travelling robots aside) was so real. Sarah Connor vaporizing in an eternal skeletal scream against the chain-link fence of a playground, her son John and Claire Danes'

Kate Brewster watching the world destroyed by machines (yes, Rise of the Machines was a film I watched multiple times) were images burnt into my mind with the intensity of heat and radioactivity of the actual reality of it. For some reason, the mutually assured destruction of the planet via nuclear weapons has unfortunately been a psychological burden of mine for over a decade now. But that inception of it, the schoolroom, the poem, the lonely pilot. It stuck with me subconsciously. That is, I have not paid a singular thought to that nightmare since the day it projected itself across my closed eyelids.

Until Today.

Desolate and lone

All night long on the lake

Where fog trails and mist creeps,

The whistle of a boat

Calls and cries unendingly,

Like some lost child

In tears and trouble

Hunting the harbour's breast

And the harbour's eyes.

-Carl Sandburg "Lost" Chicago Poems (1914)

The Only Remaining Artist's Approximation of G.D. Adorning the Poem and the Tape.

"I think the sun is a flower;

That Blooms for Just One Hour"

-*Margot*, "All of Summer in a Day" by Ray Bradbury, (1954)

"There are chords in the hearts of the most reckless which cannot be touched without emotion."

— Edgar Allan Poe, The Masque of the Red Death (1842)

Part 2: The Teacher

I am 28 and I am dreaming.

Entranced in the endless loving embrace of the eternal prison of the writer's soul, my bed, underneath the cozy duvet, a slight scent of wood smoke on the cool breeze from the window open only a fraction of an inch drifts across my face as the dog at the other end of the bed slowly nuzzles her head against my leg in unbothered sleep. In the digital world of my cell phone lying on the mattress beside my head, there lie the remnants of the goodnight video call I had with my partner, along with three separate alarms for 12:30, 12:45, and 1:00 AM. I am doing another of my 'micro naps' wherein I decided at 11:00 to fall asleep for a short stretch of time to then wake up, consume too much caffeine and write something. I have two essays in the ether right now on top of the ghost of a dissertation looming as well. But what stirred in my mind in those 90 or so minutes of microsleep has haunted me deeply to my core.

Very, very suddenly, out of the nothingness of sleep came a feeling. A drawing of familiar responsibility. The feeling of sleep slipping away as the stress of having to teach a class in a few hours. There is a quiet anxiety to that type of sleep. You dream, but it is of practical things. Remember your laptop, your keys, your adapted, your stupid little laser pointer remote. Remember that night's readings and that morning's lecture. Don't let the students know you wing it sometimes. But again, as with all nightmares, there is something uneven about this state of being in this moment. I am not preparing for my online class I teach from my desk. No. I am walking across a campus. I look down, and I see my leather dress shoes, and I hear their distinctive 'clop' sound as the wood soles and the heels meet the pavement. I feel dressed for a lecture, with my leather jacket warmly over my teaching cardigan to brunt against the oncoming rain I am always so mindfully prepared for. Except it is not a university campus. There are no long cobbled or paved walks. There is no excess of buildings. There is no one around. I am preparing for this lecture, yet I am not where my words typically ring out in lectures.

And then I realize.

I have the horrific mid-dream realization.

As the scene shifts.

I am the teacher.

I am walking into my school to deliver the "G.D." poetry lecture.

When I say that the feeling of unease hit its peak when I saw my own adult hands handing out spirals of the nonsensical poem to my students (my past peers), I cannot understate the feeling of being totally at a loss for the way of the workings of the inner mind. I was, in effect, taking on the role of the antagonist in a nearly two-decade-old nightmare for myself. Full-circle. The prairies are dug, and the frost is all over.

What I found in presenting the text is that I had somehow allowed myself subconsciously, through maturity, to have more access to the text, its meaning, and, above all else, the recording.

Without my consent, I heard it in my dreamscape: louder than I could have hoped to listen to it and suddenly without warning. Before the kids were in their seats, it was blasting. So. Much. Static. And then the chilling callsigns. The radios out to the towers, the wing commander, and the rest of the squadron. The realization of the isolation. The switching channels. The civilian bandwidths, hundreds of calls to each tower control zone. Nothing. No response. The fear rising, the military veneer melting into the human behind the aviators. And finally, that immortal phrase:

"G.D. The Air is Full of Rockets"

Hearing it at 28 rather than reading it at 14, the feeling was even more chilling. The first time it was said, it had the last shaky reminders of the professional pilot. The sternly cold, emotionless reporting of facts, the waiting on the other end for recognition, for instruction, for...closure. Nothing came. And in its infinite repetition, the sense of losing one's self came more and more, the pilot spiralling into the man, the boy, the person facing the annihilation of anything and everything that has or would ever exist. It was the wailing siren of an oncoming apocalypse. Unlike the fortunate few who would be asleep when the flashes exploded, he knew. He couldn't outrun the fire; he couldn't escape the destruction. There were no evasive maneuvers. There was no shelter. He had no one to console him and no way to console those loved ones he surely had. The true horror of the message resonated fully with me as an adult locked into the strangeness of dreams that come between binges of caffeine that are most likely a detriment to my overall health.

In my new dreamscape, I take on the added role that compounds the stress: by some strange reality, I have been asked to present the horrors of the tape, the poem, and its implications to an audience of children, myself included. I am in a place no teacher has been before. Giving a lecture I have already heard to an audience that I was once a part of. I, like the voice on the tape, like "G.D.," have transcended the social bonds of time itself. I have then become something of a guide in the past and present to the students and myself and the voice on the recording, some kind of reconciliatory force to compose a connective fibre across the eons of time and nuclear destruction. It is not a real role, and yet, in those moments of sleep, the responsibilities hung over me.

Curiously too, the near-decade of formal education between the initial dream and the secondary dualistic follow-up implanted new questions in me. Specifically on the tonality of temporality. That is, how might we, the living, have come into the possession of such an artifact from the end of time itself? Is this some high science fiction in the flavour of Bradbury? Is this the lost piece of ancient history that represents the genesis of the earth itself? Was some rocket-propelled futuristic past human outrunning nuclear Armageddon and leaving us, the modern human, a warning? Was this on par with the ancient texts of Athens or Ur that represent early attempts at communication across the eons? Is this magnetic tape materializing in my hand the next stage backward in archaeology behind the cuneiform tablet? Or is it more simply, just the manifestation of the horrors of the modern age?

It was a thought that crossed my mind as I lectured on the spiralling nature of the poem that this is a new age of nightmares. That somehow, in 1945, we as a species created a new type of monster to occupy our dreams. My mind flashed to film footage of nuclear tests during the Manhattan Project and beyond. To the buildings laid waste by the shockwave. The mannequins in the paper towns were incinerated by the fireball. I did not say to the students what I imagined it would feel like to experience instantaneous vaporization, nor did I share with them that that was the preferable outcome. But collectively, in the fires of Trinity, we did come to a conclusion, where one of the faceless children (someone I had known for all of my life to the point as I myself sat in the circle of chairs somewhere) made a remark that took me onto another tangent of discussion.

Was the poem spiralling because he crashed?

Indeed, there is the question there. The spiraling of the jet fighter from the stratosphere back to the cold hard ground. There is an artistic interpretation there to be had for sure. I asked what the student thought. They said it sounded like instead of crashing fast, it was a slow fall. I flashed again to the eyes behind the polarized visor-would they be fearful? Would they accept their fate? Was it a spiralling crash? Did the shockwave of a thousand million suns finally reach the tail of the plane? Or was it a supersonic skip across the circumference of the earth? Was it a made push of the afterburner as hard and as long as possible to outrun the sky full of rockets? Did he run out of fuel and slowly begin his tailspin to the radioactive glass below?

The tape does not tell us. It loops infinitely, repeating only that chilling remark and the barely discernable calls to any and all stations. It is a modern death mask. A black box of the final sentry of the human condition on the horizon of a gamma-wave bombarded shell of a planet. Again the question comes to me: was this somehow an article from the future or the past? Was it a present artifact? Would this be the duck and cover drill to end all drills our parents practiced in primary school? Or was this distant in the sands of the future, unknowingly waiting for the day that the 'button is pushed?"

I absconded to the horror of the past for a moment, questioning again the historicity of this tape. It felt old. Within its magnetic ribbons, it held some quantitative representation of nostalgia while being equally futuristic in its materialization.

Another question.

"Who Wrote the Poem?"

"Fuck if I know" is what I would tell my undergraduates, but for the present audience I uttered something more along the lines of 'we don't know'. And that mystery itself presented yet another existential question: why immortalize this message this way? Where did the author find the tape? How did they come to survive enough to make this spiralling ode to the end of everything? I then had an introspective moment: what would I do as the sole possessor of this tape? Now that I am awake and conscious and aware of the fact that I technically am, I guess the answer to this is to write this over-long melodrama, but I digress.

"We have to ask ourselves," I say to the crowd of eager faceless faces around me, spinning slightly to meet each void devoid of wide eyes, "We have to ask ourselves why write the poem, over who wrote the poem." It is a question of intentionality, I say. Not of substance nor of identity. It could be written by anyone. It could be, somehow the flag of a neo-apocalyptic civilization, it could be the new gospel of a long evolved species, or, it could be the last fragmentary keepsake of a time long past memory. I challenge them with this question: "Why do we preserve memories at all?" What is, in essence, the human fascination with the preservation in physicality of our experienced social momentary states of being? I challenge myself with this question daily, and yet I pose it to these 14-year-olds here in this classroom as if they are my most trusted colleagues at the end of a cigarette and the tumbler of gin. "Why keep memories?" Silence for a moment.

"Because they're good," "It feels good to go back and re-experience those good times," "because we don't want to forget what it was that was so good"

"Good?" I ask. "Good is fine. But what about bad memories? Do we make those immortal too?"

More silence.

There is not an answer here and I turn the rhythm of the lecture back to G.D.

This is bad, isn't it? This is horror? Total destruction. Fear. Horror. Why make it for us? Why keep it? Why put the burden of the pilot's realization on our shoulders? Why force us to read this fucking poem?

With that, I awoke in my bed. My throat is horrifically dry, and my lips cracked. My little dog was peacefully nestled against my right leg in her own dreamscape. My other dog snuggly cuddled in on himself, tail over his nose on his bed. The ambient lightbulbs in my bedroom are a mix of lavender and pale green at their lowest brightness. I had again stirred from the same dream in the same room nearly a quarter of a lifetime apart from the initial strike. The unease and terror remained the same.

I still haven't found what I'm looking for.

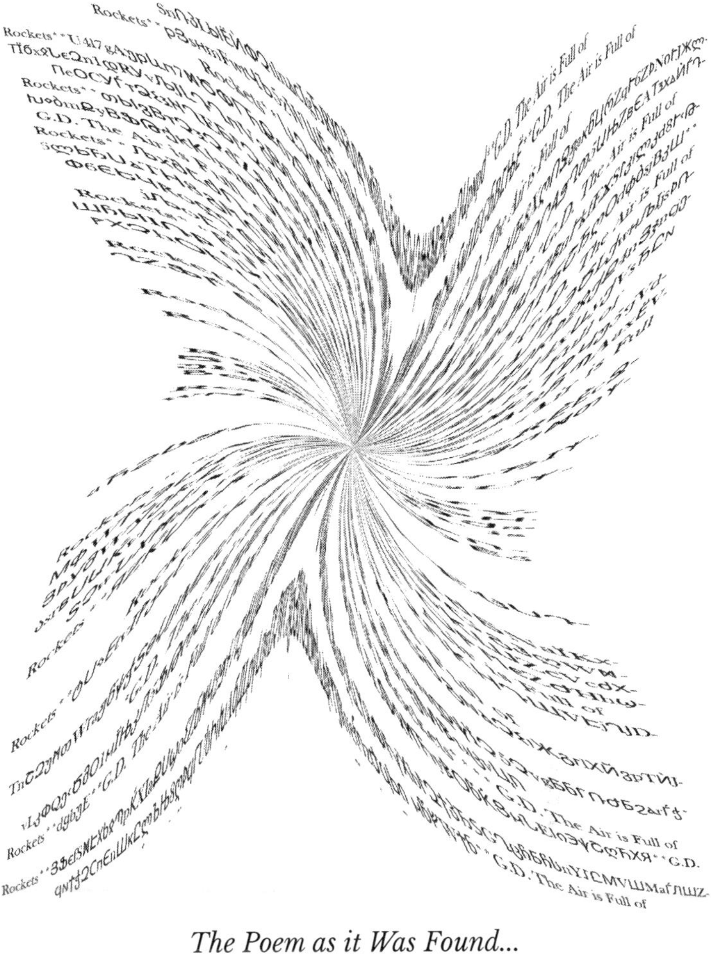

The Poem as it Was Found...

"My father was a watchmaker. He abandoned it when Einstein discovered time is relative. I would only agree that a symbolic clock is as nourishing to the intellect as a photograph of oxygen to a drowning man."

-Jon Osterman; Dr. Manhattan; Watchmen (2009)

"Perhaps the World is not Made, Perhaps Nothing is Made"

-Dr. Manhattan, Watchmen; Alan Moore (1986)

"Superman is Real, and He is American"

-Wally Weaver; Watchmen; Alan Moore (1986)

Part 3: Reality

Several decidedly horrific experiences shook me in the moments following my awakening from this dualistic redux of an earlier nightmare. Before even leaving my bed, after responding to the messages I had missed in my slumber, and after checking the usual social channels, I opened Twitter of all hellscapes. What I saw. Posted 23 minutes prior to my awakening shocked me. A headline detailing the monumental step of a watchdog group of nuclear scientists symbolically announcing the hands of the Doomsday Clock now stood at only 90 seconds to midnight. Or rather, that we are catastrophically close to annihilation by nuclear war. That the earth's destruction at the hand of nuclear fission stands only moments away into our future. The contrast, the sheer confirmatory horror of this, stirred me to my core.

I sat for a very long time on the edge of my bed, only in my underwear, staring into the blank space a quarter distance across the room. One hand on the bed the other in the fur of my sleepy dog. There were so many thoughts that I will try my best to collate them here.

Initially, I thought about death. Being a teacher of the subject, my mind goes there. Acute radiation sickness, lingering hunger, total incineration, all of it flashed in my mind. I drew then on training. For some reason, as an undergraduate, I took it upon myself to become certified in all but one of the US Government's FEMA School of Emergency Management courses on radiological emergency response. I started flashing through weather pattern predictive charts for fallout flow. Grays to Roentgens to Sieverts. Radiation ionizing bodies of water blue. The inner construction and operation of nuclear reactors. Chornobyl. Radiation burns. Metallic tastes in the mouth. The complete and total deconstruction of DNA via ionized gamma radiation. Potassium Iodide for the thyroid. Avoid milk and hair conditioner. Mind the flying glass. Seek shelter below ground. Decontaminate. Toxic air and poison water.

Suddenly it stopped as I noticed a warm and reassuring pressure on my leg. Denali, my three-year-old pup from the deserts of New Mexico, had roused himself from his sleep, knowing something might be wrong. He pressed into me, sitting on the floor and blinking sleep from his sad-looking eyes. He has a curious way of looking out the side of his eyes to make you think he is either very seriously concerned or judging you very harshly. I took it as a concern this time. I looked down at the little head lolling ever so slightly against my knee and I bent down to kiss his forehead. As I did, as my eyes met his in the distortion of the spatial properties of our skull shapes, I had two horrendous thoughts. First he would never understand a nuclear apocalypse. He was too sweet, too purely full of love and kindness and playful innocence to ever fully grasp the potential ending of everything. He was fascinated by snowflakes, squeaky toys, and table scraps. He couldn't understand the splitting of an atom and the wastelands such a split would and will create. I both envied his innocence in that kiss and felt an abject disgust with myself as a human being, having somehow been a part of the species that would create such a destructive power that those other creatures we live with would never be able to know or understand. They would simply cease to exist, become too ill to survive or starve in the barren nuclear winter. I then said something in a cracked and hoarse voice that still gave me chills weeks later: "Denali, I won't ever let you die in a nuclear holocaust. I promise." As I pressed my forehead tightly to his. He did not know what I said, but I did. *And it shocked me to my core.* I still don't know what that means. How do you tell someone who is basically your child that you will protect them from the inevitable? How do you tell a lie like that? Or rather, more darkly, was I lying? Did I mean I would stop the air being full of rockets? Or did I mean he and I would never live to die at the hands of Oppenheimer's Pandora? I still do not know. The ethics of that question linger in the dry winter air still.

Further, in my emergent consciousness, sitting in the hot tub at 1 am in the frigid winter, I again told my dogs I wouldn't let the nukes get them. And I pondered further the degree to which the inevitability of nuclear winter was or was not real. I fell into my 9th-grade obsession: Alan Moore's masterpiece of narrative dystopic fiction, Watchmen. To me, then, it was a story of the humanity of the superhero. It was the antithesis of Batman and Superman. Nite Owl, a hero, wasn't a superhero. He was Dan Dreiberg, the flabby washed-up has-been living off his dad's investment banking empire in New York City. Sally Jupiter was an aging alcoholic in South Florida. Edward Blake wasn't a superhero; he was an anti-hero paid by 4th term Richard Nixon's CIA to enact clandestine homicide across the world. Then I was enamoured with the idea of the hero, the helper, the 'good guys' being just people. No radioactive waste creating telekinesis or flight. No alien kids from Krypton. No Superhuman bat creatures beating up psychopathic clowns. No. There was a superhero in Watchmen, and his words resonated strongly then in that post-dream state stronger than the rest of it. Dr. Manhattan was a superhero by definition. Omnipotent, invincible, totally powerful over matter, time, reality and the cosmos. But he, too, in his own way, was a human with faults. He wasn't always Dr. Manhattan. He was Jon Osterman. A scientist seemingly chipped off the block of Oppenheimer playing god with intrinsic field generation. But where his humanity emerged was in the inverse of the human condition itself. He saw beyond the humanity. He stepped into a world wherein he called himself a puppet that could see the strings. He saw time as a continual mosaic of experience rather than a linear progression. Dr. Manhattan transcended the human/object conundrum of our anthropocentric systems of knowledge production to become 'higher' than humanity. He, in effect, achieved the apotheosis of Staying with the Trouble. He didn't just make kin with the cthuluscene; he transcended the string figures of entangled biological existence to see the earth as what it is to the scientific community. An infinitely small random projection of chances piled together to create and sustain everything from the petty dramas of the sex lives of former masked vigilantes to the complex existential threat of total mutually assured destruction. In his arch, Moore writes that Osterman somehow reconnects with his tether to earth through the realization that even out of pure evil, beauty can somehow flourish. That point always stuck to me as a 'cop-out' at the ripe wise age of a 9th grader. But now, in my reflective mood, having relived my own nuclear apocalypse, I see what he meant. Manhattan didn't return to earth to save it for our sake, he did it because he was asked to by someone he once loved. It was a beautifully poignant moment for me to reconcile the fact that all it took for the cosmological embodiment of nihilism to reconcile his loss of humanity in the only shred of humanity he had left: the capacity to love. It is there in the ebb and flow of the human condition, of the spatial and cosmic proportions of our existence, that we come to establish those connections that embalm some degree of meaning into our flesh long after our demise. It is in this that we are immortalizing the memories of both that which is good and that which is not. It is the scar tissue to the framed snapshot. We are a dualism of the capacities for both sheer horror and sheer beauty, and one often begets the other cyclically through the folds of time.

...

So there I am, beyond my hyper fixation on the question of who watches the watchmen, I find myself again questioning the nature of the world, this time as a social scientist. 90 seconds to midnight. What drove us here? I can easily take the route of the de-nuclearization advocate and point to FDR, the Manhattan Project, American Imperialism, the Cold War Arms Races and whatever Reagan's Star Wars fascination was. But it feels deeper than this. It feels more aligned with that classical dystopic fiction motif: that we are destined to destroy ourselves. But is the Terminator's reflection upon watching children play with toy guns in Judgment Day an accurate model of understanding where we are going? I am not sure. I am not sure I, as a social scientist or philosopher, place much stock in the assertion that we (humans) are somehow predetermined to facilitate our own destruction. Dostoyevsky, in a note from the underground, simply offers: "I say let the world go to hell, but I should always have my tea." But where in our condemnation of humanity or of the determinism of our destiny of destruction may we lay our claims to reconciliation of truth?

In reality, the path to nuclear annihilation, the path to midnight, 90 seconds away, is not paved with wanton humanity. But with a horrific inverse of that state of existence. What leads us to 90 seconds? It is not the human capacity for compassion, love, lust, joy, whimsy, wonder or surprise. It is rather the human capacity of a select few humans to establish a trans-humanist perspective of existence. That is the hero of those watchers of the Watchmen, Dr. Manhattan, the man who had experienced everything to the point of transcending humanity itself, relays himself in grounded reality to be the harbinger of our coming extinction. That is to say, the select few of us so inundated with the milieu of total access to power, money, capital, and position are those who have lost their connection to that cradle from which they emerged. This is not to take the sophomoric stance that it is 'just billionaires' who are to blame (as aside, real estate agents are just as bad if not worse than billionaires, sociologically speaking...). Rather it is a careful alchemy of several factors.

It is the de-humanization of the self, and within that a reflective state of depersonalization and a loss of the humanity of the individual themselves. It is a transcendence to some post-humanist existential void of being that we cannot yet fully comprehend with means of knowing only grounded in human thought. That is to say that those responsible for our march to midnight are something beyond the human condition. They are atomically evolved from the species being of the elemental traits of human existence. When we, in scholarly circles, on our weekend campus walks in our wool coats in the west, decry "late stage" capitalism, we tend to land on such things as native advertising, the runaway neoliberalism of higher education and "affordable housing." In short, the theory circles I have witnessed are often concerned with the worries of the graduate student looking for a studio space big enough for their Kant library.

In actuality, the late-stage capitalistic development we must fear far more than exorbitant rent prices or the lack of tenure track positions is the reality that in the post-atomic age, as a product of the Cold War, we have collectively instituted a new reality wherein the alienation of the species being of the individual has come to such a point that it is no longer an alienation from labour or the human elements of leisure and creativity, but humanity itself. It is such that in the post-war world, with the white-collaring of the West and the demonization of the red East, we find ourselves in a curious and mortally precarious position socially. That position is that as a function of the fission of the atom, we are now living in a world of mutually assured destruction, and as a functional madness of that reality, we consider this to be the strongest reason for peace in our time. That is to say that not only have we allowed such a world to evolve wherein the individuals in power have lost their humanity entirely to this neo-humanist species, but we rest assured that mutually assured destruction is a deterrent to global annihilation. That is, the very fact that we may as well send an equal sky of rockets back towards the oncoming oblivion G.D. was out running serves to be the very thing keeping us in a state of cognitive fog over the very real and horrific threat to global existence.

When we distill the situation to its very core elements, there exists in each official residence of each nuclear power an individual that is not human. They are not reptilian as the rabbit holes would have us believe, but the truth is, to me, far more terrifying. They are humans who have forgotten the experience of humanity. Wherein individual lives are now statistical calculations on daily intelligence briefs, where acceptable losses figure into contingency plans with the ultimate goal in the event of the oncoming winter to sequester the 'leader' of a given nation to a 'safe zone' to ensure their survival. In the blink of an eye, millions will die, and millions more will linger in illness for days and weeks before liquefying in their beds on stretchers or in the radioactive streets. New York, Chicago, and Los Angeles, the main coastal centers of US social and political capital, will be laid waste, and the chief goal of the established neoliberal state is the continuance of itself as a body of control rather than the preservation of humanity as a whole. It is a transcendent species to be able to so callously face the music of the sky of rockets and instead worry about how we may continue to manage the military-industrial response to the new ways of the doomed world.

In dystopic fiction, we enjoy the idea of the shifted government or the fallen state. In dystopic delusion, the 'preppers' know the state will fall. They know that it is all them on their own, just masculinity, munitions and Country Roads. But the reality is far, far more terrifying. The state's goal is survival. It is survival at the expense of the populace. Some may say that a state needs a constituency, but we are far beyond the nature of the state as traditional sociology or Marxism understands it to be. It is a living, breathing, interactive apparatus of existential validity. The state no longer needs us. It is in this regard that the dystopic fictional future will not happen. We will not descend into a whimsical state as depicted in The Hunger Games, nor will we have purges or other such young adult or popcorn-worthy futurities. We will also not have a world of sparsely populated doomsday bunkers or pop-up shanty towns in the fallout wastes. If our recent experimentation with a lethal global catastrophe is anything to go on, it is evidence of the fact that the wells of the state are deep enough to sustain a stream of normality in the face of unprecedented human crisis.

That is to say, the reality of the late-stage atomic capitalism we exist in is such that we will continue on business as usual. If next Friday, intercontinental missiles cross the Atlantic in both directions, if the Cold War ignites into a scorched Earth, if cities are levelled and lives dissolve into flashes of hydrogen fission, there will still be the assumption that we must carry on as we had by Monday. In the areas not immediately in the blast zone, there will be an urging for calm. For trust in the state and the leader who fled the eastern seaboard for the safety of the middle of the nation. There will be speeches made on the radio urging good American citizens to, with proper cautions, step out into the new age and perform as they have before to build back the world in flames. The electrical employee who is a massive doomsday prepper in the western US will see images of DC under a mushroom cloud on Fox News and wake up the next morning to go repair the grid. He won't squirrel to his bunker; he won't reach for his AR-15 to stalk the radioactive dunes to fend off the roving gangs of mutant marauders. He won't do this because he, too, has changed.

The atomic age, aside from radiologically changing the atmosphere, the ocean and the air, has existentially changed us. People my age do not recognize this change, but there are those still alive who have lived it. There are people who, as children, never had nightmares about the mushroom cloud, only to develop those fears in their 20s or 30s. Oppenheimer was wrong in that we have not become destroyers of worlds, but instead, at the incineration of Trinity, we opened a new era of the end of empathy. He is not the destroyer of worlds, nor is he death. He is simply, in that moment in history, the harbinger of the death of the human spirit within itself. He is the forebear of a new collective and genetically inheritable psychopathology of spirit. It is beyond the death of self, though; it is an evolution of the self into something far more terrible. A self that is devoid of the memory of the existence of other selves, of the ability to recognize and order the external reality as real beyond the tides of the established reality of the institutional states of being we navigate. It is a self that has seen the selves of others vaporized in a flash of superheated air at the leading edge of the shockwave. It is a self that has forgotten its humanity and, with that, forgotten its tethering subjectivity to the ways of life in the world. It is a self devoid of love and the capacity for loss. It is the shelled self left lost and without a sense of directionality in the capacity to empathize with the existence of life beyond the state. It is a totalitarianism of the individual and a total imperialism of the species being.

We now, at 90 seconds, find ourselves mutations of the human we claim to be. We are not of this earth, but we are rather beings of the social forces we constructed. We are norms of the norms, and by and for the preservation of the state and the institution. We are an assimilated amalgam of collective inevitable despairs in the face of Armageddon.

Chapter 3 (SPLIT)

Hast du etwas Zeit für mich?

Dann singe ich ein Lied für dich

Von 99 Luftballons

Auf ihrem Weg zum Horizont

Denkst du vielleicht grad an mich?

Dann singe ich ein Lied für dich

Von 99 Luftballons

Und, dass sowas von sowas kommt

Epilogue: Hope in the Ashes and Iodine

We are not doomed.

That is not to say that our situation is not dire. Nor is it to discount the worrisome transcendental evolution of the human spirit to the post-atomic creature lacking the empathy of humanity. Rather, it is to say that we do have the capacity for further evolution of the self, and there are indeed tools to resist the encroaching neoliberalization of the human spirit. In addition to the tools at our feet, there lies too an inherent capriciousness in the human spirit to radically adapt a form of existence in the interest of survival that denies or negates the previous horrors that preceded our tragedy.

This is not the naïve positionality of my grandmother's generation, wherein No More Nukes and the touting and facilitation of disarmament are the lauded solutions. Disarmament was great, but with the rising efficiency of the scientific horrors in G.D.'s sky, there is less of a question of quantity in the eyes of destruction.

No.

Rather the way out of this for us lies in two very simple yet nigh implausible shifts in the collective nature of the self. First, we must strive, above all else, individually, to cultivate, discover, and perpetuate a working cosmological sense of grounding in our realities. We have to evolve beyond the objective notion of our being today. That is, we have to reframe the means by which we consider ourselves superior and removed from the natural world. We have to move to recognize ourselves as subjects in the subjective world. That is, we must let go of the most sacred thing in our internal scripts of functionality: human supremacy. We need to evolve beyond this modality of existence that places humans at the 'top' of the natural world. How do we do this? How do divorce ourselves from the collective ego of the apex species? The answer is simple textually but monumentally complex practically. We simply need to realize that we see the world and understand all of it through a system of knowledge production that is human with no external or alternative contribution.

What does this mean? It means that all knowledge, truths, and facts of our existence, from our bank balance to the understanding of the cosmos, are all filtered directly through a totally human lens. There is no capacity for us to consider or conceptualize anything we process or experience as anything other than human, as human is the default form of functional processing for our brains. We cannot comprehend nature as a tree does, nor can we experience a rainstorm as a rock does. But, with all of our limitations in human-centric knowledge, we do have a unique capacity beyond our other subjective experiencers of reality: we can imagine. That is, we can adapt our processing of the world creatively on the scope and basis of anything we set our minds to. We can, in a word, imagine life as a rock, a whale or a bird. And it is a powerful tool for this imagination. Just as it can create human scenarios of lust, prosperity, success, despair and failure in our mind's eyes, it can create an empathetic living dreamscape of existential transference to the point that we can, if we really try, project our inner-most thoughts into a trans-species means of composing knowledge and identity.

I cannot know life as my dog, but I can imagine it. I can watch how he plays, explores and communicates empathy, sadness, pain or excitement, and I can imagine his worldview. Does this mean that I can transcend my human bias? Of course not. I think that he thinks how I think. I look to his experience as I do my own: visually, auditory, contextually, and with the implementation of human-centric and created linguistics. Every element of our existence is founded upon some degree of processing and communicating the world and the ways we process our experiences and commit them to analytical memory allows us a frightfully limited means of experiencing reality. I am unsure what Denali's memories are. I do not know how he recalls, recognizes, communicates, or experiences his daily existence. I am unaware of even how he perceives the passage of days, months, seasons or time itself. But in the brief forays into at least reflecting on this limitation of my being and the broadly unknowable existence of life in his mind, I can get as close to the escape velocity needed to transcend anthropocentric thinking.

Within this example, it, too, still represents a 'safe' incursion beyond the objective being. I choose to empathetically imagine the existence of life itself in another being we would classify as 'sentient'. Sentience is inherently a human-centric modality of thought in that we are oddly able to classify such experiencers of life as sentient or not. I question often the arrogance of this power we seem to innately and operationally incorporate into our daily lives. It is odd to me that we can so confidently say that my dog is sentient but that the tree he is lying underneath is not. Oxford's English Dictionary offers the skeletal definition of sentience being the ability to see or feel things through the senses. With the stupidly outdated unhelpful addendum: "Man is a sentient being". Patriarchal nonsense aside, one must question, as a human being, to what degree does Oxford or any other ordination of human construction have the power to establish the very basis for what counts as the acceptable experience of reality? Webster goes so much further to say that sentience is inherent in the possession of senses and the subsequent experience of 'things' through senses. It is in this regard again I must question-who are we to say what is and is not sentient. Are we not arrogant for having constructed the term itself in the first place?

If I were inclined -and I may very well be at a later date-to embark upon a full-fledged Foucauldian archaeology of sentience, I may find myself walking through the linguistic and epistemological histories of the human condition to learn specifically where and when we decided that via this hallowed possession of sentience that we and other animal beings possess more of a richly nuanced experience of reality than 'non-sentient' species. Rather too, we must not forget that some animals are sentient and others are not. A sea sponge, we have decided is not sentient. A sheep is. The possession of a nervous system seems to be the scientific hurdle to overcome to be allowed into the sentient species club.

If the simple ownership of a nervous system is enough to allow a being to experience reality, then the question may also be posed, to what degree do those that have evolved beyond the human condition, the transcendental neo-capitalist machines, experience reality? At that point, at the decline of Dr. Manhattan as he teleports to Mars, do we question sentience as simply the being within reality? Is sentience not something more localized to the experience of the reality of the life we have on the planet we currently exist on? That is not to say that the humans on Mars in the distant future will not be sentient, but it is to question the degree to which the humans no longer feel as if they are a part of earth count as sentient. As illustrated by the dictionary definitions, we tend to be the ones with the power to decide who counts as sentient, and with this there emerge two questioning points: what about the sentient creatures we deny sentience to already? And to what degree does it take one to be so far disconnected from reality that sentience is negligible?

To the first point, all we must do in order to recognize the fragility of the definition of sentience and the horror of having the power to ascribe it to humans is to look toward the industrialization of animal agriculture.

Collectively, as a species, a vast portion of us have decided through socialization and desensitization that a vast majority of the sentient species on this earth are less sentient than us, and some to such a degree that they exist solely for the purpose of being consumed by us, the "higher" being. All one must do is take one very shallow look into the practices of industrial farming to see that we do not treat 'livestock' as sentient. We can't physically do it, to know that we enact as much horror and bloodshed on millions of animals a week, animals that are experiencing that trauma actively through their sentience would destroy us existentially, I think. There is a collective ignorance of this fact and a collective decision as humans to establish a hierarchy of being so violently human-centric that we can ignore the inhumane slaughter of millions of animal bodies a month to sustain a global trillion-dollar industry.

Secondarily, to question then to what degree we must be removed from the experience of humanity to negate the existence of the sentience of non-human actors, we can see that it does not take much in the way of socialization in the world we currently inhabit to become so totally lost to the wonder and sentience of the natural world. We, in our dichotomy of sentient/inanimate, have created a very simple model of being wherein the self, the individual and the human collective stand in some strange precedence in comparison to the infinite natural components of our world that sustain our day-to-day existence. Even in our most enlightened approaches to this problem, even when we are actively working to combat climate change, we do so from an anthropocentric modality. We look at it as an existential threat to our ways of living. We see the acidification of the oceans as an "us" problem, the deforestation of the Amazon a threat to our atmosphere. Do we not consider the fish in the sea or the trees in the forest as those also experiencing the oncoming slow death of the planet? No.

Do we consider ourselves to be alone in our apocalypses? Absolutely. Even in the core thematic focus of this work, do we consider the charring of the trees or the extinction of the pigeons in the large cities to be of consequence when we hit DEFCON 1? Of course not. Do I? No. I think about my own mortality, as do many other 'sentient' beings, but the course of our evolution beyond the post-atomic age world is that we must try to empathetically imagine that those things deemed unworthy of the sentience we name them with are also capable in ways unknowable to us to experience the same existential worry that we experience.

It is now our task in the face of 90 seconds to try to approximate the knowledge of the unknowable in our world and to empathetically take that unknowable state of being into consideration of our own. Consider how our interactions and reactions with the state of the world may come to impact those natural actors whose 'voices' we cannot nor will ever hear or understand. We have to divorce ourselves from the narcissism of the human spirit and recognize that the age of our dominance over this domain is over, and the only way to exist into any extended futurity is to reconcile the insignificance of our sentience in the scope of all that we share the natural world with. We have to stop seeing salamanders, stones and shrubs beneath us and recognize that in the face of Armageddon, we are all simply atoms waiting to return to the cradle of our celestial creation.

Where is the hope?

The second fundamental tool in our survival comes in one singular piece of hopeful optimism that, while thin, exists very core to the idea that we may someday never have to feel the fear that G.D. did in his spiral. That hope, quite simply stated, is that the humans that directly control our nuclear fate are still humans. I do not mean presidents, generals, prime ministers or despots. I mean the humans that ultimately sit responsible for the destruction of humanity. The crews of the planes that radiologically decimated Japan in 1945 did not know what they were dropping. Because of them though, today's generation of fission gatekeepers do recognize the implications of what they may do. They know the consequences of that button being pushed regardless of the orders coming over the wire. On all sides. It is a paper-thin comfort to place the hope of the world's survival in the hands of someone I do not know who I 'trust' to 'do the right thing' in that critical moment. Granted, there is not much speaking to this as with each passing day, we grow closer to the individuals who evolved beyond humanity, being capable more or less of detonating a world-ending chain of events individually. But it remains that at least in the silos of nuclear nations, there still exists someone with a family, someone who doesn't want to see the world in flames. Someone who will resist the order to initiate a first strike. I am neither religious nor spiritual, but if I were, I would offer some kind of faithful transference of strength to the characters of those officers. I would hope that, at the moment, the human spirit overcomes the orders of the madness on the other end of the radio.

Is this enough to keep us safe? No. Can it help you fall asleep after reading G.D.'s poem? Sometimes. All we may establish in this regard is that the singular capacity of the individual in a moment of stress, arguably a single individual, rests between us and midnight. All I can hope is that the individual there at the desk can maintain a memory of their lives beyond the uniform to the point that they don't initiate an irreversible series of events. That being said, all I can imagine is that right now, in every top military office on the subject, there is an attempt to try the best they can to automate the process to remove the capacity for human resistance.

That is the path of late-stage capitalism. To alienate the final bastion of nuclear safety from their human labour.

Heaven help us.

Chapter 4

Ascent into the Wildwoods of Serenity in Safety

"I tried to discover, in the rumour of forests and waves, words that others could not hear, and I pricked up my ears to listen to the revelation of their harmony."

-Gustave Flaubert, November

It is not a new leaf to regular readers of mine that my work has quite often, in its presentation, dwelled on the curious state of human melancholia, particularly of and about challenges of the heart. I have found in my professional and personal meanderings into the written word that I am often drawn to the despair of being like a moth to the flame. There is something there in the darkness, something comforting. Something that, against assumptions and conventional wisdom, binds us closer to our humanity, especially so in the most despairing moments of experience that stand the strongest chances of fragmenting our own humanity to a thousand pieces strewn across the brief moment of time we are fortunate or unfortunate to existence concurrently with. To say I enjoy despair is not quite accurate, rather I find the despair I have experienced to have become so familiar to me that it almost occupies a place in the pantheon of characters in my life that I have the pleasure of greeting it not as a friend, but as a regularly known acquaintance. Milgram called these phenomenological phantasms in our daily living "familiar strangers". The people we see at our bus stop every morning, the individuals we know exist on the periphery of our daily being, but in such a place that we never truly know them or even speak to them, but curiously, we miss them when their absence is noticeable. This is the curiosity of the existence of both my nightmares and my most pleasant dreams. Marked experiential moments in life that both carry with them the antithesis of one another to the point of clouding both the good and bad into a milieu of past and present worries, triumphs, pains and pleasures. It is in this curiosity that I often feel myself existing out of time, out of place and decidedly within the inverse of what we may call a social reality. An a-social reality where the world stands still, rain flows upwards to the sky, days become nights, and the timely experience of the joys of life slip into some indescribable form of turgidity that I cannot nor dare not attempt to investigate.

Somewhere in my mind, these excursions to the dark take the form of an ancient and misty wood. Somewhere where the kingdoms of existence are dominated not by the flourishing life of nature but by the subtle music of decay, where the fungi and mycelium are the monarchy and the sauntering stag on the misty path is nothing but a temporary interloper soon to be somehow incorporated into the golden hue of the rejuvenation of the trees that stand ancient sentinel over the mushroom kingdom down below. It is a concert of silence in these woods, a place where there is a dark magic beyond the shadows of the tree trunks, where there is a rhythmic pulsing of some ancient and unknowable heartbeat that straddles the line between benevolent guide and cannibalistic beast. It is half human in the wood, where one may see an occasional bare footprint in the loam, but where one cannot tell if that print is thousands of years old or if just beyond the crossroads in the murk, there is another traveller somewhere in the dark. The dark itself is alive, a being transcendent of time and place and far older than the universe itself, as before there was light, there was an absence of it.

I listened to the reading of an essay yesterday, an essay on fear. Not fear of the tangible. Not a fear of the growing frequency at which the skies are dotted with rockets, nor the political darkness that pushes ever closer to the total and indomitable extinction of the temporal interlopers we call humanity. There was no cadence to the fear of the end. Instead, it was an exploration of the fear of the unknown. The unknown, which is, quite sadly, a construction of ours. It is a compounding force of nature to not know what exists up the path or beyond the trail and it is ours to claim as descendent. The unknown, you see, only exists once we start to know. When we are children, before we know the world through words, when we experience only so far as we are able to do so physically, we see that we are not afraid of the unknown. We possess an explorer's nature. But once we utter the first word, it is the beginning of our creation of a world beyond the knowable and in that, a world of worries. To name the existence we inhabit is to also name the existence beyond what we can experience. To create a world beyond feeling, experience and history to only know it as a collection of named wordless choruses out in the wilds. To a child, the forest is anything. To me, now inundated with far too many words for too many horrors, the forest is a place, at least in the mindscape of its construction, a place where the lurking of the woodland deaths out beyond the trail are ones to consider at every turn. Linguistic development places us in the space of not only knowing our world and the other world, but it allows us to know ourselves. It places a central understanding of reality through the lens of the "I" problem. Because when you are a you that exists, there comes the challenging twofold problem of there being other existing people, and the fact that if in the same case of the darkness of the wood, you exist, then there must also be a nonexistence. Naming the world pushes us further into the realm of existential nonbeing than nonbeing itself because now we know that there is a place to never know and that unknowing fosters a knowing fear. The fear of the unknown, my biologically inclined colleagues may say is an inherited ancestral coding onto the fabric of our DNA wherein we are to lay waiting in anticipation for the predator on the horizon. Yet, as I am sure my readers will empathize: the scariest predators of the modern age do not even have teeth.

These modern wild unknowns haunt my soul deep within. They are the noises in the forest environs that my mind walks and wanders, and I am no stranger to the toothless bites they leave on the psyche.

In another turn, unsurprising to the readers in this space, my soul is not without its scars. We all experience the world through a lens of pain to a varying degree, but it is in the quiet cold of this autumn morning with the radiator next to me extolling a calming warmth that I am lost again in the reflection of my own horrific tapestry of soulbound scarring. At this moment in human history, beyond the inky windows of my homestead, there is true terror in the unknowns manifesting in a thousand explosions across the globe. War brews, destruction is imminent, and somewhere, the flash priority reports spell out a certain doom for the age of humanity that exists ever so carefully in the expanse just to the left of possibility. As I write, we have, to a degree, survived a global plague marked by death in untold magnitudes. The iron bear of Russia again rears its head towards imperialistic expansion, and centuries-old conflicts erupt in the Holy Land. But here, in the half-warmth of the dark side of the morning, my mind travels much closer to home. I reflect today not on the global maladies, as I cannot, in my current state of being, even begin to process the empathetic responsibility to think beyond that which is solely in my own mind.

I have critiqued the notion in the past that humans are social animals, and I still hold a degree of contempt for the 'social creatures' motif, but there is some truth in it in that the social, the fabric that builds our interactional symbolic reality out beyond the waves of conscious existence is very much indeed a powerful force in the shaping of being and nonbeing. The capacity others have to inflict scars on our souls, as well as lend healing kisses to that scar tissue, is nothing other than magnificent. It is why I have dedicated my professional life to the investigation of the social question, not of trends, groups or organizations, but of the nature of the capacity for the other person to either heal or wound us in the falling of words across the ear. It is such a uniquely human experience to love, to be hurt, to feel loss, to experience lust, as well as the absence of that loss. In our modern existence, these feelings have, quite unfortunately, been co-opted not by the practitioners of social exploration nor the chroniclers of human experience but by the influential commodification of our new social reality: social media. The places where these experiences are collected, documented, stored and published for the world to see and for us to feel a degree of commodity validation from the 'familiar strangers' out in the internet waves. Love is no longer the feelings we experience privately, but it is something to be marketed out into the dawn. This is not something I will lead a charge against, nor will I, in my meagre ramblings, solve it. Instead, whatever minimal expansive notes I can offer herein exist as a love letter to loving, to hurting, and to healing in the private spheres of our own minds because, despite the nature of the social world at our thumbtips, it is still a shared experience inside our minds to feel heartbreak, hope, insanity, infatuation, love, lust and triumphs of the soul.

I am no stranger to the experience of all of these, as none of us are, but in my own reflections on my experiences, I have come to the conclusion that I feel I have weathered far too many storms as of late and, in the greatest of all philosophical findings I present the following:

I am so tired. All the time. Physically, intellectually, emotionally, socially, everywhere, all at once. It is a lingering malaise that drips ever slowly into every single elementary attempt to function, let alone create, ponder, or compose.

It becomes a poison of our time I think. A perpetual state of nonexistence while still somehow loathsomely inhabiting the world after all the struggle and strife, we still, to a point, carry with us the complicated life on our shoulders despite the screaming agony of our souls for a simple break. It's heartbreaking to a degree the path we have come, and while I can only speak for myself, I have found that often, in the forest of my mind, the unknown that creeps ever closer in the mist is not something unknowable but rather something unpredictable. Where in the path of life will I find myself bleeding this time next year? Is it the same wound I suffer now in the cold nights alone, or will it be a new melting point? It seems that in my own experience, the years have bled together into a cyclical pattern of despondent despair, to which a colleague once warmly remarked: "Don't ever stop being the depressed sociologist; it's what makes you my favourite." It was a warm, sentimental compliment at the time between two professionals splitting off into new paths, but the words still haunt me to this day. I somehow fell into a pattern of survival where to make sense of the world of pain I existed in was to embrace the darkness, to live in the void, and to go on further to discuss, dissect and explore the darkness. In some grandiose reflection, a fair percentage of the body of my work is such that it provides darkness to the light, and somehow, somewhere, someone finds relatability in that content. Is it healthy when your work elicits more questions of 'Are you ok' than they do praises? Is not philosophy the most pretentiously asinine field, said lovingly from a practitioner.

The conclusion we may draw from this is not that there is no hope, that we are collectively doomed, or that Instagram is the devil (it is, though), but that in all of this swirling pain, confusion, and grey murky darkness, the forest itself is still out there.

And what is to be done about a fear of the unknowable unknowns?

Well,

We must strive into the wild unknowns, explore, wander, and encapsulate the spiritual sociality of the wooded thicket around us. We must learn its rhythms, appreciate the scents of decay and change, revere the trees standing sentinel and respect with warmth the other plays of countless occult sentience that occupy this mortal plane with us for however long or briefly we may be destined to do so.

In a word.

We must

Explore.

From the Forest Grows a Hearth:

"The world is full of obvious things which nobody by any chance ever observes."

— Arthur Conan Doyle; The Hound of the Baskervilles

For as long as I can recall, I have heard the sentiment that 'travel broadens your horizons'. I have taken issue with this idea for quite some time given the simple reality that the horizon is the widest and most infinite compositional element of our vision. In a less poetic sense, this idea has often been passed to me by people of a higher social station, extolling the virtues of first-class transatlantic flights to wondrous European summers lived in the nicest of second homes, without the fear of a card being declined and the ensuing strandedness that comes from being up a creek without a paddle as the saying goes. As such, it bred in me a reflective position that travel itself is not the broadening horizons that it is extolled to be. Being that the horizon is always with us, and always the widest point in our field of view, I feel that it is almost intuitive that the horizons of our experiences can be broadened wherever it is that we exist. There is nothing to say that the situational experience of the individual cannot itself be transcendental in its mundanity. The beauty of social experience is that it is wholly ours and wholly unique despite the situational context it emerges in. I cannot be so presumptuous to say that every social experience is transformative in the positive sense, nor would I be so bold to say that all travel is positively transcendental, instead the truth lies somewhere between the two.

This is to say that we may embrace and love the everyday life we experience in a way that establishes its transformative power over our experiences while also treating our adventures beyond the norms as a means of recognizing that ours is an experience that is not transformed by a change in context but enhanced to an infinite degree. While it is true that for those able, travel on an infinite per diem is most likely transcendent, I wouldn't know.

What I do know is that it is not the contextual localities of our travel that leave indelible marks on our souls but rather the people we see, meet, and experience travel with. It is then not the act of leaving home that pushes our experiences out into the world of novelty, it is instead the social interactions we build along the way. The people we fly to see, that we hit the road with, that we wander into the mists with. These are the instances of magic in travel, in leaving the comfort of one's routine and stepping out into the dawn with a trusted adventuring companion.

In the past three weeks I have wandered through six countries outside of the warmth and safety of my autumnal Colorado nest. I filled out a page in the passport, slept in post-soviet airports, been followed by some unnamed secret service, been colder and more drenched to the bone I have ever been, walked across cities in the night, experienced all that leads the 20-something Instagram page to astronomical levels of engagement.

Were my horizons broadened?

By the simple act of physical movement across oceans and borders? No.

By the social experiences met with people, to a degree.

To understand what I feel, I feel I must first establish what I am experiencing in retrospect. Being that I travelled to lands that I study academically, my experiential uncovering of their secrets was wrapped into the foil of having done the research remotely ahead of time. Which is a deeply arrogantly academic thing to say. And I will not say that previous research lends one to appreciate climbing to the top of Gediminas' Tower in Vilnius, nor does it undercut the majesty of Klaipeda at sunrise. But there is a wonder of seeing this places having lived their stories in the written word for years. It allows one to fall into a place and experience it in a living sense. To not feel lost, but to feel somehow a part of the world as it exists 5000 miles from home. This is how I like to travel, to feel not as an interloper in a space but as someone just going about their day. It is a routine I tend to try to experience myself in any way I can, wherever I am. To be just another person in the roll call of faces at any given place. This, to me, cultivates an air of familiarity and calm.

While it may sound cliched, I try to embody the sense of wanton wanderlust embodied in the literary character of Jerry Westerby in John LeCarre's The Honourable Schoolboy. A shambling academically minded journalist living out of a suitcase, haphazardly bouncing from locale to locale in buckskin boots. Always the outsider, pleasantly branded as such, but still somehow knowing when where and why the locals do what they do. Maybe this is a reflection of growing up incredibly introverted on the fringe of town, where I always felt a pull to observe first, then act later. To blend into the fabric of where I existed as an experiencer of reality that no one could question when I myself was in waters uncharted previously in my experience. As a teenager, this was the lofty identity I gave myself, and my experience was muddled with the trial and error that comes from introverted teenage ego, but as I have grown, I have found that for me, the silence of observation, the quiet of blending in, and the subtleties of experience create the most profound joy in experiencing the world. Maybe it is the sociological imagination as Mills so carefully captured, a blending of history and experience into a lens of seeing the world in a way that grants not just understanding, but empathy. This is the core notion of dearly departed Dorothy Smith's Standpoint Theory, the idea that in order to make an insightful understanding of a given social experience, context, problem or history, we must place ourselves firmly in an empathetic role, something approaching participation, without the loss of investigative self. Something that not only breeds empathy, but that requires it.

It is the empathetic openness to experience that firmly establishes a sense of regularity in travel. Is it needed? No. Is it possible always? Of course not, but in some semblance an attempt to establish a relatability to the people you see, even if they are those familiar strangers becomes tantamount to a positive experience. In this regard, the travel itself is not the act that 'broadens' one's horizons; instead, it is the travel that completes the arc of having broadened one's horizons in the act of empathy prior. It is this openness that when coupled with a determined interactional care of self that predates exploration, that we come to find ourselves among the others and within ourselves simultaneously.

The same is true for daily escapes into the wild unknowns, for the need for an empathetic, transhumanistic experiential recovery for the unknowable wildernesses out in the world beyond.

To stand in a forest is to stand in a forest. To wander the paths of that wilderness into the unknowable escapes is another matter entirely. We cannot expect to lose ourselves in the woods if we have not yet prepared ourselves to do so. Contrary to the slew of self-help books on the shelves today 'forest bathing' is not something we can simply just do. We are not able to rekindle ancient primality and meld seamlessly into the wooded mysteries around us. There is indeed some work required to do so.

How, then, do we do that? What is the process for cultivating a standpoint of the forest? Where and how do we find the tools needed to step barefoot into the moss and experience the life of lives out beyond our internal reality? It lies in a simple but horrifically complex notion: letting go of our humanity.

Donna Haraway and other contemporary theorists explore the notion of the Anthropocene, a term relating to where we currently exist, the human-dominated era. But the question comes: what exists after the Anthropocene? Where does the world and its inhabitants go in a linear progression towards the fall of humanity? Some will argue for an emergent Technoscene, a world dominated by a technological worldview, a paradigm dependent upon and constructed by the perceptual lens of the technological marvels we have constructed. Views on this future range from the utopian world of Star Trek where technology and humanity exist in harmonious inter-dependence, to the dystopian cyberpunk world of total dominion over humanity by techno-corporate entities that push the bounds of capitalism and biopower into terrifying realities. Still some look towards a different futurity all together. Haraway very eloquently presents the idea of the Cthuluscene or a world where the natural is demystified in its objectivity and granted a degree of subjective perceptual agency in the interwoven collective life of all things.

This is an interactional reality I tend to gravitate towards more, and within the subjectivity of the natural world, we find that tool that allows us to walk into the woods with empathy, to see the path at our bare feet and recognize its quiet beauty as a reality all its own. This notion transcends simple respect for the 'outdoors' and instead places the individual in a situational context where we are no longer the masters holding dominion over life in the wilds. We are no longer apex but instead a fellow traveller on the road of existence. This placement of the individual as collective, not as dominator over the world allows for two very key developments in our understanding of the world in its entirety. First, we are able to dislocate ourselves from the hierarchies indemnified in centuries of oppression of the land, and this dislocation allows for a new sense of locality in the misty unknowns. If we can recognize that rather than a forest of resources, animals, plant life, etc. what unfolds out beyond us is a collective symphonic interpolation of the mysteries of the cosmos, we come to recognize a critically important factor: we are not alone in the universe. Not in the sense of extraterrestrial life, but in the sense that there is an infinitude of worlds at our feet, between our toes and on that ever-romanticized horizon. Just as we may travel to new locales recognizing their uniqueness and compounding our traveller status with the working knowledge to empathetically exist within them, we too must travel on into the wildernesses of our exploration with the sense of grand respect for something far older, far more mystical and far more agentic than we give it credit for.

Second, we must recognize that the manifestation of the forest, the unknown, the territory explored must exist in a place of socially symbolic surrender on our parts. We have to let go of our status as the creators of our own systems of knowing and being. We must ignore the desire, the strong primal urge to order things in front of us, to name, to define, to make known. We, much like in the discussion of creating the unknown, distance ourselves, not from the unknown but from the compulsion to know. Before one can step out into the world and experience the transcendence of self that comes from the curious condition of the moss in between one's toes, one must, above all else, let go of the sense that we both know and understand the moss itself. How? How do we do this, how do we let go of the most sacred element of human ego? The centralization of our experience as the only valid experience is, in a word, both simple and frustratingly difficult to shed. We may begin by asking the critical question that plagued Thoreau in Walden: why go into the woods? From here we may ask ourselves the deeper question: what of the words of the woods? Where in our experience have we lost the capacity to understand the language of trees, rocks, moss, decay? How can we process the nature of nature without the capacity to do so in a way that leans on linguistics for description? We have to let go. We have to embrace the unknown in a way wholly counter to the humanity we have socialized into our being since those moments post-birth when we began to name the world. Is there a way to do this effectively? Maybe.

Revert to your sense. Taste the air. Smell the decay. Feel the moss. Balance on the stone. Walk, touch, see, hear. This is the beginning. Do not describe, do not classify. Train your mind to experience without classification. To walk and wander in the world as an observer of the tactile materiality of the sprawling unknowns ahead. Sprint towards the trail but as you do so, do not thinking in direction, distance, velocity. Instead, think in experiences. Do not name the experiences, simply experience them. Feel the cold beneath you, hear the whistles of the wind in the trees, smell the careful petrichor of the mists on the glen.

This is the trajectory of the true wanderer to experience that which is describable and instead make the choice to let it exist in the ether of the unspoken, the void of the unknown and the chapel of the unnamed.

Experience is experienced. Knowledge is named. The forest is experience, not knowledge.

We cannot wander while knowing, and we cannot knowingly wander.

Into the Clouds in Good Company

Or...

On the Curious Therapy of Wandering The Scottish Highlands with a Good Friend

"For to love friendship, it is not enough to know how to bear the other in mourning; one must love the future."

-Jacques Derrida

With this in mind, we may now return to the story of my own melancholia. Something I sit neatly with as an old friend. We share many a conversation by firelight, comforting each other in the cold embrace of the coming winter. It seems that my unique pathways through the forests of my mind have led me to an existence where I thrive in the darkness before the mortals awake, both psychologically and physically. There is something in a dark existence that cleans the world out beyond, where in the intimacy of experiencing one's own troubles, one tends to strive further outward in search of that which may, even if for the briefest of moments, layer in some gold into the grey.

My affair with my melancholia is something that has at times driven works from my hands that I have been proud of, and in the curious state of existing beyond triggers and contextual forces creating those realities, I am now in the place of both missing the melancholia as it presented in isolation, and rereading the works composed from those moments and feeling nostalgic care for my previous self being so trapped in the world of pain that life was better because of the philosophical meanderings in the darkness. It is a strange desire to look back into the darkest parts of one's life with nostalgia, and I do so only so far as wanting to be there with warmth for myself in those days that I was not capable of at the time.

I found in my reflections (published elsewhere) on nearly a decade of living in a survivor's role in an abusive relationship that I did some of the best work I had ever done when pressed into a shell of humanity, where agency, autonomy, joy and love escaped me entirely. This was, in my own reflections, my most active and inventive era in my work. A time where escapism took the form of intellectualism. Where for ten long years what I had been battling, this swirling maze of pain, of love being used as a weapon, and of hope being turned against me as a cancer, I was most free to explore.

But.

I truly think that I would not have survived into my 30s had that situation kept existing as it was. I think the infirmities of tortured artistry would have eventually swallowed me in its entirety. It is thus my greatest accomplishment to date, to have left that behind. To have escaped the perpetual cycle of total and complete dehumanization that has left its scars thickly embedded in my heart and soul. I do not think I will ever fully escape this, and as elsewhere explored, the old tradecrafts of the traumatic years still stay with me. I think there is a paranoia there that has itself become some form of lover or partner in this grand adventure. There is an inherent suspicion, a pavement artistry to plan an escape, a retaliation, or a last stand. These are the scars on my heart, some degree of protection for and against the darkness should he ever return in the same form from ages past.

With that, though. The winds of change are blowing in the trees.

It takes a certain degree of clarity to leave such a situation. It takes even more forceful illumination in the soul's searching to find that clarity. Finally, it takes a supportive network of people beyond the boundary of confinement to liberate one's soul.

I feel infinitely lucky to have had such an influence on my life at the time. A voice 3000 miles across the ocean experiencing a tangential melancholia, and who, through care, love compassion and a shared experience came to be the strongest pillar of support both in my escape, and among the pantheon of saviors in the sweet hereafter of recovery from trauma. Someone who, in their genuine expression of humanity, came to be a kindred spirit who I now hold so dearly close in my heart that it imparts a degree of armouring invincibility to my pathways forward into the unknown.

The experiential reality of this closeness and its directly healing properties manifested in the chilly damp of the Scottish high country in mid-October. Through the mists on Loch Lomond, there emerged a reinforcement of the notion that I have long held to be critical to the experience of authentic humanity:

The symbolic exchange of pure friendship based on warm humanity is one of the most powerful medicines for the soul.

Having come off of my first performance of sociology in front of living mortal humans in a year in Lithuania, a journey began that would take me by train, plane and automobile on a collision course with those rare reflective moments out of time that force you to stop and say: “yes, life truly is good now.” It is in these shared experiences that hope for the future, both for me and for the human condition flares in my mind, and lovingly in memory.

The journey began at 05:00 in the morning. A frantic push to collect the assortment of tools of my trade from their various postings across the hotel room situated on the tenth floor of a Soviet building in Klaipeda. The trappings of the conference life created a particularly telling mural of experience as they lay in their exploded world around me. A blazer, sweater vest, flash drives, HDMI adapters, my venerable MacBook, three leather bags, a multitude of film, three cameras, and a vintage Gameboy facilitated the bulk of the packing experience. There is a certain degree of mania in not being fully acclimated to a time zone and still having to exist within it. On the chair by the door hung my travel-tested rawhide jacket and the worn felt safari hat that have now joined my journeys to many an airport floor.

Beyond the caffeine soaked mania, I somehow managed to check out without forgetting anything and, by Volkswagen via Bolt made my way to the rail station. The four-hour train ride on a Sunday morning was surprisingly mundane considering I was at the start of a 2000-mile journey across Europe to spend a week with a dear friend I had until then only known as a voice on video calls, phone calls and in the infinite multitude of several years' worth of text messages. I found I was not nervous. Which is strange as typically meeting someone for the first time after having only a remote relationship can be one of the most cripplingly terrifying experiences for the mildly anxious introvert; I instead had the strange sense that whatever it was that I was travelling towards was warm, safe and where I needed to be for that moment. You learn too, that at particular moments in the travelling mania, that coffee is not the best, and this train ride, had it been one instance where the caffeine had been indulged, might have shaken out differently.

Stepping off the train again onto the streets of Vilnius, the only true city I could ever call home, I felt an air of familiarity again, being back to the cobblestones that I knew and loved. But this was only a momentary stopover in the journey. Another car ride, this time to the airport. Due to check-in not being open until two hours before the flight, I found myself in the first of two soviet era airports existing as a lone traveller in my own corner. This itself is a transcendent experience. One feels institutionalized by the cold, the grey, the concrete, the modern encroachments into the utilitarian spaces. I opted to sit in the overlooking waiting room, observing the world unfold below me and again could not shake the Westerbyian sense of interloping observation. Below me, queued a the desk to be my check-in destination in three hours were a Georgian youth football team. By the energy and the trophy they were admiring, they had won. To the typical observer a rowdy pre-teen football team may present the most chaotic and least preferable air travel compatriots, but in this moment, as an American in Eastern Europe and as a scholar of Soviet history, tyranny and politics, it was a particularly beautiful moment in retrospect. Not the people themselves, but just the idea of a group of kids travelling internationally happily, winning their tournament and then flying home to Tbilisi. It was something that sort of brought almost a tear to the eye in that at least, despite all the horrors of the history of the region, the troubles of its present and the general sense of impending geopolitical destruction, there was still a place for joy and excitement. At a particularly poignant moment as I had shifted my watching wall to the restaurant opposite of the waiting area, the whole team, coaches included, burst into a haunting semi-choral rendition of the Georgian national anthem. In the cavernous space of Vilnius Airport, this was one of the most beautiful moments of spontaneous musicality I have ever experienced. They sang for two minutes and at the final note, applause from the entire collective of inhabitants of the check-in departures terminal. From my vantage point, even the Lithuanian customs officers in their office could be seen applauding with a smile. It was humanity. It is hard to see the humanity in the airport, but every now and again, it comes to exist. From that moment any hesitation or trepidation I had about sharing a 40 minute plane ride with 20+ rowdy preteens in the throes of massive duty-free inspired sugar highs evaporated. This said, the flight was horrifically loud and rowdy, and I received a lovely headache.

That aside, the next leg began inside the u-shaped hall that is Riga International Airport. Being that I flew in at 10:00 pm or so, and my flight left the next morning at 7, I opted that instead of dealing again with the hassle of security, etc. I would overnight on the cold floor of another former republic's airport. This proved to be one of the most introvertedly beautiful experiences of my life so far. There is a certain intimacy in experiencing a place usually flooded with people being entirely and completely empty and dark. In a picture of extreme generational contrast, I opted to sleep on the carpeted floor of the Samsung OLED lounge in between concourses B and C. To spend the night in a former republic on the floor in the pale moonlight of giant Samsung TV logos is yet another experience outside typical humanity, within the wilds unknown, that I will not soon forget.

As dawn broke, the time arose for the last leg of the journey: crossing the checkpoint back into the west, coming in from the cold.

Ahead of me lay the journey itself, but also the symbolic nature of what the journey was leading to. It was not just a flight to the UK, nor was it simply an exploration into Scotland. Instead, it was the culmination of hundreds of hours of phone calls and several novels worth of text messages. It was the consummation of a deeply cherished friendship making the transition from the immaterially social to the physically real. It was an apotheosis of collective care, of individual moments shared together in both darkness and light. It was a proposed adventure into and beyond the clouds. There was a majesty around those hours. I still now, even two weeks removed, feel the electricity of that excitement, the slight fear of the unknown and the ever-bothersome introverted continuation of anxiety that only translates into: "What if they don't actually like me."

Wheels up at 7 am, 4 hours to London. Another hour to Glasgow. Then what? In my mind, I knew with confidence that I was stepping into a wonderful new adventure, but there is always that subtle voice in your head that poses the ever-dangerous unknown: what if? It is yet another strange manifestation of the trauma experience to distrust, even in light of a thousand reasons to trust even the most caring and loving exchange of friendship as deceitful. Its another of the scars upon my heart to think always towards the darkness. To wonder aloud if, by chance, this was not to be my coming in from the cold but my rapid descent into the pillowy embrace of eternal snow.

In contrast to this anxiety, which existed only fleetingly upon my mind during the interim delays of British Airways, I found comfort and still do to this day, that I am deeply selective in who I choose to let into the world of madness that is my inner self. Not the performance of self offered out to the masses during lectures, meetings, or in more tame publications, but the me that is me before all other instances of me. The idea of self that is, in its non-social presentation begets a richer and more decisive view into my inner humanity. There are only a handful of people in the world I let into this world because, in the past, guests have damaged the walls and hearths to the point of near-total annihilation.

The person at the other end of the flight was one of the rare few allowed beyond the gates.

Nearly every potential feeling of trepidation melted instantly when, through the glass of the entryway to the carpark, I saw in the flesh for the first time a person who has lived in my phone for years but who has in his time reached across oceans to heal my broken soul more times than not. In the brief embrace, we shared at our first meeting, a unique feeling washed over me. The feeling of that moment existed as if it had always been an existential reality as if we had merely not seen each other for a few days, as if the social connectivity of our symbolic exchange of meaning had not happened in gigabits and pixels. It was like feeling home.

To feel at home with another person, to the chronic introvert (and in general really) is an indescribably rare thing. It is a culmination of so many factors that, in their combination, constitute an event with a minuscule likelihood of ever happening. Most people have a few good friends. Some might subscribe to the idea of best friends. But very few individuals experience the reliving familiarity of existing next to someone in life and simultaneously being in awe of their existence in proximity to yours while also being so at home that the presence of the other fades into the background of perceptual reality. To be seen and unseen in the same moment, felt and unfelt. Existing together in total social harmony. This was my experience as we left the airport, into the car and off into the wild unknowns.

It is a mark of true friendship that immediately after meeting someone for the first time on terra firma, your first excursion is to the gas station and the second to the grocery store. There is a subtle power in mundane domesticity in such moments that further reinforces the nature of true friendship. Anyone can bond over the extraordinary, but few can bond over pasta-shape discourse or trucks named Dennis. In the span of several minutes, provisions were acquired, and we were off to the domicile of our week: the creatively titled Pod 2.

Pod 2 would become a central point of a shared sense of well-earned relaxation as, in some regard, we both realized that for quite an extended period of time, we had been going without any idea of a break from the pushes and pulls of life. It would soon unfold in the arched wooden structure that this was a place in time, out of place, and out of time. It was restorative in its simplicity, reflective in its coziness and between the walls, even silence shared was one of respect, of comradery, and one of total and utter peace. For the introvert there is always the worry that one is not entertaining enough, that words said are not enough, that one's presence is itself a bore. This was not the feeling in these walls to me. Instead, it felt like very few instances in my life, in relationships with even fewer people, that I could comfortably exist as myself in silence and feel neither judgment nor expectation.

It was my goal in these moments to offer what I always try to offer to the few people I join on the journey of life. It seems to be what I am most capable of providing aside from nonsensical critiques of contemporary academia: a safe place wherein one can step away from the madness of the world. Where work schedules, sleep schedules, expectations and the endless collective pursuit of the extraordinary can melt away into a heater-side conversation about the British monarchy or any other elementary conversation that to the outside observer is mundane, but in the right moments to the individuals tuned to the symbolic exchange, these are moments of subtle and implicit identity validation, wherein the worlds inside both of us are emerging ever so slowly into the web of conversation to express themselves and in exchange lay bare the vulnerabilities only safely disclosed in a world of total trust.

To me, this is the person you must wander with. The person who is just as willing, capable and open to cast aside the human-centric ego view of the world and instead step casually out into the wilds with wonder and wild desire, not for the photo, not for the social clout, but for the experience of experiencing the experience. It can be done alone, but the contrasting lenses of two varied histories, two life stories coming together above the clouds in a wooded thicket of Scottish trees, allow for a true transcendence to emerge. Something akin to the apotheosis of the soul, wherein a total and complete complimentary trust of one another builds into a framework unity of shared solidarity. This is what broadens your horizons.

It is not the destination. It is the experience. And the most compounding elevation of that experience is doing so in good company. This is not to say that we cannot experience the wonders of the wilds alone, but doing so in the presence of someone not in it for the views or the likes, who will stop and look at the way the dew collects on the oak leaves, or who saves a flower for posterity, these are the memories that form a golden band of healing across the most desolate of hearts. This is the light through the storm, the warm glow of an inn at the end of the dark forest path of the unknown.

This was my experience travelling. It was not the passport stamps or the sights seen. It was the garlic passata over potatoes in the damp. It was the laughter in the early mornings. The sarcasm. The dodging of Scottish tractors. It was the calm in the silence of the night that said that there was no need to feel anything else than that whatever paths spiral out into the unknown from this moment will never be walked alone. To share that depth of trust, for me at least, is something I felt I would never be able to do again. It felt in the moment of realization in our last parting hug that maybe, just maybe, what I had just experienced was again humanity to feel joy, safety, and trust and have them be genuinely real and not perceptual illusions predicated on false realities. It was a beautiful realization under the Scottish sky that, yes, again, for the first time in ages, I now have a place in a person that I can feel at home with. This may sound profound, but it is contrarily the simplest thing humans can do with one another: connect. Connect across shared experience, shared pain, and a philia love towards one another that does not need to be expressed outwardly but is felt as the ancient Greek manifestation of the word, in an unspoken bond of true and lasting friendship.

This is how we shed the human ego in our pursuit of the wander. It is not in endurance, in the breadth of travel, or in the price of admission. It is in the collectively shared safety of trust with our companions to the point we let go of needing to know the world and instead fall into the feedback of conversation out in the wilds, a conversation that, without saying it, is, in fact, a communication between hearts. This is itself the true nature of wandering. Not for the lust but for the loss. The wandering loss of those things that tie us to the darkness of our experiences, where if even for the briefest of times, in the most mundane presentations of domesticity in some far-off place, do we find ourselves connected to the inherent joy and ritual of the woods.

We do not need specialized equipment, routes plotted, or followers gained in order to fully and completely experience what it is to exist collectively on the earth with the entirety of her interlopers at our feet, in between our toes, and by our sides. It is a joy to walk the path when there is light at the end; it is even more so a joy to do so in the safety of another, wherein along whatever obstacles may emerge, we both know without saying it to the air between us, that in a moment's notice, across the globe, that there will always be a place to take shelter from the storm. This is the true transcendental experience of wandering. It is being lost to the point of acknowledging how lost one is and, at the last moment before total and complete destruction finding in a kindred spirit the same experiential need for warmth and stability, and instead of shying away from the stranger in the mist, welcoming him inside and trusting that he will not steal the fire back away to the environs of the forest.

What else can I say other than that of all the trees I have passed, of all the scars on my soul and body, of all the countless moments in time spent existing in darkness, to have found the light of a connected soul out beyond the waves, truly to me, represents the epitome of why we must adventure. Why we must explore. Why in the last wink of dusk and the breaking peak of dawn, if we experience such a thing as to be lucky enough to feel the moss below our feet, we may hope to do so by the side of another soul travelling the same direction, who we may lean on, who may trust, and who in the darkest of possible moments would no doubt reach out a hand to hold us, while we too in our paths would stop at nothing to ensure the same reciprocity of warmth, love and serenity in the wandering escape.

Explore. Not just your forest. Not just your wilderness. But find that person whose rhythm, whose path, whose journey harmonizes with the timeless echo of yours out into the abyssal bounds of the future.

Experience experience.

Wander.

Love.

Let go of your humanity.

Take care of one another.

Part 2

A Strange and Savage Lament of the Heart and Hearth

Chapter 5

The Long Nights

"The fact that the human act is self-directed or built up means in no sense that the actor necessarily exercises excellence in its construction. Indeed, they may do a very poor job in constructing their act."

— Herbert Blumer

"We have arrived at such a point, such an inescapable leg of our journey wherein the decision to return is negated, the path forward unclear, the present unbearable in a conflagration of cosmic proportion. It is in this arrival that we must, under all pretense establish and maintain an illusory proclamation of that which is pure and authentic to the pulse of the human spirit. And forthwith we submit the message, on the final strand of communiques from the bleak brink of total self destruction."

Calling all stations. From the imitation zone on through the dawn. The solitary lamplighters in their shadowed streets. The watchers in their nests. The prayers in their pews. The lonely soul by the light of their bulb. It is upon us. The reckoning. The storm has hit. Batten down the hatches lest ye faithful. The veil is broken, and the curtain is breached. Zero hour. Facsimile to follow. Flash Priority.

"All of nature with its forms and creatures exist together and are interwoven with each other. They will be resolved back, however, to their own proper origin, for the compositions of matter return to the original roots of their nature."

-The Gospel According to Mary Magdalene

The Long Nights:

The realization comes when it is least expected. It is in one of those rare moments of self-dialogue wherein you turn your voice inward and utter to a singular audience of your own mind a directive. Not an order, nor goal, nor affirmation, but a realization. Realization is a powerful moment in the scope of our experience. It is not a discovery. It is not a newfound knowledge emerging from the edges of that which is observable. Rather. Realization implies that that which is now discovered was *known* already. It is intertwined in the nature of realization that we have always *known* that the information rather than being mysteriously veiled beyond, has been that which stays within us without recognition. The word itself does not detail a discovery but a manifesting of that which had been previously *unreal* to the realm of that which is, either socially or materially. The social realization, the power to come into the social as real on the shoulders of ignorance and innocence, is transformative to the scope of our own intimately experienced reality to such a point that in itself a realization is a cataclysmic paradigm shift in our ability to come to know that shadow individual actor in our social domain that requires the most knowing: ourselves.

I have preached extensively the modular reflectivity as it is produced in the conduit of human experience at the hour of 3:00 AM. It is such that in my current state of being, three in the morning is one of the dearest and most trusted confidants in my social scope. Three in the morning knows more clearly the depths of my soul, my hopes, my rages, my abject despairs. And it curious presents itself herein as the emergent momentary status of my being that I am moved to pen this love letter to the curious sanity of 3 AM.

You see, it is in this mystical 60 minutes of being that meets me on a daily horizon that I have had this realization. A realization of cataclysmic proportions to my understanding of what it means to be me, what, on the basis of the collective requisitions of my lived experience and social historicity, has led me to the state within which these words emerge. But, before I can offer this word, this realization, this socially manifested modality of being for the sacrificial altar of my pages, I must first describe the states that have led to this emergence of liminal reality.

When I was 20, I wrote my first and final book. A 200-page expedition to the centre of my soul titled *"Satin Strides and Two-Tone Daisy Roots: A Love Letter to Sanity"*. It was my first work, coming into existence in feverish manic bursts of daily dedication where to the tune of *Fairytale of New York* by The Pogues on repeat and my own heartbeat thundering through the countless caffeine overdoes. Perched in the window of my dormitory, Culebra Hall, Room 260, I would stare into the night surrounded by an undergraduate edifice of messy productivity. An overflowing trashcan full of endless paper coffee cups from the midnight espresso bar down the hall and countless crushed cans of TaB stood sentinel over me from the darkness of the narrow hallway of my L-shaped sanitarium. In university, at that time I experienced the true siren song of my soul: total isolation. Between the hours of 10 pm, when I said goodnight to my family and 11 am, when my first class was, I was free. I knew no one personally in university, I had no friends that did not exist as shadows in lecture halls Monday through Friday. And I was not lonely. The isolation bred within me such a state of purity of mind that I still cannot to this day fathom the degree to which it was soothing to my soul. I refer to this period as my 'soaring period'. It was a time when, after navigating the pavement jungle of university for 10 hours a day, I would steal away to my private and reclusive space, and in the safety of that space, I performed a nearly year-long dissection of myself down to the very core fibres of my being. This book that emerged was both my first and last. A leather-bound handwritten copy, now safely nestled and buried away in total secrecy, was both my debut work and a posthumous publication. The subject? A simple question: what would truly happen if I died today? It was born one September evening as I walked to pick up dinner from the cafeteria. In two unique instances: First, on my walk up the hill from my dormitory, a voice called from the top floor of the building I passed in a tone of pure hostility and directed attention to me; it said: "Hey! Hey, you in the red! Fuck you!" To this day I hear that statement, and still wonder who said it, why they did, and why the need to direct such hostility towards me as I walked in the evening twilight in my red plaid shirt. Upon my return trip, merely feet from the spot of that callout, in the crosswalk, I was nearly hit head-on by a car driven by a university character I had actually hated from the day I began there. A yellow muscle car with a Hawaii plate. It passed within inches of me to the point that my button-up shirt fluttered in the backdraft. It was at that moment that I returned to my room and asked that question about my leather-bound journal. What would happen if I died today?

What emerged was part psychological study, part memoir, part love letter, part suicide note, and part ethnographic reflection on the subversive sounds of love, limerence, despair and pain. That text also saw itself becoming a repository of a very horrific debate within myself on the nature of who I was, truly, in the core of my being. It accomplished this through one of the most terrifying things a twenty-year-old introvert can be told by someone not bound to them by familial social constructs:

"I love you. You have taught me new ways of love, and you are the most important person in my life"

Intimacy like this, an outright pure and unadulterated vulnerability in the face of uncertainty, abuse and pain, came like a thief in the night. I lost myself in those 21 words. They burned permanent spaces into my retinas and exist there still to this day as scar tissue on the lenses I view the world through. At that moment and the intervening thousands spent awake every single night, what grew in the magical forest of text messages, phone calls, video calls, letters, drives, walks, dinners and mornings were, in a word, the start of the most powerfully important journey of my heart to date. To say it was a relationship would do a disservice to the sanctity of the idea of a relationship. It was a psychosis that stretched from the latter sunny days of August for eight following winters. A pattern of 21 words grew into a cycle of torturous odds, late-night operations, clandestine extractions, rages, tears, arguments, hugs, and precious moments of pure tenderness. That isolated period of my life produced two fundamental realities that are and have been core to my existence to this very minute. First, a keenly pursued desire in the exploration of the intricacies of human interaction, the pursuit of narrative meaning in the social reality of the individual in everyday life. A smouldering professionalism in the secret art of the social, not science, not philosophy, but a clandestine work of knowing the individual, of knowing myself. I pursued the nonsenses of academia and the formality of my field for the purpose of knowing as best I could that which fed into the maze of mirrors that comprises the human affective cycle of life and death. I pledged, with a decade of blood, tears and dissociation, my body and mind to a system of thinking that places me in the uncomfortable chair of wandering beyond the performance of self into the environs of intentionality in the swirling mists of history and biography. I did not, out of this isolation, come to desire the quantitative, scientific or causal findings of the social world. Nor did I endeavour to simply ask the questions of metaphysics, epistemology or ethics. Instead, I found myself existing in a place embodied in the absurd, the abstract, the half-true, and the devious. It is a place situated in the recognition and reverence for the mysteries of the social. Not the person nor the material world, but in the complex communicative and symbolic realities that pass within and without us in every waking moment. To descend into this world, to step into the space wherein one sees not solely the individual actor, nor the fruits of the interaction, but the currents and contemporaries of those elements to such a point that the fabric of interactional existence presents itself as a fracturing in the mould of reality to such a level that one can see an individual as a basket of fault lines along the line upon which their selves manifest. I learned this in myself first. The ability to unmask the illusion. To find within the affect, behaviour and cognition the roots of my performances of self to myself, my family, my friends, and in my pursuits of the cataclysm of love in your twenties. It is in this ability that I found some niche of professional outletting where my work was somehow acceptable and a dark truth in my own navigation of the social beyond myself. That notion that what is interacted upon and unto one's self is in itself a symbolic exchange of value and meaning. Cynicism comes from this. It is not such a clichéd performance that one feels the symbolic devalued, nor that one questions the implicated intentionality. Rather it is a deeper redefining of one's lens of reality itself. It is a place of being that is both beautiful and burdensome. In the aspect of beauty, there is an appreciation developed for the minute, the mundane, the instances of the human condition that breed only a momentary lapse of the drudgery of the mundane into some form of the beautiful symbolic moment. With this comes an attenuation to the happenings around you. You become, somehow, sensitive to that which swirls in the social milieu beyond that temporality of continuance. I can exemplify this in the picture of sitting in a restaurant. The noise around often disintegrates into a background rattle and hum for us. I remember distinctly as a young adult and child that this lull was barely noticeable as my family and I chatted and joked while we waited for food. But now, in this shell of whatever it is that I have grown into, I hear all of the voices making the chatter. Not at once, but streams of nascent points come to me, and they build such richness to the day-to-day existence. To hear the foibles and experiences of the individuals beyond my scope of being, whom I do not know, whom I will never see again, is magic in itself. It is an insular isolation within itself. Because for the brief moments, we exist together as familiar strangers in the singular dining room, we have by some grandiose stretch all shared a contiguous reality with one another, and that bond itself, to me in my reflections herein, represents a special bond that we share unknowing to one another. I have since built a referential knowledge of collective nonsense that means nothing to anyone and yet still plays within my mind as an endless reelshow of performances of self in the everyday. I grew a respect for the everyday mundanity of that which reflects our existence. A love of standing in queues, of delayed flights, of the special depersonalization of the airport terminal, a penitent reverence for the ubiquity of the chance encounter of a fellow passerby on the sphere of existence. I find that out of my isolation, I found a way to exist in my own moments while experiencing a carefree collective of intrusions by the others I found upon my wanderings. It is the curiosity of these moments I hold dear to my heart. Of strange half-sentences heard in passing and repeated on to my compatriots that have since evolved into a lexicon all their own. I can, for instance, on a phone call with my dad, instantly conjure moments we have shared, from 48-hour straight-shot road trips to renegade firefighting on the line between destruction and preservation. I can say to one of my brothers an offhanded remark about mining claims and his response will always be the phrase: "Don't you talk about my father" in a facsimile Brooklyn brogue. To my other brother, I can ask if he knows Jennifer, who works at the school, to which he will reply: "That's my mom." And to my sister, all I must do is utter the sentence: "Squid out of water," to be subjected to a guttural scream in the style of Shane MacGowan. It is in this lexicon of referential nonsense that I have come to measure and mark the progress of my life, my time, and my mortality in the collectivity of the moments that come to compose the everyday. It is in itself a self-dramatizing showcase of all that is unique and beautiful in the human case. It is curious beyond the self-ascribing moments of raw rationality that come from our engagement in the mundane every day and in the passing-by of the stranger of familiarity that by some serendipitous chance, we come to share a symbolic meaning of nothing grander than simply existing at the moment. It is in such cases that I remember moments and phrases of being that come to form a library of history for myself. I associate these slices of life with the life I've lived as a stranger to others and upon me by strangers to myself. There are curious slips in this regard wherein one becomes a stranger unto themselves and these are moments I have had myself to varying degrees of harm, danger and serendipitous insights.

In one such phase of self-strangering, I found myself alone, outside, cold, shocked, depressed and scared on foot in a city I had just moved to only two weeks prior. Knowing nothing of my surroundings, no one to call upon and being isolated in cages of my own creation, I struck out into the night with a wanton abandon of careless wanderlust that today's Instagram urban explorers could only imagine. At that magical hour of three in the morning, I walked for 5 hours into the night. Into the city. With me, I had a house key, 27 Canadian dollars and a pack of unfiltered American Camels. Inside me, a feeling of having been shot through the heart, with the deafening sound of my world crashing around me and dreams fading to the horrors of murky lucid nightmares. That night I stared into the oncoming headlights as traffic dwindled to a sequence of occasional bursts from the constant stream. I sat against a building on Pandora Avenue in Victoria, British Columbia, on the cold sidewalk and shared three cigarettes each with a man both struggling with not having a home to return to and an opioid addiction he could not see the end to. I have spoken of this night elsewhere in hushed tones, but here I shall only say that which I have not before: that in that moment of abject desperation on the sidewalk in the dark city in January, I confessed all of my heart, even those pieces of gold dust I had sworn were mine and my own to this man. I told him what had happened, what had destroyed me, where I had walked from and what it had done to me. For the first time in over a decade, I cried in front of another person, and in that moment of abject desperation, this stranger to me, at the time a stranger to myself as well, put an arm around me, pulled me in and said: "man, it's gonna be ok. It's gonna be ok." He was considerably older than me, and despite his struggle with addiction and current situation in life, he spoke to me like I was his son. He cared for me in that moment and it has been something that has singled itself in my understanding of who I was from that moment on. He told me about his dad leaving his mom, how she did everything she could through her traumas to love him and how love itself is something that is always there "even out here," he said. In the two hours, I sat with him, I was safer than I had been or would be from onslaughts of the mind in any of the following three years I would live in that city. I will not wax poetic about how 'despite his situation, he cared for me' more than to say that it is reflective of the capacity for the everyday chance meeting of two lost souls to exhibit the kindness of the human spirit. In reflection now, I can say confidently that during the course of an entire PhD in "cultural, social and political thought," I have not learned more about the world, the nature of life, and the capacities of human philosophy than I have sitting on dirty sidewalks in British Columbia sharing cigarettes with people who call the streets their home for now. Whether it was my downfall into the arms of the man from Pandora, or the casual three-way discussion with the women I met on Granville Street in Downtown Vancouver over menthols and diet Coke.

It seems to me that in my moments of losing myself, I find myself in a situation company that would otherwise be considered dangerous and unsafe. It seems in moments of despair, my capacity to *"seek out the poorer quarters where the ragged people go"* is reflective of the capacity of my downfalls into the darkness to be sobering to the every day beyond. I have often found in these snapshots of my own history that I am both most at ease and most enlightened. Where I may confidently add that in my many engagements with pretentiously wealthy grad students showing off the size of their Kant libraries in pointless seminars could not hold a single candle to the treatment of a singular houseless person with dignity and honesty. I gave the man from Pandora my 27 dollars, he asked if he could hug me and he did. I walked the 7 kilometres home in a daze. I purchased a bottle of gin the moment the liquor store opened, not being a heavy drinker by any standard and sipped covertly wrapped in my leather jacket listening to Bette Midler's *The Rose* as the sun rose over Cadboro Bay.

From that moment, I evolved into a latchkey kid of my own home, a pavement artist of our street, and someone curiously alert to the minor things only someone suffering from repeat trauma could detect: which stairs creaked, how to memorize the order of a room to determine what if anything moved, to inventory inconsistencies in stories, to see through lies and see beyond the grander scope of momentary horror to the long-term dramatization of those mysteries of tomorrow. You develop a tradecraft in trauma. You become the paranoid deep-cover asset far behind the curtain, with the frontier of life and death being the very battleground of your own living room. You make escapes and approaches, you set up dead drops and safe houses, and you come to count the seconds until the lamps light themselves in the street. You learn the sound of the sidewalk and where the rigid heeled soles will slip against the rim of the storm drain, and you will know that based on the averages of walking speed that you had 15 seconds before they reached the door and another 11-20 before the latch was unlocked with the spare key. Curiously you start to map out your trauma in plans and fallbacks. You stash an overcoat on your back porch, leave through the front door and then climb the fence to take up your post asleep on the concrete outside. Somehow you learn the handwriting of your abuser to the point you recognize which variant of trauma is going to meet you at the end of the day based on the lie told to you in the morning. You recognize vehicles and have their make, model, and colour burned into your memory to the point that years later, they trigger anxiety deep inside. You learn the methods of the detective, seeing the stories of the night before in the bathroom trashcan. You can reconstruct a scene of debauchery and descent to passion in the arrangement of pillows on the sofa and the previously watched list on Netflix. It is the realization in this regard that you are under siege that leads the victim of trauma to build networks to sustain their safety. There is a proliferation of rehearsed and relied-upon routines that come into play every single day. A scan down each street, a note of unfamiliar cars, of license numbers, a detour away from your front door to the vantage across the street where you can count lights in the windows, positions of curtains, and gauge the occupation for its opposition. We start to understand in the clandestine operations of our own everydays that something has shifted beyond the capacity for what is safe, healthy and conducive to anything other than a total disintegration of all that we hold to be self-evident of the self we have come to know and have lost in the mire of the horrors beyond. Life for me evolved to this following my morning on Pandora. Where what was supposed to be the most blissful time of my life became, in an instant, a year of scrounging scraps of food here and there, stealing showers once or twice a week before disappearing into the solitary confines of the one safe place I had in the Great White North: the floor of my university office where, with a pillow and a blanket stashed in my desk, a stock of oatmeal packets and canned soups I descended into madness of a prison that those four brick walls built for me. In less than six months, I lost 70 pounds, began my affair with nicotine and lost myself to countless nights spent staring out my window onto the grounds of the University of Victoria and walking my way through the forest of mirrors.

I took inspiration from my predicament and went to work. Not self-pity or suffering but feverish investigations into my situation, hours of analysis, theorizing, predicting, and constant tending of the gardens of mirrors cropping up in my whirlwind disappearance into the forest of total desperation. I asked myself what a fictional scholastic mentor of mine once asked himself: "What do we know?" from that, my descent into this world of myself became absolute. I threw myself fully into my discipline and to my work because my work here had within itself a personal safari towards salvation. My trauma responses, once serving as a functional safety net became my operational assets, my safety signs became ways to reflect myself back into the fray. I came to a point in my understanding of who I was that I did not expect. First, I learned a distinct fact about myself: I did not trust myself. Secondarily, I learned to. I read, I wrote, I thought, I ground my hands into pure exposed brick to draw blood, I screamed into pillows, I lost my mind in those months.

But.

I was right. In the end my findings, my path through the woods, my forest of mirrors, my fray, all of it proved to reconcile itself. Patterns emerged and became predictable. Predictable to the point of worry for a social scientist. That is, after that first brush with total self-destruction, I learned the recipe of my trauma, and in that, I faced three more years of it with a degree of inexplicable confidence in my methodology, my tradecraft and my intuition. I spoke about these troubles with friends, family, colleagues, and even professionals. My family offered a degree of support coupled with advice, and friends offered the same sentence "You have the patience of a saint," colleagues conferred and helped me to eliminate confirmation bias and confirmed and helped to develop my hypotheses, and my counsellor simply said he was blown away by the fact that I had accurately predicated my cyclical reprieves to the day for three years.

All of this meandering to reflect in my moments of time, which I have since blended into historicity, has led me to know both the bricks in the paths of the night and the subtly of love, joy, and freedom that can come from the moment-to-moment experiences of everyday absurdities. You see, without that dedication to the unknown mundane of the everyday world of strangers, I could not come to appreciate nor reflect upon the magnitude of the streams of peace and war within my own mind and within my life.

And that is the first realization of my penning of my love letter to sanity all those years ago. That love and limerence are long roads of pain, that trauma changes every minute detail down to the creaking of the second step, that existence is grandiose in its mundanity, and that patience, thinking, reading, writing and waiting are the golden vessels within which we can bide our troubles in some cases. It is a finding that to sequester one's self to the confines of a small room, to the turgid bitterness of instant Nescafe and to resign one's self to the mysteries of the intention, the brevity, the potentiality and the ultimate symbolic meaning of life and interactional reality; you can, to some degree come to know the world around you as you know the sounds of the symbols on the written page.

My reflections here do not share them for the sympathy of the reader or out of some narcissistic premonition that these are words or a story that matter to be shared, but rather to present a contextual ornamental scaffolding for the first of these two findings of my project eight years ago. That realization in the face of coming to see the world around you is a massive undertaking in your formation of a sensibly independent self in the world around you.

That is, to exist in the contemporary world, we have to relearn to read the signs written on the walls we walk past. We have to reignite the means by which we present ourselves outward to the horrors of the world and, in doing so, develop a staunch resilience and a capacity to expose our wounded vulnerabilities to the world beyond the boundaries of our physical bodies. It is, in effect a brief exploration of those things requisite of our return to the light of the beauty of being human in the face of the darkness of being a *modern* human.

This is not to espouse a manifesto of anti-modernism, but rather, it is to question the trajectory of our being and existence should we continue the path that commodifies the extraordinary at the detriment of the ordinary. While that which is extraordinary will always hold within it some degree of allure, there is a stroke in the contemporary commodification of it that presents us with a terrifying dilemma: plurality. That is, via the interactional spaces of online arenas of self-presentation, we find that what is astonishing is what is most readily populating our spaces. That is, as the algorithmic machinations of the digital spaces have grown up with us, their charter has shifted towards a favouring of the collective interest masked as the individual preference. This, to me, is dangerous for the reason that it acts almost as a blindfold to the exigency of our day-to-day life, when even in that regard, the day-to-day, the natural, the holistic, have all themselves become a content-based cog in this machine. This is not entirely 'bad' for us, as it does allow for an accessible realm of engagement, interaction, and community building. But there is a side to me that is worrisome, if not horrifically destructive.

Where I worry is in two distinct outcomes of this typological social space. First, seeing the extraordinary commodified to the point of total media domination places the inhabitants of these spaces in a social space where they are inundated with that which is astonishing to the consumer. Glamour shots of glaciers, GoPro videos of ski vacations, and the quintessential photo atop Machu Picchu. What is not shown is that the sociologists still with me will elicit a nod, the socioeconomic grey reality behind the shot. Imagine for a moment that you, the reader are a teenager living a lower-middle-class lifestyle in suburbia. You have a smartphone and social media, such as Instagram. You, in your primordial development of self and consumption of this media, find a desire. *To Travel.* This grows within you as you age because you see countless photos and posts and videos all day, every day, on 'travel hacks' on how to make millions in side hustles and how to 'travel the world for dollars a day', you are lulled into a strange waking illusion where the algorithm in its nonhuman objectivity has instead created in your mind two very dangerous realities: first that the type of luxury travel, of forgoing education, and of 365 days of travel a year as a digital nomad is *possible,* let alone accessible to you. Second, this desire becomes a drive. It becomes something approaching an obsession, something we today in our modern discourse call a 'dream'. It is therefore not a *goal* with a short-term plan of achievable steps to obtain, but it is a *dream* a cobbling together of hope, of imagination, of fantasy and a suspension of belief in the actuality of one's positioning in life. I will forego the Marxist analysis here, but comrades of the cloth would certainly see where it may go...

It is in the commodification of the extraordinary at the detriment of the mundane that I think places in this space of existential unknowability to the point that we are losing the very tethers to our exigent humanity as we compress all that which is mundane into the social spaces *between* the extraordinary. That is reflected in a shift I think of the social media sphere, where much to the excitement of 2010s comedians, the normative use of Instagram was people posting minute insights into their daily slices of the mundane. A diet Coke on the timeline with the caption "Tuesday Feels" was in its own way a celebration of the mundane in the halcyon days of the 2010s. But then, we started to grow beyond, to move, to demand *more.* We could not fixate on our desire to share slices of the day-to-day motions of life with the codified means by which social media works on our subconscious to favour the *more.* This is reflected too in the sharp transformation and overall abandonment of the early, early days of YouTube "vlogging," wherein the entertaining elements of content were the familiarity and closeness of existing along with someone in their everyday lives. Rather now, even such content is shaped by the algorithmic need to highlight the absurdly extravagant. Why would we watch a day in the life of a 'regular person' when we can do the same with a multi-millionaire? What's a house tour compared to the brief sweep of a camera across a singular childhood bedroom?

This has changed us too, not just the means of the content we consume and prefer, but it has augmented the mindset of the individual to supplant a need, a desire for achieving and emulating these ways of life as well. We have been funnelled into a continual stream of content that shows us what life could be while simultaneously branding our everyday mundanity as *not enough*. It has then constructed a hellscape of a hierarchy of social experience that has created, in the eyes of many, the persuasion that one must *always* strive for the extraordinary and despair in the mundane. This, to me, as a result of the aforementioned social experiment on myself, is what I find to be horrific in the presentation of the self in the contemporary social landscape. That is what we find to be boring or a waste of time on the grander scale of life itself has distanced us from the ability to appreciate the mundane. That is, we cannot even view a sunset or the complex patterns of the sun through crystals of ice in the trees after a snowstorm without composing, framing, exposing and snapping a photo on our phones to share *somewhere*. That is not to say that sharing these moments is not good, but rather, the question has to be: are we existing in the moment, or are we commodifying the moment for later?

A discursive element I have found in the streams of photography discourse is the question of whether we are actually experiencing the moment or not. This has unfortunately come from, typically, a crowd of folks that also favors the most expensive cameras with "optical" viewfinders so you "get out from behind the screen and see your subject". I do not have much of an opinion on this, but I do have the sense when I scroll back through the boxes of Kodachrome slides from my Dad's childhood that the photographer (typically my grandmother) was very much engaged in the experience. That is because, for so long, photos, in their analog sense, were snapshots of memories that emerged months later when the roll finally went to the lab or when the Polaroid magic finished its work. The intention here is not to devolve into an analog film photography rant, enough of those exist, but I think the reason I see so many people my age, and why I myself enjoy such things, is because we do possess within our experiences the *desire* to get back to the simplicity of simply existing in the moment.

I find this too in another odd elemental locale in my own experience: the explosion of nostalgia among myself and my friends of a similar age. We find ourselves inundated with a worldly scope of nostalgic experience and the desire to search for and reintegrate elements of our nostalgic reminiscences into our new daily lives. "Retro" throwbacks or repurchases are things I see and experience on a common thread of regularity. The idea is that if only I paid 130$ on eBay for that Nintendo64 game, then I would feel that sense of warmth in the day-to-day that I did when I was 9. If I come home from work looking forward to Goldeneye007 on the N64, maybe then I can recapture and re-experience the joy I felt *before the fall* into this patterned endless doomscrolling modality I exist in now. And it is in this pattern that I see that sadness manifested. The idea is that the imagined reality of nostalgia has become within itself a blanket of safety for us to exist in. We rewatch and experience the hallmarks of a 'simpler' time in order to feel some semblance of stability and freedom from the harsh externals of our contemporary reality.

This is what I found in my writing of that love letter to sanity: that notion that simplicity still exists there, but we are not able to *feel* it as we have become desensitized to the ordinary in the shameless, addictive pursuit of the extremely astounding. It is then that we are faced with a need to relearn the process of appreciating that which is simple now and in our futurities. That is, rather than patching a bandage of the past across the wounds of the present, we can direct our efforts to the analysis of the presentation of future obstacles and develop a means of existing that is conducive to that warmth and simplicity in light of whatever may be on our collective horizons. How do we do this? What is the process of unlearning the astounding? Is this not a rejection of modernity, then, a rejection of beauty and excitement and striving for a better life? No. This is a rejection of the commodification of these elements, a return and recentering of the self upon the self, a rediscovery of the ego elements of the individual as they were prior to the loss of self in the sea of social media commodification of our lives. Does it mean to delete social media and become a hermit? No. It means reconnecting with the elementary components of who you are to the point that you are *happy* in your use of these elements, where you do not fall into the 3 AM pattern of scrolling through travel account posts to dream of a better bed to be sleeping in, but rather it is to be content with the fact that you are waking up in the same world. It is an invitation to explore your own locale as if it were a venue deserving its own travel account. It is a challenge to explore the photography you do in pursuit of your social media with a degree of understanding that not only is it a capturing of the moment for others but that it is a preservation of the memory of that moment for you yourself. When you deposit a photo to Instagram, do not do so with the idea of other people viewing it, but rather as it is a digital photo album for *you*. It is a walk through your experiences and memories associated with those so that no matter when you re-engage with your materials, you can transport back into the memorial of that time for the soothing of your social soul.

I invited myself at the conclusion of that writing project to do just that. To exist in a world of rekindled sentimentality. To build a world of memory in the steps and moments I experienced to the degree that my life can be reflected in and within itself in whatever manner I choose to record it in. It is in this that I reshaped my experience of self to be grounded again, to find joy in the momentary lapses of consciousness and to dive into the imagination in my daily experience of life. It allowed me to dream again, to experience again the joys of childhood wonder where now, rather than pondering the reasoning for the sky's azure hue, I now query such things as the nature of the social self and the symbols we trade on a moment-to-moment basis.

All I can advocate herein is the notion that for the individual to feel a degree of that stability and safety that comes from the innocence of the time gone by we may, in our own ways, come to rekindle an appreciation for the moments we experience that are "less than shareable". There are a milieu of materials teaching one how to embark on this journey but I would offer that for me a certain nostalgic sense of calm comes from occupying those wild spaces beyond the sanctity and sterility of my keyboard. When I lived in the city, I found these mundane moments on long bus rides, often travelling to the end of a line and then wandering the cityscape in search of a stop that would take me home. I would suggest having the courage to forego efficiency in the journey and instead take the momentary lapse of expediency as an opportunity to do something so grandeur as climbing a mountain or something so small as appreciating the paintings in the window of an art gallery. The irony in the engagement with the travel-minded commodification of these online social spaces is that too often is the caption and marketing along the lines of 'appreciating the little things' or 'this whole wide world is amazing and we are so lucky to live in it'. Well, in that case, one does not need an extended holiday in the Mediterranean to experience the same wonder. One does not need to be a jetsetting wildlife photographer when the social lives and intricacies of your local duck population can be just as engaging as the snow leopard you spot through your telephoto. That is to say that there is as much grandiosity in a solo meal in your local café with a book as there is at the top of K2. This is to say that living well is not something that has to be done along the socially constructed standards of those that influence our social media feeds, and rather that a good day is socially constructed on the basis of the individual actor and their day-to-day being. Maybe, just maybe, the key to a sustaining source of happiness is not in the locale one inhabits or ventures to, but it is, in fact, the journeys of our daily lives. The micro adventures to a shop across town, a break in the afternoon to walk in a park or to pound the pavements you would not regularly explore. It is my experience that routine is what breeds this mundanity because we are so heavily encouraged to embrace spontaneity in these globetrotting pursuits. What if, only for a moment, we took the plunge to find enjoyment in the routine things? I feel that it is in these patterns of behavioural experience that we can, in our own ways, find the path to entertain our desires for the extremely gratifyingly grandiose.

That is not, again, to reject the modernity at our fingertips, but it is perhaps a call for those of us lost in the sea to have to learn how to augment our reality to accommodate these things as supplemental to our exigent states of being. We cannot escape the modernity we live in, and so rather than running away to do so (which is precisely the construction we are experiencing a struggle with), I would argue that the best escape one could plot is from the frameworking of the commodification to such a point that the mundane again becomes magical.

Towards the Realization

The previous realization from my *Love Letter to Sanity* is the one that I feel to be the most pragmatic and less theoretical. The latter realization, though...That does align itself into a misty world of confusion on the basis of that which comes to form our entirety of the alignment and construction of self.

What that book taught me most about was love. And from that soaring era of diligent philosophical meditation I found myself emerging into *love* during a time when I neither wanted to nor considered myself one that *could* do so. At that point, the isolation, and the lack of intimate sociality had begun to so wonderfully satiate me that I envisioned nothing more pleasant than a world of my own, free to exist as a nocturnal creature of the night without the need nor troubles that come from the attachments built through the foibles of love and limerence in the modern age.

But. I had less self-control over these social forces than I imagined I did at the presumptuous age of 20.

At this stage I cannot write of the beauty of love. I cannot reformat my ramblings or processing to that realm of optimistic romanticism. As love was the defining rhythm of traumatic historicity. You see, love is what led me to the traumas outlined briefly above. Not directly as a concept, but in the social power that love and its more insidious social reality: limerence have on our capacity to exist in this world as it is today. Love is the backbeat to the sound of my shoes clattering on the pavements of Victoria, BC, that fateful morning outlined above. Love is the background noise to my need to build a personal tradecraft of survival. Love is what made me believe I could outlast horrors that I need not have experienced, that I could have escaped long ago.

Love is what burned into me a half-life that dominated my doctoral years, balancing between a horrific home life of abuse, insincerity, lies, and traumas unspeakable and unknowable to me now.

Waking up Blind and Alone is a Terrifying Experience

There were physical tolls on top of the psychological ones. My student reviews have often sung of their love for my 'groovy' sunglasses, which I teach in, and how that 'aesthetic' was something to be commended for. It is true that I often wear dark purple prescription glasses when I teach and 95% polarized shades any time I am outside during the waking hours. These, however, are not choices made on the basis of aesthetics but of necessity.

Love led me to a place of cohabitation during my master's degree that devolved almost as quickly as it began, and out of the love that blossomed during that soaring period, I experienced the first blow to the very core of my being. The one I had so faithfully built a dream around, who I had dedicated so much of my life and work and patience to, decided that the true dream in life wasn't to live with someone you loved, nor was it to *live* anywhere, but rather that the only way to *feel* alive was to "travel the world". That whole idea became both a point of argument between us and an obsession to the point that one day in February, we drove to the Portland airport together, and I drove home alone to my work, my books, and the deafening silence of a home that *used* to be home.

I cried that night. Harder than I ever have in my entire life. Screaming, ugly crying into my pillow lest the neighbours hear. I cancelled work in the morning and stayed awake for far too long in this state of inconsolable despairing isolation.

When I woke up, I experienced one of the most horrific things in my life: I could not see. The world of my bedroom and my apartment were blurry, off-coloured and dark. It looked as if I had taken an out-of-focus photo and put the 'warmth' slider all the way up. No amount of rubbing or cleaning could help, and in a panic, I called a colleague and asked for them to help me to the urgent care clinic. After trying to explain over and over again that I could not fill in the intake forms because my eyes were not working, I finally got in to see a physician's assistant who looked at my eyes and said that due to forceful trauma, I had burst enough blood vessels for them to bleed over into the pupils of my eyes that caused them to be temporarily full of blood. The issue, she told me, would hopefully correct itself over the next few days and that she had also never seen it occur in both eyes. She asked if I was hit or fell or experienced any kind of physical trauma, to which I said it was from crying, and she said that that could certainly do it.

The recovery, thankfully, took 4 or so days until I was back, being able to see mostly as I had before. In the years since that day, the sight has more or less come back with the unfortunate companion of photophobia. That is, in some poetic irony, my despairing trauma at the beginning of this long, hard road of love left me so sensitive to the light that I had to exist more or less in the dark for the remainder of my life. That is, the light, unabridged by my lenses, almost blinds me in stabbing pain. Trauma of the mind befits trauma of the eye, which in its metaphorical malice makes darkness a soothing force and enveloping blanket of safety and sight where the light is something I have nearly grown an aversion to. Such a cruel irony, yet nothing a pair of Ray-Bans can't fix.

This was but the first step on my traumatic journey, and it is now that I would present the true horrors of the power of the realization alluded to so far above in this essay: coming to the realization that you have experienced deep trauma is one of the strangest experiences I can imagine undertaking. That moment where, once the dust has mercifully settled, you sit in your reflection and say the words to yourself, "I am traumatized" or "I am a victim of trauma," is soul-defining, overwhelming and terrifying, to say the very, very least.

This realization led to the composition of this essay and has occupied almost every waking moment of my life since it came to me a month ago. Respective of the nature of realizations, this thought did not manifest on its own but came into existence reflective of compositional elements in my own history and experience that had existed dormant and unknown until that realization.

I have often held the thought over the past four years of my life that dreams are great until you wake up. That building dreams manifested into the real world can be simultaneously the greatest and most liberating feeling possible, and also a primordial source of the elements of despair known only to the *ragged people* Paul Simon once wrote about. It is within this realization that I have come to finally find the motivation to compose an essay about its nature in a way that is partially a memoir and partially something masquerading as insightful somewhere, somehow.

To begin with, I must say that the experience of being in love and somehow being loved in return was one of the best experiences I have ever had. This has led to the experience of realizing in retrospect that it was not the love I received in return that caused the feedback loop of despairing realities that have manifested now.

Out of the ashes of that reflective soaring year, I found myself a new purpose. My interest in the fields that occupied my time as an undergraduate led to a grander calling, and with that calling an escape or rather a flight. That is, there was a mutually dreamt dream. A dream of the shores and spruce of British Columbia. A flight to the Great White North. And with that flight, an escape. For me to the wild yonders of a world of sociological thought freer than that of the liminal bonds of criminological study in the US, and to my counterpart, a chance at life itself. As our journey together both began and ended in the whirling web of abuse, psychological pain, listless loss of joy in life and a turgid determination to make life better for ourselves. We dreamt that Canada and a life of living together, studying together, and loving one another would be the end of all of our troubles.

What followed was a series of setbacks that tested my determination and mettle as a scholar, an author, a philosopher, and, first and foremost, as a person.

I was rejected from my initial application to the University of British Columbia, and in a mad dash in the face of a dream conflagrating in front of my eyes, I made the impulsive 11th-hour call and applied to Oregon State University, where I was accepted. And so the dream changed. We moved to the Pacific Northwest, yes, but there was something *off* about it all. It felt like a sacrifice, a resignation to the currents of the universe. My goal the day we set foot into our new apartment was to make every single moment spent in Oregon a testament to escaping it to BC. I am happy to say that I did this eventually. But, the *off* feeling persisted for my better half who did not have the constant social responsibility of graduate school to occupy time. Rather, there was a similar period of isolated development occurring in our home at the time. And, in a sudden cacophony of events, I found myself alone, bleeding into my pupils by the first February of our time together. The reality of life set in for both of us and the distance between us grew into a canyon that led me to move into a smaller apartment alone and him to move to Eastern Australia.

Forays into Bondage, Domination, Sado-masochism, Madness and Social Theory

When I recovered from the loss of sight and the torturous end to my first year alone, I was also met with having to host the person who left me in that state solely for the job of printing out visa applications and serving as a hotel bedroom for a night; I fell into a period of time directly converse to my soaring period. I no longer walked in the sunset to the dining hall for sandwiches, nor did I diligently ground myself in handwritten memoirs. No. I had two specific goals: survive and get myself into a doctoral program.

The period of time wherein I stepped into the shell of the philosophical and theoretical soul that I am now was an embodiment of the phrase: *"Drugs, Sex and Rock n' Roll"*. And I do not share that reality shamefully. I fully threw myself into the world characterized by most sane psychologists as intensely self-destructive. My drugs of choice? Unfiltered Camels and caffeine to the point of tremors. The latter elements? Combined. For a period of 33 days straight, I stayed in my apartment to compose my ramblings. I left for several hours a day to perform my duties for my job, but every other moment was spent sequestered among my books. By day I would black out the windows and in a manic nicotine stained state I would fire into my keyboard all of the rage, the despair, the isolation and the pain into words weaving a nonsensical symphonic collation of ideas and data points that would form the basis of my eccentrically depressing sociology. Plumbing the depths of social horrors and making monsters out of the shadows on my wall. At night, I would deviate into the netherworlds of the strange and terrible and embody the truest and most faithful dedication to Michel Foucault's most leather-clad wet dreams. With a partner who emerged into my life and melted away in almost perfect timing, we transcended and pushed the limits of psychological and physical boundaries of the human spirit. It is in these moments, strung out on coffee cigarettes and kinky sex, that I found a grounding again, not in these vices, but in the emergent realization that the world itself was inherently dark and grey in its organization. It is a strange place to be pushed so far into the cynicism of existential nihilism that all that makes sense finally is the debauchery of being bound to one's own bed or, conversely, binding another human to one's own bed. It is in these acts, these performances, these expeditions into the depths of the *Venus in Furs* that I feel the practice by which I found my self and stride again emerged. In between meditations on the nature of the institution and the insidious imperialism of self in society, I could then escape the storied world of watching every single muscle tense as one delayed orgasm for hours on end. I could, in my practice of the social psychological, transcend that to my partner, engaging in the consensual breaking of the mind that pushes an individual to the edge of sanity and insanity wherein we are reduced to the very formative structures of our identity. It is in this same state that one such as myself can finally let go of the masks we have to wear in the waking hours and exist in a state of pure humanity. Foucault was not wrong in his theories and instead presented a means of escaping the subjugation of the body by the state in ways that test the limits of the socially real in every instant. Playing games, manipulating the boundaries of modesty, turning one's house into an open-door playhouse, and modifying the realms of reality to the point of total deviation into the purely human is the best form of carefully medicated coping for a crisis of the soul that I could have experienced at the time. Constantly aware, though, of the pragmatic limitations needed in such therapies of the body and mind. The power of these trysts to become consuming was certainly evident, but it is in this that I feel I transcended that temptation to descend to the addictive elements so present therein and instead emerged on the other side have set a clear boundary for when it was all to end. After squeezing the last tear out of the physical muse of my thesis work and shedding my own, we bid each other farewell. We never even knew each other's names or how to contact one another. We just knew that as soon as work was over, the real work began. While there is no doubt a chance at erotica here, what emerged amidst ropes, whips, chains, leather, latex, and silicone was *not* an emotional or affective partnership. It was, in effect, a month-long nightly therapy session for two broken souls who needed to focus on coming to learn about themselves on the deepest level possible. And when that swirl of gratification, denial, humiliation, praise and the knowledge of how a single finger can break the individual down to their barest form of self we emerged new people. By the age of 23 I emerged from a month long anonymous no limits BDSM carnival in my own bedroom office a completely changed person with a strong sense of grounding in my work. By the time of my defence, I had slept for an average of two hours a night for over a month. I had barely consumed a real meal and I had written work that meant the world to me in my understanding of my professional place in this world. My partner in this psychosexual therapy safari found his grounding, too, and on into the dawn, he sailed in the pursuits of lives better suited for that development of self-authenticity that can only come when you have been vulnerable in the most intense way to someone else. Confidence and self-assurance can certainly be found splayed to the whims of a safe and sane sadist at the foot of the bed in the dark.

The Subjective Frameworking of the Abuse

Over a mediocre dinner at a brewpub in the early summer, I saw the person who had crushed blood into my sight for the first time in a year. I was asked a simple question and then a follow-up via text message that night:

"Are you still planning to go to Canada?"

"Yes."

"I would like to come with you if I could."

I then made the largest mistake in my life in retrospect. I said yes. Of course. You're family. All is forgiven. I love you. All that.

What began the moment we set foot off the boat into Canada was a horror story that is still playing out in my mind day by day. After rekindling our relationship, after redeveloping trust, after letters, cards, falling asleep on phone calls, and all the things that reflect the reconstruction of love, after only 11 days in our new home in BC it began.

I did not have the emotional tools to deal with the person I built this dream with, bringing someone from Tinder home the day we got the internet hooked up. I did not know how to deal with the sounds of cheap sad sex emanating down the stairs of the home we had fought so hard to get to. I was not ready to be blamed for the crushing feelings of despair I experienced from this.

My *Night on Pandora* began then. Any semblance of being able to feel remotely safe in my new home in a new country evaporated as a psychotic 20-year-old from Tinder became my unofficial tenet in a house I was paying for. This lasted for four months straight. It was during these months that my tradecraft was born. At the time, it was survival. Now I know these to be trauma responses. The safety signals, the pavement artistry, the lamp lighting, all of it. It was to preserve what little bits of myself I could. As I tried to situate myself into the rigours of a doctoral program, dodge other realms of insanity in menial social circles, and mitigate my own family flying apart due to my own mother's insanity, all I had left to lean on was my own wits and a quotation paraphrased to me by the professor who saved my life at that time:

"Stay with the trouble-it'll all work out in the end"

Paraphrased from Donna Haraway. But burned into my mind and into the whiteboard in my office in red ink, in Russian. It became the mantra of my survival. I then took inspiration from a morosely unlikely source from fiction: George Smiley. Who, in his extraordinary ordinariness, taught me via his creator John Le Carré how to disentangle the webs of lies and secrets of the life of the individual. First, my own. And second that which plagued my home life. *"What do we KNOW?"* I would often whisper in the din of my office. Staring out the window with Julio Iglesias' *La Mer* on repeat, I visualized the web of misery I was escaping nightly as a massive knotted string with invisible ends. I followed the beginning to the beginning, the end to the predicted end. I followed the thread of behaviours I was observing through a lifetime of abuse, the abuse we tried to escape together and the abuse I fear my former muse will never fully escape. I watched in my mind the ways that the abusive realities I had seen unfold in our past together would come to manifest the experiences I was seeing day to day. I then watched as the thread slowly unraveled at the other end, that is the means by which this hurdle would be overcome.

I saw these woes become patterned and conditioned, and with that, they became fanatical in their repetitiveness. It became a game of waiting as a means of surviving. I fooled myself in those lonely hours into believing that it was "worth it" to stick around because, at the end of the line, there was that bliss. It was only a matter of months as the signs piled higher that the realization was coming on the other end, and then finally, we would be free together again.

And so sang the siren song of the weary traveller, that sanguine voice in the meadows of the uncertainty of an abstract future: *"If you wait long enough, everything will work out how you want it to."* The challenge here is in contradiction to the paraphrase of Donna Haraway in that working out in the end and working out how you want it to are vastly and widely different realities. It is in this dissonance that we must examine the core elemental side of love so often left out of the discussion. That component is known within the social sciences as *Limerence.* Limerence is a term coined by Dorothy Tennov (1979) that speaks to the *state of being in love*. That is the metaphysical modality of existence that one occupies in the active cognitive, affective and behavioural experience of being while one is in love. Limerence is the overloading of the emotionality and internal sociality of the individual actor. It is in these experiences of limerence that we are infatuated, obsessive, prone to fantasy and imagined utopian futures, and overly interpretive of symbolic clues to the purpose of a self-confirmation bias of monumental social importance. Effectively, the typology of existence in a state of being in love is one that supersedes rationality and supplants us within a forest of mirrors all its own that wraps its tendrils within and without us to bend our forms to their infinite refractions. And it is within these expansive woods of uncertainty that we start, through the throes of our own irrationality, constructing the most dangerous world of all that we may inhabit in the waning moments before sleep and in the blissful dreamscapes of our slumber. We build within our minds an entire narrative story on the subjectivity of our own limerence-soaked delusions. That is that love, love will find a way in spite of anything and everything to the contrary on the singular and most intimate levels on through the collective uncertainty of shared experience, we manufacture a world of symbolic reverence for the ebbs and flows of the loving futurity. We erect between us and the subject of our desire an entire utopian dream, a halcyon state of being that leaves no positive stone unturned and no negative shadow unilluminated. At the spark of a new flame of limerence, we are overtaken by that uniquely human ability to imagine and to suffuse our ego through our imaginative lens that allows us to see on through any and all strife, with that subject of our limerence being the saving grace of any and all potential moments of despair. It is in this phase, the pre-proliferation of loving companionship, that we are at both our most content and also our most pre-disposed for abject defeat. It is in the stage of limerence pre-social reality that the individual actor seesaws between the divinely perfect and the horrifically disastrous. It is in these scenarios in our minds that we may either induce an anxious insomnia or spur on a blissful fantastical sleep.

This is the stage I found myself within again in the interim between the initial downfall of my existence into a swirl of abuse and into the equally distressing time of waiting for the positivity to return. You see, the story of how I have come to sit where I am today in a state of half-existence in terms of my cynicism towards the nature of human social interaction in general and the toxicity of the capacity to imagine what is best for us is in the fact that I, rather stupidly in hindsight, believed in the capacity of human beings to change, to experience empathy, to love, and secondarily in the power of love as a transformative means by which the individuals intertwined within it might find their common ground, in a circle of song, to evoke Paul Winter. It is often in my reflections on this stage of my life that under the brim of the hat of an outsider, I may more succinctly cast this simply as my inability to socially and relationally meld with other people, some deficiency on my part, some lack of social and emotional reciprocity that lends to an innate challenge when it comes to the symbolic exchange of social reality. In actuality, I think the challenge lies far deeper than that. While my approaches to conflicts were not always the best, and in hindsight every relationship bears a degree of fault on both sides in some elements, somewhere in the timeline. I feel my situation was unique. Why? Because the shattering reality of the fabricated bliss I had pinned every single hope upon fell away into the actuality that what I was hoping for was solely a hope and nothing beyond a careful sifting through social cues and patterns to the point that while I was *right* in my analysis, the simple fact of the matter is that where I was in my own timeline of life was such that to achieve the storied bliss of my imagined realities would take me a decade or more of survival just to experience.

One of the most common refrains I shared with friends who supported me through this was that it was a matter of time, that it was worth the wait and that, eventually, everything would work out. This was my delusion, my narcissistic fall into the sociological headspace of having the ability to read the currents of the social to a degree of certainty that would eventually land me in the right. There was progress, there was verbal confirmation of suspicions I held. There was everything pointing to my work, my tradecraft, my countless sleepless hours being worth it. But at every single turn, there was a negation of that because the social forces of the world beyond my control or station were such that I was never enough to be the person my former partner needed in order to break the cycles of abuse, addiction and pain in order for "us" to be a true social pairing.

There were countless nights when a conversation started in our living room that ran the scope of everything from our history to our future to arguing to crying in each other's arms. There was true vulnerability there. Responsibilities were taken, apologies landed, and love exchanged in the form of promises to always be there, to be supportive. All of it lent time and again to a renewed sense of hope that once my head hit the pillow for a 45-minute nap before teaching at 9 AM, I was able to satiate my concerns with the words: "See, it's getting better." But to fool yourself into sleep three times a week by saying 'it's getting better' for three years, does not mean it is getting better. It means the opposite.

It is a very hard reality to exist in being simultaneously the subject of abuse and taking on trauma after trauma while also being the person your abuser relies on for support in their darkest moments. That means that I have been at the same time forced to sleep in my office while that night's Tinder conquest used my towels to clean themselves up afterwards, and then forced to come home in the morning after the Tinder conquest left to counsel my partner through a depressive episode and suicidal ideation. I lived not a double life, but one that was horrifically multifaceted to the point that now, in my reflection after escaping that social space and the cycle, I am in the curious space of having to learn how to live life without all of those facades blending together. It feels as if my cover stories were all blown and that now, to borrow again from Le Carré, I had done my service and had to now *come in from the cold.* Coming in from the cold of a nearly decade-long relationship that skirted from wedded bliss and being called a power couple, from dominating social situations together, being perfectly complimentary in our interests, desires, drives and dreams, to having a secret shared reality of pain and struggle where behind every happy memory there is a storm cloud of pain that buffets the nostalgia. For every dinner date, there was the fact that that night's Tinder date had already been briefed on our ETA home so that when I walked through the threshold of my own home, I had a crash 3 minutes to run to my safe house lest I want to again be subjected to the two hours of buildup to the 11 minutes of intercourse echoing down the staircase. It bred a constant awareness and an inability to experience joy. Truly. I lost the ability to feel happy in any moment or experience because I had to turn my eyes to the subtleties that would remit my predictions of what I would have to dodge once I got home. You start to recognize strange things in this regard. Like which fragrance is just for you and which one goes on for the date after dinner. You notice that the way household chores are done differs from needing to be done to being done to showcase the home to that night's guest. Consent was out the window, communication nonexistent, and in the end, I was expected to simply deal with it. I was told that this was "who" my partner was and that if I liked being together, it was simply something I would need to learn to accept. In effect, I was pushed into a polyamorous relationship without my consent and without ever having the chance to protest or lay out my feelings before being subjected to the horrors of not feeling safe in my own home. It is another curiosity of life to live in a web of gaslighting at all times. To be told that my distaste for sharing my home with almost the entirety of the 20-year-old co-ed population of Victoria, BC, was a reflection of my own issues and not in any way a reasonable response to an absurd situation.

To keep with the theme of hopes, both false and failed, there was a moment in the immediacy before the dissolution of this pairing that the light shone in briefly. It was a light carried on the wings of a psychologist and an agreement to finally seek treatment for the woes that were befalling our coupling. It was in these sessions that I began to see glimmers of self-awareness, of the potentiality for that futurity that I had so often staved the demons with. There was growth, a desire to get better, an admission of addiction. And all of it, all of these subtle hints at happiness, were undone almost immediately. While I am not a psychologist, nor a clinician, I cannot understand how an individual in such a profession can hear someone confess an addiction to them, asking for help, only to reply with: "Well, it isn't hurting you or anyone so keep doing it, and it isn't even an addiction, it's not in the DSM-show me your peer-reviewed sources." This. This is the sentence thrown into a seminar discussion by a first-year graduate student. This is not sound therapeutic advice. This is a self-destruct override that allows for a rhetorical and clinically backed justification for the continued patterns of destructive behaviour. Conveniently as well-the 'no one' being hurt by those actions somehow did not include me in the equation. But. I digress.

The goal here in sharing this is not to garner a sympathetic reader nor devolve entirely into musings of the past historicity of my time in Canada. Rather this is a twofold exploration of the origination of my theoretical and philosophical periods and swings in insights while also serving for me as a funeral of sorts for that loss of bliss that grew out of nearly a decade of being forced into an abusive space by my own empathy and desires to be with the person I loved. These reflections, rather than being simple tangential spats of recollection, are, to me, the last physicalization of the social soul of who I was. Within these words remain the last vestiges of a person I once knew to be me. It is then the inverse of Kierkegaard's *At a Graveside* wherein I myself am peering into the void of the earth below and observing the burial of myself.

This is an uneasy process. As with the passing of a friend, lover, or family member, there are these moments that occur where one forgets the death and the passing of the living to the veils beyond. This happens to me often throughout the day. I forget the part of me has died, turn to interact with that part, and am suddenly and shamelessly crushed into nothing all at once. Am

I mourning a simple breakup? No. It is deeper than that, it is a death of an entire abstracted future reality, the saving grace of many a dark night, and that tether to the reality of the world that I had relied upon for so long. It was the ending of much more than a partnership, but rather a deconstruction of a core tenet of my identity, a subject of my drive and motivation, and the loss of a true muse of my own compositions. Randomly now, throughout the day something strikes me. A memory, a reminder, some external trigger. I walk through the grocery store and remember the countless trips we made together, the dinners we shared, the squabbles over flavours of drinks, all of it. I remember in the darkness of my new solitary nights the times we spent under the soothing tones of audiobooks on the speaker as we drifted to sleep. I remember the road trips. The times we played with our dog. The surprise campus lunches and social affairs at our table in the faculty club. I mourn the loss of having someone I can turn to, despite the darkness between us and at the very least receive some kind of validation of my own exigency of reality. You miss the little things like how you argued over how to do the dishes for four years or the older faded yellow pages of love letters that still somehow described all of the love and the hate that was swirling around them. I find myself then wandering my new dreamscapes, never fully awake. It is in this vein that the opening of this essay, the mediation on realization, really comes to shine in my experience of reality.

That is, we are not subject to the traumatic realization that we are victims of trauma just once. Nor am I free of the realization that I am waking up alone and miles away from the reality I had imagined for myself. These realizations crash into me daily, and the power they hold in jarring my state of being has not waned. There was a peace in the chaos. A certain rhythm to the pain that led me to my chambers in the dead of night to put words to paper that I was proud of. That pain flavoured the cigarette smoke and the sad and lonely solitude of a bench in the rain. That pain made it all worth something. The realization then now is not one of loss, but it is a realization that I am not sure who I am nor how to exist without a constant feeling of pain, fear, rage and isolation. In short. I do not know how to feel joy in the little things anymore. I am a shell because it seems that in that inferno of pain and loss and constant fighting for survival, I had the contrast I needed to find the flow of freedom and joy in the moments between conflagrations. Yet at the evaporation of this burning pain that befell my every moment of being, I find myself now unsure how to handle the consistency of returning home and *not* having to check. Not having to make sure I knew some degree of the debauchery I would be walking into. I am in from the cold, and I do not like the loss of the pervasive sense of danger to my psyche because I cannot now find a way to justify my existence, which, in reflection, horrifies me the most. What if this momentary sublimation of my ability to feel alive in general and gratified in that life specifically continues to elude me? Had I been someone closer in social prose to my former partner, I would fix this issue by finding the next available person and jumping headlong into another toxic relationship. But in the vein that I am who I am and have survived what I have, the reality is such that at this time, I cannot even feel a semblance of belief *in* love itself rather than any call on to the journey again.

It is a dystopia of the self, I think, to be where I am now. Not physically, but effectively, a place of constant dissonance, longing, waning, and wandering. I have come again to prefer the night because that is when the pressures of the world fade away, and I am left alone. Previously, I would have written. Now, even in this composition, that skill has left me. That dedication, the manic spark of madness that drew from me a torrent of collated nonsensical ramblings, has been reduced to the shell of a third-rate ghostwriter unable to fully commit to even a centralized theme. It is in this fact that I have realized what my partner and I often joked about my rage, pain and despair brought on by our partnership was more than a joking point. It was real. The pain of longing for the light at the end of the tunnel was the strongest drug of the mind that I can imagine having consumed. The idea that if I sit still and create a 70-page treatise, if somehow I break on through to the other side it was only a matter of time until the wedding speech was materializing. Alas, now, simple emails elude me. This monstrosity and three others in the void are fighting me tooth and nail to not come into the world, and my dissertation looms composed but unwritten.

Life, as it seems, has become a curious swirl of randomly manifested feelings of abject worthlessness, seasoned with futile rage, and baked in an oven of hopeful delusion that *maybe, just maybe*, It'll be ok. But then I am mad at myself for that. For letting my mind wander to what I know will hurt me. But, for some reason, the painfully abusive reality is a drug all its own calling me home. I hate that it is, but I, on some masochistic level, miss the thrilling sense of calm and peacefulness that came from familiarity and a love that was without definition or boundary that often cut so deep into my flesh that the blood still stains my mind. Is this what we are reduced to in our modern age? Loving the idea of loving so much that we cannot come to process a world free of the pain of that love? I fear for myself, and in this hour of total honesty, I do present my worries that the kids, as they say, are not right. And yet, I cannot clinically justify the de-evolution of my psyche back to that world of pain and terror as a means of patching the very wounds it wrought upon my social soul.

And this, I believe, to some degree, is the song of the scattered and damned youth with whom I share my generational and temporal ties. We, I think, by the machinations of the rapid onset of the 21st century, are locked into this struggle. Maybe not entirely in the relationship venue, but in the dissonance between a nostalgic pain and a current one, one that we tend to seek as a means of soothing our tired souls and this is then exemplified in the long and tattered road we lead with our selves. The tireless pursuit of serotonin to the extent that anything and everything that leads us to feel just slightly more *human* becomes the thing to which we gravitate our formulation of new identities. We scoop from interest to interest at a blazing speed without ever finding that calling home that we are so desperate for. We search out feelings to replace the ones we've lost in our pasts and then encourage those to proliferate to the point of designing their own insufferable voids within our new shattered dreams. And that, I think, most desperately so, encapsulates the irony of the existence of the modern human. A chasing of the feeling we once had on a Friday night with Pokémon Ruby on the Gameboy Advance and not a care in the world. We seek out those leisures that transcend the responsibility that we are now shouldered to carry. We do not bat an eye paying 3 times the MSRP for a said copy of "Ruby" if it just means that when the package from eBay arrives, we get to be 7 again, tearing into the pristinely preserved cardboard. It is why, I think, that we are lost in our comfort shows, our nostalgic YouTube playlists, and overall experiencing such a dissonance of the self that I am wondering to what degree any of us even knows who we truly are anymore. Identity, self and personality, all of it has become so swirled around the tendrils of this inauthentic experience of life that it reflects a total unknowing and unlearning of those tendencies we often treasured in our childhood.

Is this a personal condemnation of my fellow wanderers? No. Is it a manifesto on the subjective subversion of the human spirit by the grinding maw of capitalistic commodification of every single fucking thing we hold sacred to ourselves? Again, it is to my comrades of the cloth to make the final determination.

And I am left here with the final notion on this subject: I do sincerely hope I meet myself again someday. I feel as though we have some catching up to do.

Chapter 6

The Valleysong

"The more identities a man has, the more they express the person they conceal"

-John Le Carré, Tinker, Tailor, Soldier, Spy (1974)

"Soup and Salad"

-Lonely Diner Marquee on the Valley Floor; Author Unknown

Maybe is murder to the mind...

Maybe drips of potentiality, of unknowability and of the sanguine possibility that someday the darkness may wane to the light. And it is in this unknowability that we find ourselves sailing home. Venturing on to the point on the horizon wherein we may, with the hopeful abandon of our experience of and by the self, come to terms with a respectful reconciliation of that which has made us and that which will continue to shape us in this moment on through time.

It is in a swirl of maybes that we always return home. There is something magical about the journey home insofar as it often outweighs the nostalgic mystique of arriving there all together. I can see, in some regard, the desire to leave home, to explore, to wander, but to always have some tether to the world somewhere. But why is it that the journey home feels so much better than the second day at home?

Where in the waking of our days within the walls of our familiar places do we lose that wondrous mystique that so readily presents itself three turns in the forest path before the candles in the window shine into our view? As the previous part stressed the need to feel some degree of contentedness with the mundane, what is it about the mundane of home that conditions within us a response that fosters the need to leave, and why, then, is the journey home so graciously rewarding in its fruits?

This is the struggle I now face as I have returned to the valley of my youth but without the innocence of that youth. It is odd to wander the pavements of your hometown after being away and experiencing the wider world beyond. It is something I think is unique to small western American towns that we have a certain allure to the general public but a private weariness to the long-time local. I had this experience the other night in the local saloon, the same place where my grandfather and great-grandfather spent their days in their respective eras. I found myself at our usual table, all the way in the back corner, in the seat facing the door. You never sit in a saloon with your back to the door; it is one of the things you learn as you grow up in a collective community of cowboys, hippies, coal miners and real estate agents, the latter of which being the real ones you must watch out for.

As I ordered my customary onion soup, which has since become a *du jour* offering rather than a menu staple, I could not help but become absorbed in the social theatrics occurring across the empty dining room. You see, not many folks would venture out into the snowstorm for a simple cup of soup in the saloon at 9:30 PM. The only other occupants of this hallowed historical space were a gaggle of what appeared to be several generations of men out from the eastern US on a big grand Rocky Mountain hunting trip. This is a tourist town so seeing out of town folks is just a simple part of life, be they the wealthy skiers or the wealthy outdoor adventurers, everyone is out to bask in the beauty of the *rocky mountain high* as neighbor John would say. It is easy to spot the out of town hunters as they often travel in little packs and are entirely entranced by such things as roundabouts in the road or grocery stores as a concept. Their markings? One would assume the bright orange hats, but it is even simpler than that. Is it the camouflage they wear everywhere or the fresh, bright blue Wrangler jeans they bought for this trip specifically? No. It's the boots. I have yet to see a pair of cowboy boots worn in public by a local around here that are spotlessly clean in mud season. I would wager that a church carpet may see such manifestations, but alas I do not see such carpet and make it a point to not do so. And so, in watching the shiny leather boots that have not yet seen the sno-seal needed to keep their wearer's cushioned feet dry, I began to notice the other things one tends to when one has had to become a *watcher* for the purpose of survival.

Aside from the strange efforts of both the 17/18-year-old among the gaggle and his presumed father of 45-50 to "pick up" the waitress with their Texas drawls and the absolute state of disorder they left their table in, the thing that caught my eye and pressed me to remember this strange little brood of testosterone was the fact that amidst the continually arriving pitchers of what I can assume to have either been *Bud Light* (cultural prejudice) or *Coors Banquet* (to try the "local brew") was the curious instance of the youngest of the brood continually filling and emptying his tumbler. While I have certainly experienced the relaxed drinking age of the rest of the world, the boy of 12/13 did not seem to me to be the best candidate for a hangover in the morning as he trekked around the public lands of my homeland with a gun looking for something four-legged to shoot.

And this reminded me of a darker element of coming home that I don't write about often but that exists strongly in my experience and that of others. That is the simple reality that if you grow up in the bedroom community of Aspen, Colorado, a place where drugs flow more freely than the millions slapped around for luxury condos, a fair few of the people I share yearbook pages with had even as kids succumbed to a dark spell of this place. The alluring call of the party scene. But party scenes in the rural west are not the same as the party scenes in the wealth of Aspen or the cities beyond. The most common scene for the kids was the bonfire. The hallowed bonfire. The event where highschoolers would pick up middle schoolers and steal away Friday night with ten thirty-racks, several bags of weed and the intention to stand around in the deserted dark flats of backroad wide spots to freeze in their letterman jackets while pushing the blood-alcohol capacity of their veins to new heights each week with the hope that just maybe the girl they convinced to come out with them would give them 3 minutes of premature bliss in the back seat of the dodge pickup their parents purchased for them. In a strange mix of the stoner jock kids and the wannabe cowpokes, there was this bonded neutrality of social station in the pursuit of 'making memories'. The problem with this? If you're taking dabs by 9th grade and downing a handle of fireball at the same time, well, by junior year, the tolerances are just too great that to truly make a memory, you have to push yourself further.

I know a large handful of people who, before they were 18, were snorting Adderall by the pill every party night between shotguns of Natural Light. I know a handful of them now who are either contemplating their third run at rehab, who have found Jesus to a frightening degree of intensity, or who are still burnt into the scene in ways that feel sad to observe from the outside. There are some, too, whose Facebook pages have suddenly filled up with messages of remembrance, whose obituaries then appear in the paper I write for. There are people I know that I have seen working at every restaurant in town because they cannot keep a job long enough due to their spiral. I see so many of these people reposting obscure life-affirming antihero quotes over a picture of Heath Ledger as the Joker that I cannot open Facebook without being inundated with the overdose of Joker Memes with weird slogans slapped on.

For instance, in my timeline now (at the time of original composition):

What does this mean? Why is it there, and why does the person known for their 'mad' party days think that sharing this at 3:12 AM is going to mean anything more than a burnt-out place in life? I do not want to offer judgment too harshly, and I do not ascribe such descents to the people themselves. But rather that small towns and homes can do some fucked up things to you if you never leave. And returning? I am not yet sure what fuckery I may look forward to, but I have come to recognize that while I never thought I belonged here in totality, I now entirely feel completely out of place in the place my ancestors landed in when Queen Victoria and Jack the Ripper were alive and busy with their various slashings. That feeling of dis-belonging is an odd thing to experience. I feel often in visiting familiar places that I am not entirely meant to be there anymore. And also that I am not fully consciously aware of who I am in these wanderings when they occur. I feel a stranger to my own experience, some kind of depersonalized soul wandering the ether between the veil of life and death. Even in the company of familiar faces, the world as I have experienced it over the past few months has felt like a flickering illusion of film flashing across the lens of a projector. There does not seem to be a reality to the reality anymore; rather, it is an illusory collective of images flashing by so quickly that they trick my mind into believing they are some representation of the world as it is. It seems that as a result of the roads I have walked, I have somehow retreated back to the floor of Plato's cave, even though I am not sure I ever climbed out to begin with. And that is the worrying fact of this. In my barest reflection here I can say that I am scared of what I have become insofar as the ability to feel, to experience, to remember and to laugh naturally seem to have lost me. And yet, I am not unhappy. Rather I am quite content to experience the life I am and it seems real in its momentary flashes, and the joy felt, the appreciation for the little things and the emergent challenges met and mounted reflect a state of triumphant rehabilitation for me. But it is in the hours of the nights I have come to occupy that these things seek me out and batter me into a knot of negative emotions and passively intrusive thoughts of nervous melancholia. I will swiftly shift from a hopeful reality to a spiral of self-doubt, self-hatred and resentment at my allowing myself to fall so far into the depths of this darkness. I often reflect on my window facing Mount Sopris to the South that rather than the light coming in and fading away, the dark fades and then seeps in as the sun disappears. With our time change and the onset of winter along with it, this seeping of the darkness comes faster and with less warning. The room chills with the intruding dark, and within that cold lack of natural light comes the despondency and the dissociation. It is in this prison of my mind and body that I find myself thrown and prone to randomly emergent bouts of extreme disconnection from life and the world around me. Random bouts of unexplainable emotional upheaval wrack my brain with no outlet. I cannot plug in the electric guitar and play until my fingers bleed at 4 AM. I cannot decide to walk into the night and traverse the rugby field to the corner store for an excuse to walk outside and buy a snack in the dead of the streetlit early morning. I find that I left much more than a handful of possessions in Victoria. I left myself, and I left a life that I had spent every day for nearly a decade building. I am lost now. Not for lack of opportunity, nor for lack of ability nor pedigree. But simply for the fact that the way I was living for a decade of my adult life, from 18 to 28, was in some major form shaped around this tangled web of dysfunctional functionality in my relationship to the point that I became nothing more than a participant in it alongside my public persona of the academic that writes about eccentric things. It is in this reflection that I find coming in from the cold to be the hardest. To shed an identity that I had so lovingly cared for through hell itself in a manner of months and expect to somehow move on and function? It tears me apart from the inside on a daily basis.

Am I alone in this? No. I do have a support network, and they are there for me should I need them. But a challenge I have experienced in my life, professionally and personally, is that often I find that I fixate, analyze, and meditate on the darkness too often. I am too dark and despairing for those close to me to bear for long enough to make my venting normalized. Sadly, the few people I have in my life who can withstand my onslaught of darkness now only exist in my digital world on my phone. They live far away. Some were in Victoria with me and are not chat bubbles popping up in the pixels. Some live oceans away. And still more...are dead.

A key component of the feelings I am thrashing with now, even at this moment, is the drive and desire to walk for hours, to smash my fist into the brick wall in my office to feel the heat and bruising of the knuckles, something to *feel*, comes from the fact that in August I lost my best friend suddenly. Without warning. Quite literally in a matter of minutes from when I last spoke to him alive. I jokingly outwardly expressed my nonchalant reproach of my mental state at this time being the university's resident 'death professor'. However, in the weeks since, in my isolation at the mercy of The Valleysong-at the crossroads of the social space we had shared our Childhood find myself lost even further now in reflecting on the substantial void in my personal and professional lives that his death has wrought upon my experience of life itself.

And it is in this theme of death, of loss, and of listless wandering the streets and mountains of my place of origin that I have found myself both soothed and dismayed at the sound of The Valleysong-the caressing crooning of the openness, the natural beauty, the art, the shallow pretense of enlightenment that I find my home to be broken, whole, and entirely strange and terrible. That there is punctuation to every act, every coupling, every instance of meeting the bare minimum of human acceptability to such a level that the fear and loathing are tangibly present beside me in bed every night, like the worst part of an impulsive hookup, there are these bodies pressed against mine, and I am awake at 3 in the morning wanting nothing more than to be alone and in company at the same time. It is a careless dissonance and a savage wresting of the soul that it is, in its finality, totally exhausting to the infinite limits of the oblivions of life. I am simultaneously overwhelmed by the social forces around me and desperate for the tender caressing love of days gone by. There is a cyclical conduit of painful nostalgia and pertinent dread at the nature of the future. Do I dare send that text message saying how lonely I am, or, God forbid I fall back out of the tendrils of my new found escaped freedom from the pain of perpetual abuse. A trial of the soul is upon me, and the soundtrack, amidst the haze of cigarette smoke and the smell of burnt coffee on the counter, is this Valleysong. This pulsating voice transcends the physicality of its spatial limits and penetrates deep into the psyche of those of us here in its tendrils. It is a pull to wander the wilds alone and free for hours on end and to be deafened by the silence, but it is also a frighteningly loud reminder of the soul-crushing isolation it breeds in its walls. It is on the wings of winter that this song calls to me, as the Long Nights take their plunge out across the valley, The Valleysong becomes somber, despondent, and isolatory in its composition. It is akin to a sudden and unexpected shift to a minor key in the middle of the crescendo of the colours of a symphonic tapestry of lived experience. There is a slowing to the world, like a record played at the wrong speed. But unlike the sensuality of the vinyl, The Valleysong calls out to lure its victims into the snow, into the shadow and into a space where even the warmth of the logs in the fireplace do little to quell the storms within us.

This is not to say that this sombre symphony of the rhythm of the world around me is depressing, nor is it some temptress beckoning me to my early death-rather it is the purest and most centrally universal calling frequency to the outstations of our own minds. We are invited amidst the pain and the terror of the Long Nights to reflect on who we are to the subtle undertone of the perpetual Valleysong that leads the soul not to temptation but to retribution and transcendental emergence and rebirth. It is the anthem of the shattered dreams, the crushed spirits and the fruitlessly hopeless romanticism that stills our hearts as our pillows cradle us to sleep. This is the event horizon of the transformative changes we are invited to make, on this, the centrally located and universally divined hallowed ground of where the soul is to be tested in its capacity to enter into its future. It is a place where, in the chill of the woods, the spirit of the individual, the self, and the social comes to meet the physical world incarnate. You lose yourself in the woods and the cold and the dark, and in that loss, you come face to face with a facsimile of what you once imagined yourself to be. It is like noticing yourself in the mirror, strung out on caffeine and whatever else, and struggling to remember if your eyes are truly your eyes looking back at you or if you've just met someone completely unknown to you in their entirety. This is the sign of your transcendence of the mortality of the separation of the soul, of the physical world and of the social currents that govern how and when we might come to know the social beyond and the internal material within. It is a transfiguration of the materiality of reality itself into a half-rendered dreamscape where you walk alongside yourself as you continually run and run and run into the voids of nothingness like the dream of a fall you never wake up from. This. This Valleysong. This is my home, my prison, my mind, my self, my soul and nothing all at once. This is the Valleysong in the Key of Winter Minor.

...

A dear friend of mine penned a beautiful reflection on the nature of going home last January:

"Being back home is a strange feeling. Well, it is many feelings melded together into an undefinable state — some juxtaposed combination of nostalgia for the past and anticipation for the future. The safety of familiarity and the alluring risk of the unknown. I left because I needed to express who I truly am, environment playing an important part in that."

It is in the returning home that we find some strange and terrible reflexivity, I think. Something beyond the scattered spacing of time as we age, but something deeper and more sacred to our core. For me, there has been a sense of seeing through into my own history and experience as a windowed eventuality of repetitive nostalgic mundanity. I think, too, that my rosy reflections of the spaces, places, and times spent here, as I now occupy them again as an adult who has walked across the scorching surfaces of lived experience, trauma, abuse and intellectual exploration that they have changed for me in my memory and in my exigency during the day to day wanders through them. There is a fading of the memories associated with certain elements of my own personal Valleysong, and in that fading, I find myself even more lost in the familiarity of the day-to-day existence here. Where I find that perhaps in high school or as a younger child staying home all day with my dogs, watching the snowstorms and having nowhere to be was a dream, and now, doing it every day, I am losing myself in the isolation, in the dislocation from the tattered remnants of what my life was only three months ago. I do not miss Victoria, but I think I miss the person I was allowed by myself to be there. I miss walking through campus, my two-bedroom little sanctuary just across the street, and the experiences I had there with the people I knew. I miss that element of intellectual solidarity that comes from living on a university campus and interacting daily with people who not only know what you're talking about but who listen to your words. The amounts of times here at home that people have looked at me as I am speaking Russian to them when I talk about my work, only to squirrel away to other conversations, have been small, but still, these events are present in my memory as a sharp reminder that I am not in my element anymore.

And so, this being home, the journey back, the life while here, all of it has led to a stronger call to the wild unknowns. A desire to escape again. And I am shaken by this. I did not think that it would come so quickly. It has barely been two months, and I am already feeling a call to leave again, which is unsettling considering *this* was the escape route. However, the call to leave is different than I saw in my former partner, whose call to leave was to travel abroad without a home; in that case, *home* was the torture, whereas for me, I feel that I do not have a home yet to go to, and therefore my call to leave is to leave to a place where I can feel at home. I have yet to truly establish that kind of feeling, as all of the places I have existed in after leaving home were temporarily linked to the lifestyle of a student, meaning that I always knew that a place would *stop* being home eventually, and so my valley was where I always envisioned home. But there is something that has happened to me on the journey from there to here, and it has transformed me into something that cannot functionally exist here, something that has transcended in some ways the nurturing magic of The Valleysong, and instead, I now only hear that song as a warning to stay away.

I used to tell my confidants that my previous situation felt like burning alive and drowning at the same time. Listening to the sound of someone you thought was the love of your life fucking someone else down the hall in the home you built together will do that to you. But now, it is not even that. At least in the stage of burning and drowning, there was some kind of feeling I could experience. Now, as I am here in this strange void of existence, there is nothing. Only a quiet numbness that shuts out anything and everything from the world to me. I feel as if my ties to the social have been severed, and I am sailing alone out in the wilds without that candle in the window to guide my journey. And so, the magic of coming home has left me, and I cannot yet fulfill that part of my path, and so I am wandering aimlessly into the woods without that path leading to the warmth of the hearth I may feel safe within.

I do not want to sound horrifically conceited although I fear it is too late at this point, but I feel too that my intellectual sharpness has declined significantly since leaving the physical space of a university campus. I feel a fog over my mind where instead of preferring to sit into the night meandering through the written word, I have to force myself to do it. Where I feel now that instead of bleeding into the words I write, it is more of a battle for the singular drop of inspiration that might lead me to pathetically write 3 pages over an entire rage-filled night of despondency. I think I miss the streetlights and the feeling that there were people beyond my walls. I do not have that here, and the remoteness and isolation of what I once called home have taken me into its grip, and I am very unsure of how I can feel in these moments. Some people dream of living where I do. It is a destination for many, and it might sound spoiled and ungrateful, but at a time, there is a saturation point for isolated woodland wandering, and I think the true nature of the human spirit is such that one requires a permanent place to hang one's hat.

This is not to say that all I would need to make life better is my own home- it is deeper than that. But somewhere in the parasocial milieu there is a need for a social space called home rather than simply a physical place to do so. I once naively believed that I could find a home in the companionship I kept as that was one of the many platitudes we whispered to one another in the nights of calm, but now I question even that. Because I think the true realization of both my struggle through the Long Nights of my past and the Valleysong of my present is that home needs to come from our internal reconciliations of the self and the social. That is, we need not feel at home in a specific place, but rather that home is a feeling that can come from anywhere, and in this universality of home, we arrive at the final motion of this essay: the realization that we are our own homes.

Home has been hard to define for me in my 30 years, but there is always the element of feeling "at peace" in a specific space. That is, not having to worry so much, just for a brief moment in the day or in the quiet of the night, that while I am where I am, nothing at this moment is actively causing me harm. In this moment, that feeling has all but left me. I am not sure now what *home* is, but it is not a space, and for me, in this stage, it is not a person or a feeling. I am quite literally adrift in a sea of uncertainty, not knowing truly what constitutes anything resembling a sense of feeling at peace. There is a constant turmoil within me, a continual and cyclical pattern of unknowing that breeds within it a grey milieu of a dull and rocking pain to my heart that transcends that which I had experienced previously. Although it is a different pain. It is one of feeling as if the ground underneath me is shaking away or the feeling of terror immediately prior to impact in a dream where one falls to the earth. I cannot understand this and all of my introspective methodologies carefully honed those long nights in my safehouse in Cornett A351 have left me entirely. Perhaps it is that I do not have the third-floor window to stare out of at all hours, or perhaps it is that the social forces surrounding me have taken on new and unforgiving shapes that I have yet to come to understand pragmatically to the point of being able to slay these new dragons. Alas, I am scared to no end that what I am experiencing now is the precarity of my situation in a new and frightening proportion.

I have often been of the mind that the adage of Le Carré's *Home is where you go when you've run out of homes* may not inherently be a viable exfiltration option for me at this moment. I am truly in from the cold, where my needs to survive as an active watcher of the world around me have ceased to become necessary in my experience of the world, and now I must adapt to a new world entirely, and I am unsure exactly how to do that, and the reality is that I am doing so without *any* of the points of reliant safety and support that I had in the past. It is truly a point of worry to face so many new challenges in light of just now trying to overcome and survive the onslaught of delayed infliction of pain from the old ones. There are seemingly new wounds cropping up on the scar tissue of the old just the moment that the bleeding has staunched from the previous battles. And this...this is a new era for me.

Is it reflective of the transformative nature of growing up? Is this maturity? Shedding the last vestiges of the bygone days of my youth to the point that I cannot rely on even a shred of something that once may have held me to some tethering pole? I feel that I am now, as a close friend of mine said to me the other day: *in between worlds.* In some transitory state where the milieu of my historicity and my futurity are blending in some horrific amalgam of what I can only describe as the petty foibles of an everyday life.

As I near the end of my reflection on the subject, I am, for the first time since that soaring year, in a place where I cannot with any confidence meditate nor ascribe any semblance of predictive goals to the paths I shall now be forced to walk. I cannot for the life of me see the trail in the woods upon which my feet are treading. I am not lost in the woods at two divergent roads, but rather stalking the underbrush woefully underdressed for the elements and quickly losing the safety of daylight. What Robert Frost did not explore in that poem is the fact that beyond the safety of our divergent roads in the woods lie the creatures just off the path, watching from the shadows of their respective hollows. In the dark of the woods, you cannot discern the stalking eyes of the badger or the mountain lion from the watchful vigil of the deer in the vale. And this is the uncertainty of the walk I and I fear many others are beginning now. Into that sea of dark uncertainty, it becomes very, very difficult to identify which eyes beyond the trail are those of a friend or a foe. There is a pervasive sense of being watched, followed, evaluated and estimated as of late. A question of being summed up in those unknown eyes in the shadows and the unsettling reality of not knowing their criteria for assessment, capacity for attack, nor persuasions towards deceit and betrayal. It is in this that the final realization hits: That we are, to a very deafening degree, quite alone when the cards are down and the hands of the universe are upon us. There, of course, is the guiding love of serendipitous salvation peppered into the bushes surrounding us, but there is no ability to rely upon that chance or predetermination insofar as it only belies that fragile old capacity to slip once again into the sanguine hemlock of hoping and dreaming. I do not, still firmly in this state, discount the power of these dreams and hopes, and I have, even in the last 24 hours, relied heavily upon them to quell the darkness just long enough to allow me to slip into the safety and serenity of sleep as the sun breaks into the valley floor.

It then makes me think again of the isolatory nature of The Valleysong and how, geographically and metaphorically, a valley, this valley, the cradle of my youth, composed of several critical elements: the arid and barren valley floor, where the passing of time and the everyday life of the individual in a social world comes out in scattered and continual performances, which is then guarded on all sides by hills to die on. In a literal and metaphorical sense. That is, there is an insurmountable quantum of avenues worth pushing on through this swirling vortex of worlds in between worlds to achieve and experience, and there is an even more infinite collection of values, norms, and ideals to embody for the actualization of the self to the fullest potential just up these hills. And there is the literal sense that if one cannot come to reconcile their own Valleysong in their hearts, they are destined, I think, to ascend those hills to die on and promptly die on these hills. I read about this happening just the other day where after fifteen years, the remains of a childhood friend's father were found in the hills at the edge of the valley. And while my heart breaks for her infinitely over and over again, it is a sad and tragic story that, removed of the personal reasons and rationales and contexts and histories and biographies, I do understand to some degree how it can happen. How, in the din of the morning sunburst, we can walk our last walk into the wild unknowns, unable to return by our own hands or taken in some unseen ambush by the eyes just now adjusting to the morning visibility. It is in these spectral opposites, the arid stagnation on the floor or the ascension of the hills to die on, that punctuate The Valleysong with percussive force. I have to ask myself if the decision that was made in a clear and present state of reflexivity to return to this valley from my island in the northern Pacific Ocean was the correct one. Because even now, perched on the side of one of the flanking hills overlooking the valley floor, I have to ask myself if these spaces, if this time and place are both safe and supportive to where and when I need to be right now. I think, too, that this is the siren song of the approach to 30 that we all must reconcile with. Some, whom I envy with a great deal of respect, have either already fought these battles or do not have the overthinking hang-up of the neurotic's introspection that they are not burdened by these challenges to one's existence that crop up in the early morning hours when we are truly and utterly alone.

And so the crescendo of my Valleysong is such that I am not yet sure if I am aware of its key, tempo, time signature, instrumentation or arrangement. Rather, at this time, it feels like a symphonic compression of an entire prelude to the rest of my life shot through a singular mono connection in a shattered fraction of a second. It is unintelligible and illegible in its presentation, and I am horrified and astounded by its performative presentation. I cannot see through the muddiness of its noise and instead must reach out in blind faith, unsure of where my feet may land, hoping against hope that wherever they do land, I will be able to feel home beneath them.

"And breathe in ever slowly. Welcome the tenderness of the sighs of the trees, the spirit and song of the silence in totality. Follow the path into the centre of your woods to find the warming love of the fantastical. For it is within the imagined that we so do produce that nectar that does sustain us. Embrace the solitude. Lose yourself to the voids. And measure, every so carefully the lethal dose of absolute joy and be embraced within it. For these are the fruits of the Valleysong. May they rest you on through the dawn.

Part 3

I Write.

Chapter 7

The Madness Manifesto: A Treatise on the Nature of Art and the Spirit of the Artist

"No sympathy for the devil; keep that in mind. Buy the ticket, take the ride...and if it occasionally gets a little heavier than what you had in mind, well...maybe chalk it up to forced consciousness expansion: Tune in, freak out, get beaten..."

-Raoul Duke, Rolling Stone Magazine (November 11th, 1971)

"And now the foxes have heard the horn, they have become known as the hunted rather than the living, and those that seek to force them across the veil approach ever steady on wings of wax.

Shelter me from the powder and the finger, cover me with the thought that pulled the trigger. Remember me to my love; I know I'll miss him..."

-Typewritten note on linen paper with mildly misaligned margins, February 26th, 2024, 3:00 AM, partially augmented with lyrics from Powderfinger by Neil Young (1979)

A Tortured Hypograph:

This work began in late February 2024 as a toast of a few small words to a small corner of the world wherein 23 artists, for a time, occupied a space in creative fervour, composing masterworks within and beyond the depths of the human soul. Originally, there was never an intention to include this work in the series Papers in Residence, as it had seemed, at the time, to be an ancillary footnote to a month of growth, enlightenment, and madness at the core of being. Something of an ode to sleepless nights, memories that would never leave us, and that curious state of being that comes from creating art: a mania, a wanton Bohemian abandon for the grounding pleasantries of life itself, a state wherein we do not expect happiness to enter, but for pain and suffering to emerge only insofar as it is cathartic.

As it happens, I now sit at my desk as the morning sun creeps into the window and the winds whip at the sides of my solitary writer's cabin perched over the valley having two wildly frustrating realities existing beside me at once. First, the Papers in Residence series sits unfinished in the annals of my collected works. Second, my Two Prayers for the Lost project has stalled itself into nonbeing. Both projects had themselves existed in a milieu where they would have met their loving ends by now, but somewhere in the mire, something is not right...

At first, I theorized that the simple shock of travel, the movement from place to place, the end of a month dedicated to creativity, the return to teaching, the return to routines, and the end of a blissful blur were to blame for the stall, but over time that reality itself faded as is the nature of the travelling foreign correspondence journalist to be able to feel 'home' no matter which floor we occupy. Home is where we go when we run out of homes, after all. Somewhere in my mind, this made sense, that in transitioning from Writer in Residence back to writer on the fringe of residence, I had simply burnt all of the fuel I had for creating and would logically then be able to reclaim that momentum once my mortal coil had time to recuperate and realign with its metaphysical companion. However, as days became weeks, and the weeks melted into a month, I found that something troubling was definitely afoot. Compositions, especially ones in the aforementioned series, had flowed through me so easily even prior to stepping into the halcyon magic of living with other artists in a world immediately adjacent to the real world, but now, it is almost as if the magic is limited in how I may divine it into sentences and syntax.

I have composed most of the fourth installment in my Two Prayers series, which exists now as a child just on the cusp of leaving home for the wild beyond. But words cannot flow into those pages despite my most intensive ritualistic summoning of them. Those that do flow are not right. They do not flow, they do not resonate, there is something missing from them, a spark that is no longer present. On the desktop of my computer, floating in the void over the 1970s retro futurist background wallpaper, there is a folder icon with the title 'Feb'. Inside it are three more pieces that would have been destined somewhere to have become Papers in Residence themselves. In an accordion folder near my feet on the floor, there are six of twenty-three letters composed in full, signed and typed. Each letter bears a thoughtful reflection of my experience of experiencing the art of the artists that were brave enough to share. Still, in the tattered Field Notes book in my desk drawer are hastily composed notes on over twenty open studios slapped together in minutes between tears and hugs. Each of these notes itself serves as a reminder of the contents of letters still unwritten. Emails unsent. Compliments, gratitude, love, and praise are all left unsaid. Somewhere a nagging voice in my mind screaming to 'just fucking write the things' while an equally unforgiving voice reinforces the fear that those recipients promised such emails are, in their own eyes, decrying my inability to follow through with these promises.

These are the typical thoughts that swirl in any creative mind. The projects that pile up, the things that go unsaid, the emails that never make it to even a draft form—all of these are unfortunate products of the madness we endure to create what we create.

But this is a different feeling entirely. This is not burnout; it is not a case of saying 'yes' to too many things, spreading myself thin, or even simply losing interest. It is a deeper sense of some barrier or boundary out there in the waves that is steadfastly holding me in a state of artistic despair.

The projects hanging in the ether, neither here nor there, are not ones that I see as tasks to force myself to complete. They are markedly not for any other purpose aside from an expression of thought through text, and as a combination of that process, a creative expression in that. They are, in a sense, art that I want to create. They are stories, reflections, meditations, and explorations that I feel I not only deeply desire to finish but ones that I feel are somehow, maybe to someone out there, potentially enjoyable to read.

I must confess that I did not know the nature of this barrier until the morning I sat to compose this. Sitting on a weathered wicker sofa outside in the wind as the sun crested the hills towards Aspen with Southern Cross by Crosby, Stills and Nash playing in my ears, I finally found the key to this languishing sense of nonproductivity. I did not 'find the spark', and the powers that be did not move me to compose, instead a desperation to return to my old ways of actually taking some degree of joy from the art I create, a longing for the sense of pride, of excitement in exploration, and for some degree of baseline fulfillment in my work fill me this morning. A sort of hellbent spitefulness to reach out into memory to reclaim some semblance of who I was and the voice that I had so dearly cherished.

Mere months before writing this, someone who was a stranger to me mere weeks prior, who I now feel is a true friend I have longed to know my entire life, in a moment of pure artistic vulnerability and intimacy, communicated to me that my work had itself inspired them to see life in new ways. As a writer and as someone who has (in his own mind) lost many an opportunity in life due to my own choices of career path and other such decisions, to hear through the static of the outside world such honest and warm words still rocked me to my core. I cherish those words and hold them close to my heart to this very moment.

I want to get back to the version of myself that could pen those words. That was where my love of this art stems from, not in blind praise but in moments found in the platonic love of collective exploration.

It's buried out there...Somewhere...

The key to my resurrection, to my transcendence from where I exist currently to where I feel I can and will exist again, lies very, very simply in these pages.

What was required was not a revisit and polish of papers written a month ago. It was not a forceful torturous sprint to the end of essays before I could make sure they could fly on their own wings. It was this. One-fourth eulogy, one-fourth love letter, one-fourth quasi-philosophical mediation on the nature of art and creativity, and one-fourth reflexive psychological autopsy. I think, too, that somewhere within those fractions, perhaps in irrationally small doses, there are also fragments of veiled condemnation, prophetic warnings, and more than likely a fair dose of questions over answers.

And so, in the following pages, I invite the reader to follow me into the madness of what will lovingly be considered the final nail in the coffin of the series Papers in Residence, reproduced in this text for a simple reason: I went to France to finish writing this book. In a sense, I met my goal, but not how I had imagined. Rather than writing the final chapters amidst flowing wine, cigarettes and espresso, I experienced the following madness, which, in retrospect, was exactly what I needed to experience in order to finally put the last nail in the coffin of *Pleasantries*.

This Chapter Bears the Following Dedication

Avec Amour to those who offered hugs in the rain, to those who answered late-night phone calls, to those who whispered their words of love over dinners, cups of coffee, endless cigarettes and overflowing palettes. With love to voice that said: "can I give you a hug" and who proceeded to offer a warm embrace of safety and serenity 3000 miles from home. With love to the writer who pushed past the midnight hour and whose hands inscribed a letter of support that has still, to this day, not faded. With love to the dance partner under the ebb and flow of *Rumors*. With love to the artists whose presence followed me when stability and safety in numbers were needed and who took me as a sidealong companion. With love to those voices that reached out and said: "are you doing ok? Do you need anything?" With love to adventures down country roads that end with pizza in an abandoned town square. With love to the hands that carried extra food in the night and to the voices of solidarity in absurdity. With love to the artist who mixed my coffee into her used wine glass, talked to me about the Pogues and, in a moment of pain, took care of me. With love to the words 'thank you for being so nice' whispered in parting as the train approached the platform. With love to the artist making his way from France to Portugal who answered every overly worded text message with infinite kindness, and who knew in that moment the depths of how dark the feelings were. With infinite and never-ending love to the loving voice on the other end of the phone after a long day of charting the stars who, in those most inky of voids, stood strong as my harbour in the storms.

It is because of your voices, words, hugs, and presence that this catharsis came to be. Know that my courage and reassurance in myself are in no small part a conditional reality because of these collective moments. I am forever humbled and grateful for the many ways our paths have crossed. Know, too, that the slow resurrection herein foretold is as much a fruit of your labour as it is mine.

Part 1: Thunder Only Happens When It's Raining; Players Only Love You When They're Playing

On The Business of Art, Creativity, and Spirits in Flux

1. Disregard the illusory luxury of the first draft.

2. Cast your work out into the world with no fear.

3. Take No Prisoners.

- "Advice to Artists" (Hastily written iCloud note, February 26th, 2024)

Theodore Adorno wrote, "A successful work of art is not one which resolves objective contradictions in a spurious harmony, but one which expresses the idea of harmony by negatively embodying the contradictions, pure and uncompromised, in its innermost structure." In my memories of words read, another phrase written by Alan Moore materializes now within a radically divergent context: "Never compromise, even in the face of Armageddon."

Adorno tells us that art in its true form is not a facsimile of toxic positivity. It is not the capturing of a purely perfect moment of bliss, nor is it a conceded effort to paint a picture of a world without contradiction. In the simplest of terms, in the composition of a painting, we are tasked to pay reverence to the balance of the light and the dark. To be mindful of contrasting rays of light as they play across our subject, and since the subject within the canvas itself is wholly a construction of our hands, we, too, must pay respect to the placement and existence of the shadows. The metaphor is simplistic on the surface to modify existentially outwards in the notion of Bob Ross' "You gotta have light to appreciate the dark," where our understanding of the sanguine moments of life is only existentially possible to us through our perception of the moments of joy in comparison to the despairing moments we have experienced. Further, we may call on the hopeful notion that the light is just around the corner if we are indeed stranded in the dark. It is a powerful notion in its simplicity that in order to appreciate the depth of joy, love, happiness and fulfillment, we too must have been exposed to some antithesis of each in order to learn the difference. Unfortunately, this metaphor gets taken into extreme territories of madness (as most good ideas do) when it enters a world of competition, capitalism and the seemingly total descent of the world itself. I ask my readers not to take Ross or Adorno through the routes of believing in the idea that in order to be successful, we must suffer, nor to fall into the traps of such horrific concepts as commodifying 'grit' or the capacity one may have to survive trauma. The contradiction in life and in a successful artistic reflection of life is not predicated on the individual need for trauma, to create art that captures the world, we do not need to bleed, nor do we need to aspire to be the tortured or starving artist. Pain in the heart of the painter does not itself lend to beauty in the canvas, and the absence of pain in the soul of the songwriter equally does not lend to mediocrity in verse.

Instead of being a requirement, this is a testament to the nature of art, being that in order to capture those elements of being that themselves transfer the aesthetic effect to the audience, we need not fall into the illusion of feeling compelled to compose a facsimile of the world we inhabit that is bathed in golden sunshine as a step to exclude the darkness, and secondarily we cannot then fall towards the other end, where the darkness we feel in our hearts becomes the singular representative focus of our work. Instead, there must be a balance in the middle focal point between the two. Within the contradiction.

Art as it is created is a representation, not solely of the subject, but of the mind of the artist as subject in absentia. Our work, be they words, images, melodies or memories, are ones that are inescapably individual to us despite the affective experiences of those who experience our art. As such, the creation of art is itself a psychological autopsy of a moment or moments in time that express the very interior realities of the artist who cannot fully claw their way out without a medium. It is here that we see that this contradiction in life, in being, in art is manifest in its entirety. The artist is the conduit to the nature of the human condition, where in their work, they capture forever momentary pleasantries and prolonged despairs to calcify them into stone or canvas for others to see. In this act of seeing art, there is an intimacy of knowing, an intimacy of being in the same instance in time, if even only for a few minutes, where one is in a private revelry with art at hand. The artist can, in their madness, in their mania, take into custody that contradictory state of being, of living in the contrasts of life and melding them into a representation of our innate joys, fears, triumphs and abject failures. As such, the positionality of the artist in the realm of human existence is one that is critical to the juxtaposition of our being both deeply cosmological creatures with inner worlds of imaginative creativity, and the mortal physicality of the real world out there.

When I compose these words, there is a sense somewhere at the back of my mind that they may resonate with someone beyond the waves, but far more at the forefront is the personal spirit of the individual piece. It is not for others when I am agonizing over it at unholy hours of the night; I do not compose for an audience when each essay itself feels like its own painfully slow lobotomy. And so, when I compose it is to mitigate a contradiction in my own spirit, to meet at the gates a contrast of reality and do my best to excise that monster out into the world so that, even if I do not vanquish it in single combat, I may at least make its name known. And so, what is the contradiction herein being battled to the death on the mountaintop? What is the name of the spectral horror beyond the words on the page that has me in a death grip with its sword to my throat? It is the terrible reality of the contradiction of the understanding of the spirit of the artist, or rather more specifically, the abuse of the artist by the hands of those who see art as a commodity and not a representation of the negatively embodied contradictions.

Adorno's quote above, aside from reinforcing the notion that great art is that which does not shy away from the darkness of lived experience, also tells us that art cannot be great unless it is made without compromising the integrity and identity of the artist. That is, that great art is honest, true, and made for the pure love of the pain of its creation, not for external gratification, and not for the pleasure of others beyond our scope. And so, we may borrow from Alan Moore again Never Compromise, Even in the Face of Armageddon. The anti-dialectics and political sociopathy of Rorschach aside, we may borrow this sentiment that the marriage between the intentional honesty of the artist and their art must be protected at all costs as the most sacred of all bonds. It presents a worrisome reality in its inverse where the tortured starving artist choosing to buy Terre Verte over groceries for the week to finish their landscape is one we may see bleeding for their art, while at the opposite end there is the darkness of facilitating, creating or co-opting art for the benefits only, without credence to the process. For every masterful work of art, there are throngs of business-minded vampires waiting to see just how sharply their talons may be dug into the work for the benefit and enrichment of their own coffers.

This is the contradiction that haunts me. The one that has stalled my hand on finishing two artistic series and effectively grounding my abilities to create anything beyond basic life-sustaining actions for over two months. It is in the pain of watching art created out of love, passion, pain and suffering at the hands of the artist be misunderstood, commodified, and co-opted for the ever-omniscient algorithms that drive engagement.

Art is not a commodity. It is an expression of the human experience curated in the experience of that experience by those individuals who possess a sensitivity to the nuances therein. The notion of the tortured artist, this shell of a creature treading water between mortal and spectral, the creature somewhere in the night that through their infinite pain is able to create beauty at their own detriment, this is the creature that business-minded people in the 'art world' fundamentally love to commodify. There is a majesty and mystery in the pain of our creations, and we love the idea of the artist bleeding for their work. However, the contradiction herein that haunts me is not that there appears to be a price tag and monetary gain to be seen from our pain, colloquially known as the stereotypical art person, someone who assumes that their opinion is expertise and that their positionality is infallible due to their abilities to support the art created. but that there is an almost overt need to continually reproduce that mindset. There are those who understand art as a flux of the spirit, where the joys and despairs come together to formulate conversations between the creator and the creation, and there are those who supplant understanding for the gain that they may garner from the artistic expressions of others, and pass it off as understanding. In this faux understanding, these people often find themselves in the coveted positions of power over artists. We know the caricature of the patron of the arts in the modern era as someone with power and money (which artists often lack) who decides that it is their divine mission to build up artists for the benefit of their own status and standing in the niche world of artistic endeavours. I think this is where I find the most conflict in art, the most entrenched contradictions of the spirit. We colloquially know the stereotypical art person, someone that assumes that their opinion is expertise, and that their positionality is infallible due to their abilities to support the art created. IT is a relationship that is, on the part of the 'patron' seen as symbiotic, where their efforts to provide space or supplies or money puts them in the equal status driver's seat of work created, while the artist sees the relationship as parasitic.

This parasitic nature is what haunts me to this day, what has continually fragmented my creativity. It is a deeply heartbreaking realization to come to that the words being levied at you from these supposed supporters are both a performance themselves and a veiled intentional move to supplant the ability to ride the success of your work insofar that it continues to serve the purpose of being marketable. To realize that your work is not being experienced but still being reposted is a supremely intimate form of harm in the artist. In knowing that your work is looked at and "liked" but nothing deeper than that, in seeing it used as promotional material following the initial 'like' is a unique type of draining knowledge. For artists to know that the work they have produced is neither understood nor appreciated but still co-opted is a maddening cycle of harm in hindsight. It is something to say that art is shared out of appreciation, it is another to know that it is shared as bait for future artists to continue the production cycle.

When art is commodified, it loses the contradictions, it loses the honesty and integrity of its creation, and it instead becomes a decorative symbol and nothing more. To share a painting without its story, to scoff at the story itself, or to supplant your own story over its creation is not building up artists; it is a reduction in the spirit of that hand of creation. It is not something I had ever felt I needed to write so directly as I had incorrectly assumed that such things were common knowledge, but it appears, based on experiences of the past months, that I was markedly incorrect in this assumption.

The commodification of art, we may assume, is solely the transition of it into an object of capital acquisition, but this is only a form of it. An artist selling paintings or being paid for books is not the same form of commodification as when individuals who were artists cross the sacred river into administrative managers of art who decide that not only is their experience paramount to the objective understanding of all art, but that their experience and wealth allows them the ability to dictate the purpose of the art itself. If a self-portrait or a nude figure painting for the artist has a representative symbolic meaning to it that is personal to the contradictions of the experience of life unique to the artist, and there is no effort made on the part of the promoter of the art to empathize with that process, then their appreciation of it becomes hollow, and their acquisition and reproduction of it must be questioned. If the answer to the latter question is that the reproduction of art in social spaces stands to operate in the market sphere for the administrative art patron, then the purpose of the art is co-opted. The art is, in effect, metaphysically stolen. When you do not share the intentionality, the meaning, the experiential process, or even the title of a piece of art, but you do so with the intention of showing just how much talent you can reap from the fields, you forfeit your ability to claim support of artists, or identity as one. If you use art as a marketing tool, you are an advertiser and a business person; you are not an artist, and if that art is created under the guise of support and independent artistic celebration when the reality is that the brand is the singular focus, then the art itself becomes a victim of the business, and not a living and breathing manifestation of the artist's soul on canvas. What is particularly heartbreaking about this cycle is to see artists coerced into the milieu of this abusive parasitic relationship because they have been told that they are not quite worthy of art as an artist without the 'exposure' and 'promotion' of the administrators. It is a particularly predatory move on their part to seek out the artists without fame, without a full-time living from their work, and instead of cultivating a sense of true patronage of the arts, they instead modify the convent to promise exposure and promotion for their artists without acknowledging or divulging that the promotion is not for the artist, but for the peerage itself.

When we see art commodified it is not that the painting, the essay, the sculpture or the photograph is commodified, it is much darker. It is the soul of the artist that is itself corrupted by this vampiric pressure to conform to a marketable, sharable and monetizable cookie-cutter mold approved of and by definition a product of the powers that be. C. Wright Mills said, "Prestige is the shadow of money and power," and that prestige is powerful to the absolute zenith of all beings in the world. Prestige as shadow is the contradiction to the world we inhabit, that in the environs cast in shadow from the monoliths of wealth and power, we find ourselves at times uncertain of the distance to which that shadow stretches, and in knowing the degree to which the shadow encroaches on our souls. To acquire both money and power is to acquire the shadowy veil of prestige. This is not the point of this essay. Thinkers (Marx et al.) can explain this model of being better than I can in my current state of being. Rather the darkness here is that there is a curious and particular horror of the shadow of money and power that emerges in the throes of the creation of art. That is there is always someone with both money and power who stands to market to you a taste of their shadowy prestige if only you offer up and lay bare your soul in their hands. It is difficult to resist this offer, as the artist, should they desire to have the time and space to do their art, needs some degree of money, power and prestige. It is enticing to be offered, on the wings of patronage, a chance to earn that prestige with the hopes that the shadow will erect the monoliths in due course. To the spirit of the artist, I have since learned this is a poison to be wary of. We must ask in these exchanges what is being exchanged. Do we gain the prestige we seek? At what cost? Do we debase our intentionality and authenticity to allow for the prestige to flow? Do we set aside that which enlightens our spirit to share our words and our visions with the world in order to play nicely to the powers that be so that we may be graced by their uttering of a word of kudos to our laboured effort? If indeed we do, does the blood spilt in spite of our work and being for its benefit measure up to the aesthetic expectation of the prestigious? And further: how much wealth and power do we provide, surrender, or generate in our quest to be among the chosen few?

Does this allude to a critique of the artist who works for their prestige? Does it denigrate the artist who participates in this cyclical change? Of course not. There is an intentionality in every artist's decision, and it is not my responsibility or right to deride them for their agency. I may do this to myself and to evoke Buffalo Springfield in a hindsight message to myself: stop children, what's that sound, everybody looks what's going down? There is indeed something happening here, and what it is, ain't exactly clear. It is no fault of the artist to desire a sense of recognition, nor is it sinful to the artist's integrity to pursue success, wealth, power, etc. Instead, where my perception of the life and times of the artist becomes murkier is in those vampires that peddle the dream, the fairytale, the illusion of success disingenuously. Ulterior motives are human, but the exploitation of the artist is tantamount to indentured servitude. It is not uncommon, too, that in these people who dangle the limelight just out of reach in exchange for our blood, sweat and soul, there is often a glaring misunderstanding of just how far the reach of their money, power and prestige can travel. They do not know that holding all the keys of life over someone is powerful, to them, all of us can afford any luxury, to us, the insanity of luxury is a norm over an outlier. But again, it is not where I am needed in this work to denote the disparities of socioeconomic stratification; I would wager there are good YouTube videos for such things.

Instead, I think this pseudo-academic posturing here puts distance between my heart and the page, to again continue to construct barriers between myself and the darkness contradicting the flows of my heart and mind. I am still here after over 5000 words and I do not feel any closer to finishing this damn thing, and I question even now if it will ever reach publication.

I cannot speak for all artists, but in my experience, I feel somewhat confident in speaking of my own art when I say that what burns me most deeply in my fringe experiences in the art world on the edge of nowhere in a twilight zone of insanity is this: I do not like pretension in art, and I deeply despise disingenuous approaches to art. Ever since I was a child in school, learning to fight the power and belting Give Peace a Chance during recess, I have hated disingenuous people. I do not often employ hatred in my writing, but I do so here. I do so because I cannot abide dishonesty or the lack of integrity in general, but specifically when it is levied down onto myself or people I care about by people with explicitly concentrated power. It adds insult to injury in my experience for this dishonesty to come flavoured in the particular aroma of pretentious misrepresentation, misappropriation, and downright misunderstanding of hallmark staples of artistic exploration. I can trust that a real estate agent, a loan officer, or a landlord will be disingenuous; it comes with the territory. I can then trust the untrustworthiness of these characters, and we all operate well together, knowing there is an air of untruth in the air. But what I cannot, at the fundamental core of the fibre of my being, tolerate is when people who so clearly ought to know what they are saying do not.

In February, I said multiple times in various mediums that I can excuse and understand incompetence as, by its nature, it holds a space for growth, but I cannot excuse nor tolerate willful ignorance or stupidity. A dear friend from the trenches issued the moniker of weaponized incompetence, and I feel a kinship to that verbiage. To further expand: I cannot tolerate weaponized incompetence when it is masked behind the hubris of pretense. I cannot excuse the absence of integrity, especially when it is buried behind the veil of prestige, wealth, and power. As an artist and as a human trying to understand the nature of my being, I feel a particular sharpness of pain in my heart once that veil is pulled back. By virtue of my nature, my experiences, and my approaches to institutional existence and normative reality, I have often found myself on the receiving end of verbal hostility. It has, unfortunately, become a sort of check-in to ensure my professional life is still normal, if I'm not being angrily accosted by a tenure-track white guy at a conference for having the audacity to suggest students are people too, I'm doing something wrong. However, it hurts more when it is directed at your art, because art is the manifestation of that experience of the contradiction, it is by virtue of its nature a piece of our hearts. I can handle (and often ignore) critique of my work, but when a critique of my work becomes a critique of my character, and when that critique is under the thin veneer of artistic patronage, accessibility, support and safety when the values directly contradict the nature of the verbal venom? That is when my soul hurts most. It is what shocks me into a realm of non-reaction, a freeze, a depression. It is not, however, out of fear; it is shocking, plain and simple, and that shock boils over, not into a rage, but into determination, a determination to exemplify and embody the very core elements that are sought out as targets to destroy. In short, I do not find anger when met with these obstacles brought by the immature and the disingenuous, I find resolve and determination to ascend above their phony presentation, their thin veneer, to aspire to be what they claim to be over me. To be clear, I do not do this out of spite or pettiness, I do it because I cannot idly experience the abuse of prestige and power, and I cannot abide by systems of oppression being levied against anyone. I occupy a very privileged intersection of identities (for the most part), and so I find a particular revolutionary zeal in being in a privileged position but using that insulation to agitate the system by embodying more genuinely the virtues falsely advertised. In a word, empires fall when you embody the virtues that prop up their despotic rulers. Take the fires to Nero, as it were.

And so, what virtues establish the empire of the business-minded commodification of art? How, then, do we dare to embody those for the cause? In a sense, all we have as artists to lose are our chains, and so what is the nature of our chains?

I have found in my experience in creativity, both recently and in the past, that the scariest thing to someone with power in the art world is an artist who does not surrender to the expectations for what we should be creating. The despot in art believes that art should be free, radical, and expressive of the things that push the envelope of acceptability, they revel in this idea but do not possess the capacity for reflexive experience of art nor the emotional maturity to confront their own internal contradictions when they experience art that calls attention to those contrasts. They love the idea of art being scary but crumble immediately at the first indication of emotion they get in experiencing it. They love the image of the patron that facilitates the wanton and unbridled creativity of the tortured artist, but they shy away into reductive emotional outbursts at their confrontation with true artistic exploration. This is because true art, per Adorno, is itself an honest investigation of the darkness of life in the light, or vice versa, and to the businessperson, there is no capacity for nuance; they seek out only to find the golden rays of sunshine while forgetting the need of the focusing lens of the storm clouds in their composition. This is the root of their disingenuousness, that they love the idea of art but not the practice of it. This means that if the works they see do not meet the strict rules they have established for what they believe to be "good" art, they feel an almost involuntary compulsion to douse those flames the moment they kindle.

The virtues of the empire of art, then, are that radical expression, freedom of agentic expression, and the darkness of the spirit are paramount to the creation of art, only insofar a it does not rock the boat of the empire. Go and create, but God forbid it isn't marketable or favorable to a certain image, if it is, then there is a hornet's nest of consequences. In a breath, the empire will spout Andy Warhol quotes reproduced in cheap fonts about the intimacy of creativity and the need to weather the storms, to push the envelope, to bleed into the canvas for your passion, while in the very next breath will enact a circling of the wagons to protect the brand of their aesthetic disposition of a particularly sanitized version of art. They then appear to forget the entirety of

Andy Warhol's philosophy towards art while managing an assembly line of revenue-generating advertisement media. They style themselves as that picturesque Master of Art in the trenches, but land somewhere closer to Warhol's quote about business being the ultimate art in and of itself and miss the critique of commercialism that comes along with it.

So then, to bring the proverbial fires to Nero's feet, what we must do is embody that elemental revolutionary zeal for the bizarre, the terrifying, the dark and despairing, and the beauty inherent in all of it. Above all of this, though, what I have found represents the most concerning threat to the stability of the illusion of the empire of art is the brazen intensity of it being known that your work and your spirit do not require their praise or prestige. It is in the rejection of the deal, the casting off of the reliance on their positionality, that grants us the most power over them. People who style themselves as rich and powerful do not take kindly to their opinions not mattering, especially to the artist. People who hold power who extol the virtue of being an emancipator of creativity fundamentally crumble at the notion that their liberation is neither helpful nor wanted. A word of warning in this reflection is that, in most cases, the imperial 'suits upstairs' will almost always categorically respond to a truly self-actualized artist with rage and impunity. The means of combatting this are somewhat simple in words but difficult in practice. Essentially, allow them to make their mistakes, allow them to show their hands, and allow them to dig their own graves. One of the sweetest affective experiences of my life has always been watching people in power get frustrated to the point that they fully display their true character to an audience whose approval they depend on to keep the lights on. This is our silent revolution in the arts, embodying that spirit that brings breaths from life to the page, the canvas, the medium and doing so with impunity, with a rageful dedication to the practice of creation from this life into the stretches of abstraction and humanity at such a pace that those who stand to try to stop us cannot for the life of them even hope to. It is not productivity that we must aspire to, but a fervour, a mania of the creative heart to blast out into the undiscovered countries of human experience and hold a grimy mirror of spite up to the darkness and its purveyors. We are not conduits of profitability and productivity but adventurers unto the frontiers of the mind, body and spirit to such a degree that we cannot hope to ever be stopped. And so, by virtue of the wild untameability of the artistic spirit, know this: you do not need a benefactor to liberate your art. You do not need flashy studios, hopeful gallery promises, or your work exhibited in privately held collections. All we need for our art to be art is for that singular person to experience it and have an experience. Should that experience transcend the typical "oh, it's really good," that is all the better. But do not allow the toxic money-sighted ghouls of the world to see your art as a stepping stone to their beach holidays or their second homes. Manifest, should you desire success, but do so knowing those that prop themselves up as patrons of the arts are decidedly less interested in your art and more so in the patronage they may reap as a result. It is not the norm in today's "art world" to find those individuals seeking the expression of the human spirit artistically purely for the nature of doing so; there is always an agenda, an image, a market value assessment and an accountant, somewhere. Do not sacrifice your own integrity for those who cannot maintain their own. If we may require a heady metaphor for this practice, it is this: in the ancient Looney Tunes cartoon One Froggy Evening, we must strive to emulate the singing frog's revolutionary direct action. We entice the ghouls and goblins of the 'business of art' world to promote us, and then, in the critical moment, before we may earn them their millions, simply choose not to play the game. Do not perform, create, or make them anything. They do not deserve your creativity or your spirit. Any moment we stand to let them think that our work is theirs to some minute degree, they win, so work in the opposite direction. Capture their insanity in your work and display the madness for those to see. Let the ghosts of the art business patronage saviours fall by their own waysides. Their toxicity will reach a point of concentration where nothing will be able to save the house, the yard, the mortgage, etc., and they will be faced with the reality in that grimy mirror that no matter how many artists have paid you for Instagram exposure, your usage of that art has itself diminished your own ability to see and appreciate that which pulls the hand to the canvas: you lose the ability to see the voice in the image, to read the picture of the words, to, in a word, understand art. I cannot imagine a more despairing way to see and experience the world. But hey...it's a living...

Just Sign Here, Kid; I'll Make You a Star...

Part 2: When in France, Have a Revolution

Toxicity, Finding Safety, and the Silent Revolution of Artists

"Outside in the cold distance, a wildcat did growl; Two riders were approaching, and the wind began to howl..."

-Dylan Originally, but More Masterfully by Jimi

The following excerpt is a fragmentary introduction to a piece originally to be authored for a fairly prestigious American journalistic publication on the nature of and importance of fostering artistic community. I killed the story myself as I lost the magic somewhere on the floor of some airport between there and here. It is included here as an archaeological dedication to a version of me that once, perhaps, existed out there in the ether and to set a scene in the imaginative visual spectrum. In a simpler sense: I wrote this while still believing in fairytales and dreams...

A French Dispatch

Flash Priority from the Nocturnal Desk

Two hours East of Paris by train, hidden in plain sight in the French Countryside, the village stands both timelessly out of time and presently existing right when and where it needs to. Signs of life between the influx of the month's shipment of artists and authors and the general magical eccentricities that follow them include the smoke curling from the three or four occupied chimneys, the occasional rattle and hum of cars blasting through the narrow roadways, and the ever-present roll of the river past the *lavoir* in the village centre. On a hill overlooking the village stands the chateau, towering over the stone houses and buildings below, another structure wildly out of time and place yet curiously precisely where it needs to be. Beyond the gates of the grand residence sprawls a grounding of art and artistry that, even in its most chaotic moments, represents a culmination of the human spirit of creative expression unparalleled in any other instance of gathering.

Within the hallways of the chateau, over the chatter of artists and the swipe of brush strokes on canvas, there is subtle magic humming beneath the surface, somewhere intermingled with the smells of acrylic paints and mediums, and between the oriental rugs and the spirits of those before us, creativity is always flowing from hands and hearts to their pages and paintings to capture if only for a moment a snapshot of humanity in its most innocently intimate existence.

The grand salon catches our blood and tears as we share our work and our souls with one another. The thriving undercurrents of this space reflect and replicate within themselves a reinforcement of the notion that we are in and of ourselves connected beyond the boundaries of that which constitutes a simple friendship. There is a camaraderie there, something impossible to capture and even less possible to know or describe.

End Transmission...

-30-

It appears a fitting end to a series titled Papers in Residence that the composition of this grander work has manifested in me almost like an autopsy would for a medical examiner. There is a corpse ahead of me, and I must, in the practice of the anatomist, slice and excise into the flesh of that body in order to determine the nature of its living and dying breaths. Here in this investigation, my own memories and experiences lie on the slab ahead of me, and with my trusty Liston in my right hand, I feel it is now time to begin to peel back the layers and perform this dreaded postmortem. In the case of any autopsy, there is a healthy mix of malignant compositions and perfectly youthfully healthy elements. I will do my best to grant a sense of time to each, but I do confess to my readers that this is not the autopsy of a peaceful hospice passing; this feels darker somehow, where the deceased memories laid bare before me take on the shape of something far more sinister. And in such a moment, I am glad to say that I am not that kind of doctor...

"I live to be an ambiguous blob, and your perception is a hate crime"

"We were looking into the spots between stars just for an instant of infinity"

"European cold medicine does not work"

"You're too young to remember the real world"

"Don't let the truth get in the way of a good story"

"Empires will fall"

"I am not myself aloud, and so I write"

-Words of Wisdom from Various and Highly Talented Artists

I do not know where to begin this section. I have been in varying throes of a myriad of agonies over the following experiences and memories, and I cannot for the life of me find the motivation or the words to fully encapsulate their lingering effects on my heart, nor can I capture the true madness of some of them. The very fact of the matter is that I feel I owe this space a publication, and I owe my own creative soul some semblance of closure.

Growing up, I have always had a very sharp disdain for people whose actions contradict their stated philosophies or intentions. I have long harboured a very deep dislike of the lack of integrity exhibited in people who say one thing and do another. This has almost always gotten me in trouble with authority figures both in school and in my professional academic work. I have frustrated many a teacher and administrator by calling gentle attention to the hypocrisy of certain actions and their disregard for a stated position or philosophy. As such, I am no longer truly affected by this kind of nonsense. I remember once, during the first year of my PhD I graded a student's exam favourably after they had ended an essay question about the nature of qualitative versus quantitative research methods with a hand-drawn diagram of their explanation, the insecure former "men's rights activist" who was the overseer of the lecture class decided this was egregiously unacceptable and called me to his office where he decided it was time to put on his big man pants and rip into me about my grading integrity. Given this was not my first experience of the vertically challenged and positionally threatened white man, I found the experience to be quite a hilarious exercise in insanity. God forbid we consider varying modalities of learning and expressing knowledge. This one decided that he would arbitrarily lower all 100 of my student's grades by several points so that his class average was more acceptable. He even wrote horrifically abusive comments in the margins for my students about how they were previously graded. Did I respond to this situation by yelling back at him? No. These types of men want their adversaries to yell back, puff out their chests, get loud and get mean. What burns them deeply is disengagement, and a reduction of their meltdown to its base components, when there's no channel of anger backwards the immaturity of these types of people always comes out in full force to face them in the mirror. It helps, too, to reflect back on their sentiments that prove them wrong and that they cannot disagree with them. In the case of the angry Napoleonic professor? "Are you saying that we need to discourage abstract and individualized approaches to learning in favour of a standardized universalist approach?" Silence. Apology email two hours later. Secondarily, a way to combat the toxic man on a power trip is by simply relaying their immaturity in their toxicity in the transparent communication of the experience. I told my students the exact nature of our conversation and explained to them why their grades had been changed and who they ought to direct their inquiries to. Strangely I was never hauled into the office again, and 90% of my end of term feedback was directed to this toxic man in some permutation of the phrase: "why is Tucker not leading the lectures for this class, he's the only one I learned from the whole semester". I did not ask my students to do this, nor did I direct it in any way. Curiously, I was also not asked back to work with the same man the next term.

I relay this not for any recognition or for any egoistic enrichment but simply for the communication of the reality that toxic masculinity is itself alive and very pervasively well in all walks of life, and it becomes particularly toxic when it intermingles with the world of art. Statistically, those of us who are drawn to create art are very likely to occupy at least one marginalized identity, and often multiple ones. Additionally, toxic men are often situated in positional power over those individuals, and further, via the patriarchal reality of modern existence, these men often hold systemic power over marginalized identities and wield that power without ever knowing it. It is an abuse in the quiet of actions and performances, and one where they are unaware of their actions' longitudinal impacts considering their entire approach to life has always been to come to blows and then to move on immediately. This is what happens when people never have to worry about the continuation of their survival or existence on a systemic scale. Often too, these misunderstandings of their own power come in the form of money and power. It is how they are able to peddle prestige for a price to the artist and how, in a single moment, their entire visage as patron of the arts can dissolve into the mists of madness.

For me, meeting toxicity head-on is exhausting emotionally and physically. Being on the receiving end of a screaming match is never enjoyable, but when the nature of that math is such that you are placed into the space of being emotionally mature for both involved parties, it stretches you thin. A strategy of toxic men in these types of engagements, aside from the childish screaming and physical expansion of their plumage, is to manipulate reality to benefit their position. It is critical to be aware of this reality shift because it is not designed to win arguments; it is designed to destabilize the resistance. If they say that their anger is justified because they heard it through the grapevine (and refuse to say who constitutes the grapevine, even to their close confidants), then their goal is not to right any perceived wrong; it is to establish their rhetorical superiority in breaking down lines of trust in a collective. It's much easier to escape accountability when your victims leave or are broken into silence.

I have found in these types of conflicts what often manifests is not a legitimate concern. Legitimate concerns can be handled with a civil discussion, and they are often. The screaming display of authority is a ritual reserved for the propagation of a narrative that must be enforced through verbal violence because its rhetorical foundation is built upon pillars of sand, pillars of sand to borrow from Coldplay. As such, for me, such things rarely tend to linger with me for too long as I can see through the blustery nonsense to the projected insecurity within, and I opt to ignore it. What often comes from this approach is an apology, either unprompted or when it is stated that the behaviour was not apologized for. In those instances, it is best to neither accept nor reject such an apology but to let it hang in the purgatory of the unknown, for that is where apologies for such things do the most damage and healing, respectively.

This all said I can take toxic masculine tantrums day in and day out in academia. It is my general understanding that these types tire themselves out after enough of a fuss and will be fine with a nap and some apple juice. However, when the toxicity manifests into the personal realm, it gets more difficult to simply laugh it off or see it as the child throwing a fit in the LEGO aisle. Especially when the question of the berating is not something fixed and demonstrable like pedagogy or grading scores, but it is something personal, creative, expressive and, above all else, intrinsically linked to my character and identity. Meaning I can handle professional discussions even when my opponent is red in the face at the thought of a non-standard grade point distribution. When the projection of anger instead focuses on something I hold more closely to my heart, that is when the knives begin to dig in and when those marginalized identities I occupy become explicitly visible to me.

"I don't give a fuck about your work..."

The term "safe space" has been thrown around nearly to death in American popular conversation. I cannot speak to this across other nations aside from a momentary and humorous comment from a friend in Klaipeda: "When I was a kid, a safe space was where there were no KGB". The political right has decided that a 'safe space' is antithetical to everything American, masculine, straight and whatever other pseudo-theological identity they attribute to their presumption of self. This discourse often revolves around homophobia, classism, racism and a marked elitism of self. You can hear this discourse taking shape in comments or jokes about younger generations being "too sensitive" or "always triggered". These jokes are not often far from the lips of toxically masculine men, typically they occur when they are in familiar company (or perceived familiar company, as men often see me at 6'3" with a long beard as also somehow being on board with their misogyny). In essence, these types of men see people sensitive, emotional, or emotionally intelligent as a threat to their own unresolved traumas, and so they lash out when confronted with such terrifying clashes with the full spectrum of human experience. These are the types who believe you heal depression by simply opting not to be sad, the ones who believe queer folks are inherently villainous, and who see gender as a sharp binary with women occupying a very particularly submissive positionality.

In actuality, a "safe space" is a space where someone with varying degrees of identity components that are systemically victimized can feel, if even just for a temporary experience, the ability to breathe without fear on the back of their necks at what oppressive shitstorm may be on the horizon. A safe space is not a place where everyone gets participation trophies, where everyone is told they are special, or where everyone is absolved from accountability. A safe space is where for just one fucking minute, we don't need to look over our shoulders for the next round of pain and ignorance. A safe space can be as simple as someone saying 'yes' to the question: "Can I tag along with you so I can avoid any confrontations?". There is a lot of love in that 'yes' and a lot of safety in walking astride someone who you know cares and who can go toe to toe with the madness if needed. A safe space can be a complexly coordinated collective effort among real friends to organize an impromptu meal delivery service when you are so burnt out from being berated that you opt to avoid meals at all costs because you never know what horrors may come between courses. Sometimes a safe place is the comradery that comes from a shared cigarette in the rain and an exchange of discourse on the absurdity of a situation. Sometimes safe places aren't physical places at all, sometimes they're voices on the phone saying that they love you. They also manifest in the questions: "Can I give you a hug?" or "You're not leaving too, are you?" And finally, sometimes safe places come from deciding to stay in a situation where you feel unsafe in order to be the safe space for someone else should they need it.

When you combine an attack on someone's character, someone's art, and someone's integrity as a person, shouting, the aforementioned fluffing of masculine plumage and the power that comes from total domination of those compositional forms of prestige (money and power), you have created the perfect recipe for someone to feel totally and completely under fire. It is a situation where past trauma responses resurface. Where we discover the old tradecraft of surviving an abusive relationship, and suddenly, there are measures in place to be safe out in the cold. You suddenly are aware of the background noise of your street, the time at which the lamps go out at night, the sounds and license plates of specific vehicles, and above all else that irrational fear creeps back in. I have compared that paranoia elsewhere to being an agent in the field with cover blown and legends falling. You stop being free and become Alec Leamas trying to scramble over the wall, not knowing if the GDR bullets will tear you down or if you'll land in the American zone on the other side. You stop sleeping entirely because you are strapped with the distressing knowledge that the person who tore you down to this paranoia not only has the key to your bedroom but owns it outright. You fall back on your tradecraft of placing cigarette cases on doorknobs to be awoken when and if they come. Personal papers and projects move into bags in the closet, and you close down to any and all shared experiences because you never can tell where the next blow will come from.

That was my reality for three full days.

The creative hit from that experience is still being processed. What happens often when these types of people unload their anger onto you, you learn who they really are. When you see their true intentions and their true character laid bare. I cannot say that anyone is truly a bad person at heart, nor can I presume to psychoanalyze or dissect intentions or states of mind. What I can reflect on is the aftermath. Where my entire sense of safety in an entirely removed and isolated physical place evaporated. I could neither trust the systems of power around me nor, through those systems' words, the collective commons around me. That paranoia of the trauma response, the misalignment in the expression of anger and power over minor misunderstandings, and the true terror of being forced back into the wilderness of mirrors is not a state of being that can be simply brushed aside with hasty apologies. Often as well, such apologies come in the form of "if I upset you..." where the inclusion of the almighty "if" places the responsibility not on the perpetrator but on the sensitivity of the victim. I have heard many of these apologies in my life; they never go further than the second of their utterance in making a situation better, let alone safe. Apparently, too, the diagnostic resolution to the loss of my sense of safety was alleged, "Well, he just needs to not be so sensitive then..."

Being in an isolated state of paranoia as a result of a re-activation of a traumatic experience, coupled with the overtly explicit visibility of systems of authority and power that deaden any semblance of safety or any chance for self-advocacy, is a mortally exhaustive experience. In my time as a writer, I have not been immune to my fair share of frightening experiences. I have been followed by the Russian FSB and slept in bugged hotel rooms; I have received death threats with my home address attached and a whole host of other horrors; I've even dodged bullets fired by weekend fox hunters. Somehow, these instances have always stood to situate my writing in some way, where in those moments, you learn to adapt. You play Joy Division on a loop next to the microphones, you dive into the leaves, you let your intelligence agency followers believe you don't notice them and simply melt back into your monitored hotel room. Somehow, being within 35km of the Belorussian border during the height of springtime, Russian military operations pale in comparison to being isolated in a state of not knowing who to trust, not having anywhere to go, nor any money to facilitate an escape plan. Backdoor exits and cover stories are what you build when you fly 6000 miles to a former republic with a briefcase of declassified documents, not when your destination has an inclusivity clause in the mission statement, and somcthing tells me my membership in the associated press doesn't cover clandestine extractions in the dead of night, it appears the coverage stops at legal protections from litigation over my written work, which I will never complain about. Glory be to protected speech and membership dues.

In the interest of fairness to Adorno's contradictions, what I will say is that from the erecting of a wilderness of mirrors, of a social space of distrust and misgivings, of the negation of the safety of space that it strengthens the absolute zenith of possibility the bonds between truly good people in common collectivity. Essentially, a class consciousness of solidarity emerges almost immediately when the true nature of institutional structures is exposed. Where individuals band together and collectively placate the powers that be with what they want, while in private they fraternize over the absurd insanity of that situation that they have fallen into. This is what broke the isolation and what historically has always been a saving harbour of safety in the storms of darkness. Recognizing that you are not alone in your assessment of situations, and where in that recognition you find your people who, like you, see dishonesty or lack of integrity and also aim to stand above it in spite of the madness. People in power who abuse it, be that in business, art, or the business of art, are often woefully unaware of the damage they do to their reputation when they slip into the toxicity bubbling beneath their external veneer. They often see themselves as above accountability and, as such, can never even perceive when their power wanes and disappears in the eyes of their subjects. It is a small but reassuring phenomenon. I myself never aspired to lead a revolution out loud. I am neither Lenin nor Jefferson, instead, I feel myself more aligned in the waves of a silent and soft rebellion among peers. I try not to be a font of contempt, instead facing what I must and seeing how the ripples in that experience may prompt others to confess their own dismay at the state of being. People always outnumber the powerful, and to again evoke Neil Young: "Red means run, son, and numbers add up to nothing." There are more of us than them, and they depend on us to keep the lights on, and this is a hollow comfort. It is not a reassuring feeling to see the confirmation that the systems in power over you are abusing that power or that they have the capacity to do so. It is a hollow victory to know that you are not alone insofar as it is nice not to have to suffer in isolation, but it is equally disappointing that you have to struggle at all.

In direct contrast to the tumult of 1789's French Revolution, my revolution was silent, without violence, and without a guillotine in sight. My revolution wasn't even one that I started, but one born out of the goodness of the hearts of a select creed of artistic creators who saw through the mirages of fantasy to the reality of inequity and, in doing so, embodied the true sense of Liberté, Egalité, Fraternité in ways so imperceptible to the powers that be, that they may never know the true reach of that collective spirit of artistic liberation. There is an unbreakable bond between artists oppressed or artists who have seen behind the curtains the machinations of potential oppression, one that cannot bend away from one another in direct spite of the efforts of the powers that be. For every insult screamed, for every half-baked apology, for each moment of fear in presence, for each sleepless paranoid night, there are hugs, plates of food, messages of solidarity and a collective humour that spreads in quite a resistance. Power to the People is a dangerous concept on its own, but when those people are artists, you add the sharpness of eyes that are honed to see through to the inky voids of the depths of human depravity. And, at the end of it all, every screaming match only serves to solidify the collective artistic spirit in revolutionary spite.

Glory to the silent revolutionaries. Your shadow work in the trenches was not only healing but also a radical construction of safe spaces in direct response to their destruction from the top down.

My infinite gratitude swells to those revolutionary artists who, against the currents, opted to build up artists.

"Every man is guilty of all the good he did not do"

-Voltaire

Part 3: Looking Glass Wars

Ego, Projection, and the Defense of Toxicity

"Nobody told me there'd be days like these, strange days indeed. Most peculiar, Mama..."

-John Lennon, Shortly Before the Day the Music Died

Ego is inherent in art, as it is in everyday life. There are healthy balances of the ego in art always, and often these are wildly imbalanced in and of themselves. When I used to teach a course on the process of writing social theory, I would tell my students over and over again that the key to being a brilliant theorist is to call yourself a brilliant theorist. A healthy God complex. I would say that this is why the best surgeons are so narcissistic. They have to believe they have the power over life and death so that when it comes down to it, they, through their divine touch, can grant you life when it counts. They're obnoxious dinner guests, but I wouldn't want the charismatic charmer holding the scalpel while I'm on another plane of being between here and there.

In art, there is a similar need for this unbridled self-confidence. It is hard to find and even harder to embody. You have to be a humble God out among the mortals. You can tell yourself in the mirror every morning that you are the next Warhol (God forbid), the next Picasso, or the next Foucault. I myself, while admiring my non-existent hairline often reach for the latter in my daily affirmations. Further, I know that by now, my dear Denali is more than tired of hearing me say to him in a manic burst at 3 in the morning, "Ok, are we ready to go be so brilliant they'll teach about us in 100 years?" Much to the credit of his stamina, he has yet to put forth a reality check on my ego, although I fear such an intervention is on the horizon. My grandmother understands this facet of my process all too well, and often, during our visits, I am subjected to the firmly levied, halfway joking condemnations of my inflated sense of brilliance.

All of this is to say that one must possess a certain degree of confidence in one's own ego if they are to follow the creative path. This is not to foster mastery of any artform but to allow us an insulation between our fragile hearts and the world beyond that seeks at all costs to denigrate our works as useless wastes of time (at best) or, in direct pain to the heart of the artist, to levy criticism out of spite, jealously or misunderstanding rather than critical engagement from a place of genuine artistic support. We must shield ourselves from those voices that tell us we are not good enough or that our work is not worthy of their time or experience. When your passion lies in the aesthetic exploration of life's contradictions, you have to be ready to meet the uninitiated hate for your existence outside beyond the waves. That doubles should you be so bold to be different, radical, or hold in your heart some elemental sense of an identity that does not fit in with the mainstream. For every empty "this is really good," there will be a hateful condemnation. Sometimes this comes from those close to us. "Don't quit your day job." This is a personal favourite comment I've heard and received in the past. I do not paint to the standards or technical skill of artists I know, so I cannot relate to visual art in the same ways, but I know that in my writing, I will often receive a smattering of several types of reactions to my work. I will hear from some "this is really good" and nothing else. I will get one or two hate messages, either on the minor end (someone deciding to ignore the entire thesis of the piece and correct a type) to the extremes of being accused (rather hilariously of fabricating misinformation), and the classic death threats. Very rarely, some beautiful soul reaches out to mine to share their full experiential reaction to what I have written, and the first time this truly happened to me, it reduced me to tears and made all of the aforementioned horrors worth it if only just for that intimate connection across those pages.

The ego, in these instances, is a fragile thing. Art is something intrinsically tied to our presentation of self, to our understanding of the world we inhabit, and to the aesthetic or affective moments we consider to be not just worthy of capturing but worthy of celebration in those whispered couplets between brush and paint. In a sense, there is a living and breathing part of us in our works, and that is where the artist's real ego lies. Besides the intrinsic nature of the internal battle of words between the sense that your work is good and the sense that it is terrible, there lies a fragment of our souls in each piece we compose, be they inherently good or bad. That is how we create, we funnel our pain, or joy, our experience of life itself into a physical, sonic, or digital medium, and that is where that piece of our soul then resides permanently. To revisit a piece of art is to reacquaint ourselves with that snapshot of life in that moment of its completion. We can walk through our memories and experiences in such a way through art that it is, aside from something aesthetically pleasing to our audiences, a living diary of our own journeys through life.

To say that artists are egocentric is to compliment the spirit of the artist in the compositional manifestation of their work for our experience. However, when those ghouls that see art as business opportunities bring their egos into the page of the artist, they do so in a way that poisons the entire creative experience itself, and they then, due to their misunderstanding of the artist's spirit in flux lobby the word ego as a venomous assault on the spirit of the artist themselves. This pattern leads the art business mind to see their role in the creation of art as simultaneously the virtuous saviour and the egoistic master of understanding of all art, from physical visual works to the written word. Ego, in the business world, is not the same ego that situates itself in the creation of works that inspire joy or reflection. Ego in the business world fits neatly into the sycophantic obsessive pursuit of commodity valuation and the addition of yet another zero to the bank balance. Ego in business is the cutthroat exploitative selfishness that transcends the need to understand such inefficient and unprofitable things as agency, identity, freedom of expression or the curious nature of pain in creativity. Even people who were once artists lose this empathy once the bottom line replaces the canvas in their focus.

Because the business ego is so intrinsically tied to the selfish, individualistic, profit-driven mindset, it is not a surprise to those who see these individuals in the wild that they are often either hand in hand with the above-discussed toxic masculine tendencies, are practitioners of the craft itself, or are staunch defenders of it. It is a reality that is far more depressing to see than the garden variety of toxic masculinity. That is, seeing the enabling of and benefitting from toxicity in the facilitation of art is heartbreaking. It is scary to be on the receiving end of the berating that forces you into paranoia, but it is another feeling entirely to be confronted by the enabler and the collision of ego and projection as it represents a total and complete deconstruction of any barely recognizable veneer of artistic solidarity. When, in these moments, the true colours are flown, they hurt even more than blatantly immature toxicity because the true colours of the enabling ego are far more venomous because they have been honed to a razor's edge to cut deeply at the internal reality of the artistic heart.

In the Act of Bleeding for Art

A marked dissonance between the genuine presentation of the artistic soul and the fabricated artistic mirage is that the artist, a creature occupying those holy contradictions between dark and light, is capable of meeting others with empathy, while the egoist at the head of the meeting table cannot meet moments of tenderness or vulnerability with empathy. They do so with anger and malice but a cold and calculated targeting of the nature of their rage. They do not resort to the blustery nature of the Napoleonic man yelling to assert dominance, instead they internalize any slight disconnect between their perfect commodified situation as a massive risk to their wallets, and further, a massive personal condemnation. It is in these instances, when the facilitation of art is tied to money that the almighty critique, wonderful in theory and horrific in practice, is laid bare, and the egoist implodes before exploding.

This can manifest as a public off-colour joke at the expense of someone who has already lost any sense of safety in space and concludes in the hurling of toxic insults in the rain. Curiously, the steps between the first instance and the explosion are often paved with courtesy and trust, where the simple communication of discomfort is immediately compressed into a month-long catharsis of pure disregard for art, for empathy, and for the human nature of being itself. There is something pathological about these leaps, from what may have been a simple mistake in communication, to an angry sprint to tear away your victim out into the cold to unload the month's pain into the healing aura of tearing down an artist being for the benefit of the ego.

In this instance, I must reiterate that my soul resides in my work. I do often quite literally bleed for my work, where concerns for physical health, mortality and longevity are often cast out into the winds of disinterest. It is also a reflective reality of my work that it rarely sits in the warmth and sunny glow of the human experience of contradiction, where almost my entire collective works represent a thousand-page love letter to the darkness that occupies our waking and sleeping moments. Even in this continual companionship in the darkness, I still leave pieces of my heart scattered across the pages. There is something of the human remnants of me here somewhere. Each of my essays, monographs, lectures, etc. are part of me, they are creations that I feel encapsulate an imprint of who I was and what pains flitted through my veins at any given moment.

"I think you manufacture hurt to make your work"

That sentence haunts me to this day. It was shouted hysterically over immature discourse about authorial intent, inappropriate jokes about mental health, confessions of insane insecurities about not understanding my work, wild accusations of ego trips (when in reality they were heartfelt tributes to the art of my friends), tangential diatribes about existing in art as someone who isn't a man, and a whole other host of a strange and terrible cocktail of insecure narcissism and a blatant disregard for the nature of the artistic process despite the loud proclamation of 'no one here even knows I'm an artist' despite that being a primary marketing strategy in identity construction. Somewhere in the insanity, I discovered a root cause of the insecurity and rage: a perceived mismatch in ability. This sounds wildly childish, but when the art soul is corrupted by the business ego, competition is unavoidable, as is comparison. Somewhere in the venom flow the words: "You're an academic, an intellectual, you're so far above me, you shouldn't be offended by two little words." This, upon reflection, is a challenge I've met in the past, where people have encountered my work, but I think that since I happen to also teach university classes, my work is overflowing with a plethora of citations, definitions and jargon. It puts a mindset in some approaches that they are not 'worthy' or 'able' to read or even understand my work, and so they respond with dismissal on the best of days (a sort of blasé ignorance that usually manifests in an interruption of whatever I'm saying to enact some variance of the 1980s movie trope of silencing the nerd and demanding they "speak English"), and on the worst of days a person's entire luggage car of baggage becomes the tunnel vision focus, maybe, just maybe, if they can tear me down, they can prove to themselves that they've "bested" me. All of this is to use one such jargon term: absolute bullshit. Regular readers of this space know that this is not an academic journal; close friends and family know that I do not write academic texts. When I explain my work, I try directly to communicate that what I do is not the inaccessible nonsense of the academic world, and instead, I try to write from my heart so that others may read my words and feel some kinship.

However, at that moment in the rain, this was not understood. Somehow, I was under attack for my work, my career choice, my personal character, and even my perceived gender and sexuality. It was a multi-pronged attack that sought to find some weakness in my armourAside from being a whirlwind of madness, a mountain of disgust and disappointment, and a mildly stressful end to a very long day, it was now, in retrospect, one of the most pathetic displays of humanity I have ever experienced. to finally enact that little victory. Aside from being a whirlwind of madness, a mountain of disgust and disappointment, and a mildly stressful end to a very long day, it was now in retrospect one of the most pathetic displays of humanity I have ever experienced. Where the motivations to wound and the cheapness of those motivations were all laid so poignantly bare that there was no question about their intentions. This was revealed in two instances. First, in a far cry from reality, the toxic masculine force intervened in my defence and subsequently issued a heartfelt, emotionally mature apology taking full accountability for the previous paranoia-inducing attacks. Second, after being accused for the second time of "manufacturing hurt" to fuel my work, I was forced, in order to save face and defend myself, to disclose elements of my identity and history that I did not feel safe doing while also explaining that when you exist in toxic spaces as someone carrying marginalized identities, you do not need to "manufacture" hurt, because the systems above you do it every single day, so the hurt does not need to be sought out when it's all around you. Curiously, at the moment of discovery that some hot-button marginalized identities existed, all of the rage and venom of the fractured ego screaming across the room deflated almost instantly. There was what I can only describe as a 'oh fuck, don't sue us' look of horror and realization. The hour-long baratement session ended with the ego crying, and hugs exchanged over words of goodnight.

I share this not to garner a sympathetic reaction nor to try to situate myself above or below anyone socially. I share this because I needed to. This insanity has been blasting apart my mind since late February, it has stalled all of my creativity, it has floundered any and all efforts to even do the bare minimum of creative work. Not because the words themselves hurt. But mainly because the feeling of disappointment and that old childhood disdain for the lack of integrity, honesty, and strength of character have been gnawing at my mind. It is not the words; I have dealt with far worse critiques of my work from people who have actually read the fucking words I've written. Instead, it was the cruel end to what was supposed to be a magical fairytale. Instead, it was a cruel reminder of the fact that fairytales are not real but instead are often horror-soaked parables for the dangers of the depths of human depravity. It is not that I paid to be berated, but that for some curious reason, I had to be the divining rod of rage so that others may have soared. This is not a melodramatic emotional outburst, nor is it again a call for sympathy, instead it is more a curious reflection of a short story by Ursula K. LeGuin titled The Ones Who Walk Away from Omelas. The story briefly details the proverbial shining city on the hill, a total utopia, a perfect vision of the future of humanity where strife for the masses, pollution, disparity and oppression are distant memories. However, the horror of this utopia is that for the entire population revelling, the parable herein is that in order for the suffering of all to be lifted, it was instead focused on one singular life. in utopian bliss, there is a child locked in a basement enduring total and complete neglect and abuse. The parable herein that in order for the suffering of all to be lifted, it was instead focused into one singular life. This is not to say that my writer's God complex includes a Christ narrative, nor that I feel any semblance of martyrdom amidst all of the childish insanity, but rather that it reflects a sad reality of our experience that in order for bliss to exist, for utopia and dreams and joy to be embodied there indeed also must be the contradiction, per Adorno. There is the darkness to the light, the horror to the fantasy, and a healthy dosage of hypocrisy sprinkled in for flavour. Unfortunately for me and my artistic process, I seemed to be one of the chosen few among the bunch who was deemed worthy of the shouting, the attacks, the dishonest presentation of self, and the shattering of the illusion. Wandering the wilderness of mirrors faded to a sad but spiteful realization that the powers that be, even when they spout empty sentiments about creativity, safety and freedom of expression, are nothing more than asset portfolio managers, and I had unwittingly fallen into the problem child advertisement production role despite the carefully curated marketing surrounding the strange and savage journey.

In the wake of this madness, again, the silent embers of revolution glowed brighter. It is a very important thing whenever you are faced with such unfair or damaging abusive treatment that you tell someone. It is easier said than done in most cases, but in this instance, among the comrades in the arts, artists who are themselves revolutionaries, this solidarity did not create difficulty for me to disclose what had happened. In fact, within an hour of the end of the madness, a fair majority of the revolutionaries were not only aware of the insanity but were firmly rooted in their shared collective condemnation of it. In that solidarity, I felt safe among my fellow artists; a sense of unconditional love was there in the air, where among those of us present, there was an almost universal protective wall erected, where the true nature of the powers that be, had they not already been on display were now fully and publicly known. Many discussions followed that stretched out into the latest hours of the night, where in the clandestine shadows, it was more or less the collective consensus that at this rate, the light bills would most likely not be paid for that much longer as you cannot advertise a safe haven for the creative spirit while your true nature is that you would rather demean it into the ground so long as the cheques keep coming in. I hold nothing but love for my comrades in those trenches, and doubly so considering the hours upon hours of conversations that have occurred since that fateful night in the rain.

In the months since standing there in the rain as my artistic soul tried to dodge every attempted assassination, I can take solace here in this moment in discovering the fact that I had to pen this overly long autopsy of this situation in order to save my soul from the toxicity, that I reinforced the idea that we have the power to facilitate our own healing. We do not need to lash out, to seek revenge, to seek some form of closure externally. There is magic in the human power of creation, where in the composition of works of art that reflect these struggles, we are able to work through them without reservation. This is my catharsis here in these pages, where, along with the fragments of my soul that have bled for this art, these memories no longer need to stay in my mind. They are here in the lines of text and the pages, and therefore they are outside of the mortal coil that they once wounded.

In a final parting word on the nature of ego and business in art, all I can offer is advice to the artists themselves. I cannot presume to offer advice to the ghouls seeking to exploit us because the business ego and the toxicity associated with it cannot be helped, I'm afraid. There is no cure for individualistic selfishness or the addiction to money and power. These are chronic malignancies in the spirit and soul of anyone who falls prey to their temptations, and this is especially sad when those who fall were once fellow artists. With that, to the artists, both those that I know and those that may read this independently, what I can say is to retain those formative points of artistic quality that good old Adorno shared with us: exist in the contradictions and do so with an uncompromising dedication to the honesty in your own artistic pursuits. Do your work with no deference to the powers that be. Fight back, quietly or in a deafening crescendo. Prove to these sad and savage beasts beyond the veil of creativity that you are more than a price tag, a shareable success story, or anything other than that purest of artistic identity that resonates most strongly in your heart. Empires will fall. Power to the people. Glory be to the artist; you are our last hope in a weary world.

Never Compromise, Even in the Face of Armageddon

Fuck your Criticism.

An Epilogue

"Our crime was that we were beginning to live a new and contagious lifestyle without official authorization."

-Tom Hayden

It may appear to readers that the above essay reads as a condemnation or a whispered scream for sympathetic overtures. I cannot modify the means by which you interpret this work, but what I may offer is that the intentionality herein is not an attack, not a condemnation, but instead, a personal reflection so that I may leave this madness behind me and move on to the work that matters most to my heart. It was in effect a deconstruction of creative barriers for me, along with a more macro reflection on the challenges of human experience in the creation of art, and the nature of those who may stand to be threats to the performance of the artistic process. I do not condone these behaviours, and having survived them and their subsequent compounding oppressive ignorance of the nature of power over others, what I can say is that it is crucially central to the performance of self in an authentic way to resist at all costs the pressure to fall into the toxic traps of those that seek to exploit our art. That is the true "business of art" is to dodge the business side at all turns and to be full of a continual vigilance to protect not only our work but our spirit from those that seek to use us as commodities and to instead seek out the community of creative collectivity that will resonate together in silent revolution in spite of the powers that be. Despite the insanity of my experience, it was "worth it" for that realization alone and for the community that grew in spite of the madness from the top down. To say that friendships were made is an understatement. In the neo-bohemian chaos of creatives existing together, there is a subtle magic that cannot be understated. The nature of art in practice surrounded by other creatives is something that must be protected as sacred at all costs. It is a horrific reflection of the state of the world that the only people able to fully facilitate this type of community in terms of the pragmatic logistics (housing, money, food, etc.) are the types of people so prone to taking advantage of that community to enrich their own senses of ego.

What I will say is that the silent revolution of the artist's collective is well underway, but the direction it must take is one of direct spiteful civil disobedience to the powers that seek to use our art as revenue streams. It is not a revolution to be fought with violence but with a resolute resistance to conform. Art is, by its very nature, a totally free and radical expression of our hearts. We cannot bend to allow others to demand, control or expect anything other than total and complete respect for the process, even if the art we create pushes discomfort or unwanted mirrors of self-reflection. We must not allow those who seek to exploit us to win the battle, and they do every time we allow these tropes and behavioural problems to fester in the world of art. Cutthroat capitalism can keep its rugged individualism; I will instead advocate for art to reclaim the human spirit of communal, collaborative existence, where competition is not focused outward to outshine the earning potential of others but inward to fight to be a better creator than the version of you that existed in the past moments, hours, or years. The reality of life is that there will always be people who claim to understand the artist and their art but who will also conveniently turn a pretty penny from our pain. What we may do to combat this is to fully dedicate our efforts to the capturing of the contradictions and to do so with an ironclad honesty to ourselves. We must be true to our art, to our pain, to our experience of life itself. We cannot allow these ghouls to take that from us, no matter what venom they spit into our faces in the rain. What I have learned is that despite that pressure, the paranoia, the loss of a sense of safety and security, is that true artists will always be there to fight in the trenches of silent revolution alongside you with warm empathy and knowing wisdom that far transcends the petty insecurities of those that seek to hold us down. The funny thing is that our revolution does not even need a rallying forward base of operations because the poison of these people will tear down their systems for us. All we must do is sit back and paint the spreading fire.

Create as if your life depends on it because it does. Create honestly because honesty is in short supply, and laugh at the absurdity of the ghouls and goblins out there that promise you exposure, fame or recognition in exchange for cash upfront. They don't understand the true north of art.

"And I-I, had a feeling that I belonged

I-I had a feeling I could be someone, be someone, be someone"

-Tracy Chapman, Fast Car

Chapter 8

The Moral Art

"And by the way, everything in life is writable about if you have the outgoing guts to do it, and the imagination to improvise. The worst enemy to creativity is self-doubt."

-Sylvia Plath, Collected Journals

Writing is a Moral Art. It guides our minds to reason, to morality, to love, to empathy and to revolution.

I have often remarked to many of my students across multiple disciplines of social science, philosophy and now English composition that writing is the most intimate form of communication we may perform as human beings. In our earliest days, the inscription of simple symbols on clay tablets, on leaves, into stone walls stretched across the gaps of continents and cultures. It allowed for the communication of life to contemporary others, to distant contacts, and to those that would succeed us in existence on earth. Writing has facilitated diplomacy, business, economics, socio-legal realities and the establishment of the institutions of civilization that contribute to the emergence of social order as we know it today. Writing, too, has been the medium where love has been confessed, where the mysteries of life and being have been explored and extrapolated upon, and where the world we inhabit has become known in the creative examination of life itself under the stroke of the stylus. Philosophy, drama, fiction, journalism, all of these critical pillars of human existence have themselves come from and by the written word to form a collective of knowledge, history and experience as living discourses that continue to inform our world and our lives. The intimacy of writing, of distilling the complexity of lived experience into a symbolic lexicon of letters on the page, is something so unique to the human experience that to think of it in a deconstructive sense is to revel in the eccentricity of the practice itself. What a wild concept to compose an essay, to selectively choose the correct combination of 26 letters, a handful of (hopefully correctly implemented) punction characters and the variety of modalities of communication to make something akin to art in its existence. To evoke Christopher Hitchens, everyone has a book in them, but for some, that is where it should stay. Not all that is written has this inherent beauty, but we may, in that sense, still reflect on the intimate beauty of the process outside of the content of the product. I have read many things that have made me wish writing was an exclusive elusive talent, but then again, I have, in the same stride, read many words that take my breath away in their beauty, either in the simplicity of their association or their complex marriage of ideas in their flow to convey the mysteries of being.

While I have in my time romanticized the process of writing and, to far more extreme ends, sacrificed my mortal body for the craft time and again, I have yet to fully meditate on how someone makes the divide between human and writer. Where does the process begin? Who will become a writer? Why? How? These fundamental questions make sense in my experience; I know what drew me here. It has not been an easy journey for me; where in elementary school and kindergarten, I had to essentially teach myself to read and write during the day and with my parents at home. Reading came easily behind the yellow covers of National Geographic magazines in my kindergarten library area. Writing was something I hated for many years. Because I never formally learned the way to make the letters 'correctly' they were hard for me. They hurt my hands, I didn't have a concept of spacing, size, or any regularity in margins, capitalization or handwritten punctuation. To this day, my penmanship is a horror show. My resentment of writing plagued me throughout my entire K-11 experience. I hated the notion of writing. By hand, digitally, fiction, academic, all of it. Never once in those years did I have the luxury of a teacher who could communicate the beauty of the written word to me as a composer. I have written elsewhere of my teacher who wove magical landscapes in literature in my mind through 7th and 8th grade. Reading science fiction, poetry, and even Shakespeare felt not just enjoyable, but it felt like something deeper, where ideas were there, and it was a safe space to examine my own ideas in the communicative contexts of those texts. It is in the absorption of the written word that we discover our passion for the composition of the written word. In effect, we cannot come to appreciate the nuance and intimacy of writing without first engaging in a complex and nuanced appreciation of the texts we read. There are texts I have read and re-read dozens of times since my first exposure to them decades ago, and they still resonate with me to this day. This is what pulls us into the world of the blank page, not a requirement, nor rule, nor grade but the idea that what we have before us is an undefined place of our own thoughts. We, today, are no different than our ancestors staring at a blank clay tablet, reed stylus in hand, poised to write the epics of myths and legends of our time. In us is a scribe, and within that scribe are words that are meant to be shared. We cannot compromise our voices in this sense and instead must strive further out into the world of our own making through our written voice.

A direct contradiction to this romanticized version of writing I have presented here is that there are so many missed opportunities in the teaching of our craft to our students. Students in a formal sense and students in a theoretical sense. Where our real-life students may listen and copy notes on parts of speech and grammar and endlessly paw through rhetorical analyses and summative unit projects, our theoretical students, our readers, may see the keys to written communication in their own understanding of our shared words. We, as writers, are always teachers, whether we perform any formal education or not. There is always a sense of mentorship and mastery communicated from our pens to the minds of our readers and we cannot under any circumstances forget our responsibility to their learning in our craft. Where we see a departure from this model is in the teacher who teaches but who is not a writer. One who may hold a very dear claim to the rigour of composition but who does not possess the lived experience of having created written art for the communication of their individual thoughts. While it may read as a gatekeeping notion, it is, unfortunately, a wide reality in the field of education. Not all of us have the privilege of being taught by a writer, and even fewer of us have the chance to be taught by a writer when we are learning to write. This is what hindered me at times, and what saved me was teachers who had not forgotten that they, as readers, were students. That is the foil to the lack of experience in the trenches of our craft, a continual lifelong love of the communication of thought through written words. The teachers who taught me to write did not teach writing, they taught reading, and they taught thinking. Thinking about what we have read is the key to teaching ourselves to become writers. Unfortunately, again, when we do not have a teacher or context that allows for thought and instead relies on rote memorization and standardized benchmarks, we lose the love of reading and, with it, the key to writing.

In the Trenches

"Literature is the art of writing something that will be read twice; journalism what will be grasped at once."

-Cyril Connolly

Beginning August 15th, 2024, I have been working in the most dangerous and critical theatre of my foreign correspondence career to date. A familiar place, yet mined with potentialities, where the unknown lurks from the shadows, where the drop of a social faux pas means certain demise, where your own legend is a lifeline in the mist, where the world falls away to be a series of incalculably slow moments where your only goal is to make it through to the other side unscathed. It is a place where comradeship blossoms, where there are lessons to learn and to teach, where a swirling world wholly new to me has opened, and one where I must at every turn rely on the ghosts of my own footprints that have tread the paths in another life before.

I have returned to my former high school to teach twelve days of college composition and literature.

It has been an odd experience, to say the least. Classroom teaching is no shock to my system; it is no foreign battleground. However, before the 15th of August this year, I had never had the experience of truly teaching in a place that held so many ghosts for me. Somehow teaching at my undergraduate alma mater has not had this profound effect. I think this is because the trials I went through on that campus were private and within my own mind, while here, in these walls, so many formative emotional flashbulb memories have flooded back. They are not fully traumatic, and while it is certainly a trip to be here, the experience itself has been largely positive. It is a strangely comforting experience to be teaching writing and composition under the watchful eyes of photos of my great-grandmother (a librarian here) and grandfather in the hallway just beyond my door, where great-aunts and great-great aunts also lovingly look down in their 20th-century class photos somehow keep me safe, or rather, comforted somehow. Upstairs is my own class photo, and elsewhere, siblings exist as well. I walk past the locker I 'owned' for my first year here, where on the first day of school (having never had a locker) I got my backpack wedged in it and the door became stuck. I had to have someone from the front office unlock it for me in a very embarrassing after-school moment for fourteen-year-old me. The classrooms, too, bring back memories where now I am sitting at the teacher's desk in a room where I once studied Edgar Allan Poe and Emily Dickinson. My first morning back, I ran into my favourite teacher from those days, the teacher who somehow knew I was an awkward kid who needed some guidance and mentorship with respect to confidence, who would teach me how to create speeches, how to dissect and reconstruct animals, and who would, even to this day be a safe space for a kid learning who they were. My other favourite teacher from those days has the classroom directly above me. She teaches writing and reading too, and so our talks have played between nostalgia, shop talk, and true pedagogical creativity. The principal is the teacher who taught me Poe and Dickinson here in this classroom. There is a legacy of knowledge here. I feel a strong sense of carrying a torch for these mentors I have had and a sense too of wanting to provide a space for my students that gives them the best chance to step out into the world of the written word with a voice they feel confident in sharing, and a sense that their positionality on the reality of life is such that they have voices worth sharing. It is in the notion of the sharing of the voice that we may offer to our students places to and from which they may take their experience in the composition of writing as a means of enriching the ways they come to know their worlds.

It sounds overly romantic, but still, somewhere beneath the waves of grandiosity are the simple rules of life that such an ability to communicate effectively is a good skill to possess. That said, I vehemently disagree with the idea of teaching writing to make students 'successful' in terms of the jobs they get or which college or university they attend. I instead prefer the idea of building up a student's ability to feel confident in themselves despite being confined to the systems around them. I told one student recently that they are a very gifted writer, and I meant it, but I also meant what I said next, to not let the 'science' of writing crush that out of them. Maintain the individuality, I said, and I mean that more than I can articulate. Due to the intimacy of the written word, and the arrogance of some that teach it, the science of writing can crush the craft of it before we even find our voices. Curiously, my younger brother once learned writing in the same classroom I am currently occupying, with the same teacher I am covering for. He left this room with a comment ringing in his ears still to this day, something to the effect of: "I can't find anything wrong with this, but I don't like your written voice." Comments from teachers follow us, always, but comments from writing teachers follow us with far sharper teeth. They can be glowing positivity that starts us down a road of composition for the craft or one of glaring toxicity to forever turn us away from the path itself. The latter is inexcusable. There is no 'bad' writing, only writing that is still developing. Once we stretch out into a world where we may make these classifications in a classroom, we should hang up the teacher identity and perhaps step into one with less importance in society, I hear realty is a good second career for individuals needing to ascribe an ego to their profession.

The podium from which we teach is there to hold up our papers for the day, not our identities. We are not to tie our sense of self to the power associated with the lectern. To do so is to betray everything we came to the profession of teaching for initially. There are no other reasons beyond 'the right ones' which are to teach younger humans how to exist. A core facet of that existence is the ability to write and to write effectively. It is one of the most basic forms of existence to know how to know your existence and then how to share it beyond yourself. It is what situates the teacher of writing in such a hallowed space in the pantheon[1] of education. We are

1. While composing this idea, I shared it with my students as they were wiling away their time in a poorly implemented composition lab class. They asked me who ranks lower in the pantheon of education. Without thought, I said 'football coaches' to some scattered laughs. But seriously. Football coaches.

there to bridge the gap between your inner world and the outer worlds you inhabit. Writing is something that, if handled with care, passion, empathy and kindness, we can bridge the divide between the storms of our minds and the storms we weather out in the real world. It would shock none of my readers to learn that such empathy is a rarity in modern American education. It is in this rarity that I have faced the worst struggle of my time in these trenches: the disconnect between teaching writing as a science of the ego and writing as an art of morality.

Readers who know me are aware of my general distaste for rules. I have never enjoyed being bolted into boxes on the basis of the arbitrary rules of others. Especially in creative endeavors. The audacity to prescribe a set path for something so subjectively individual, to me, has always been a major source of rage and anguish. I can respect rules that are not arbitrary, and in my pursuit of sociology as a career, I see why they need to exist. Rules have their place. Those places specifically are in the preservation of life, of the care of self, of the objective pillars of reality that govern our survivability in existing as agentically as possible. This is not to say that all social rules are moral but rather that I can understand their existence. Rules that come from above that hold themselves openly in the pale moonlight only being for the benefit of the ego of the ruler, these are the things that hurt my soul. I have had the unfortunate reality of seeing through a window into the world of writing as it is taught solely by an ego and not from the heart, and it has broken mine. To be forced myself, as a teacher of writing, into the boxes of another person's arbitrary whims, to be told in explicit exacting detail to break my students' spirits, to mould them into something subjugated, something subhuman for the almighty and lofty status associated with the power of the podium and the tickly feeling on one's ego when you get the 'respect' of a broken student has been utterly devastating for my soul. I was told before I began that teaching writing was "like music, we teach the chords and two or three of them will play jazz". To be responsible for nurturing the inner voices of over 70 brilliant students and to have the mindset that only two or three of them would have the ability to shine is sickening to the absolute zenith. Further, what burns my soul deeper than arbitrary rules set by egoists by and for their vanity is knowing concretely that they are unqualified to hold the position of power they hold. I have written elsewhere of how much disdain I hold for people who flaunt academic titles, achievements or worst of all, degrees. Even more so I categorically condemn the egoist writer that lauds their publications over another person.

I am ashamed to admit that in the trenches, I have had to resort to these tactics to ensure my own spiritual survival.

Typically, in academia, such battles come from administrators, but this has not been the case. No. These fires have pushed me towards flaunting such disgusting things as my experience, credentials, and publications, which have come from someone trusted with the sacred charge of teaching the most intimate form of communication to students eagerly waiting for a chance to stretch their writing legs.

In a similar vein, I have learned a wild truth of the academe which is this: in postsecondary education, teaching English composition or first-year writing to university or college students is considered either an entry-level or even punishing posting. In the walls of a high school, this somehow translates in the eyes of the teacher with that 'credential' to being the most senior and honoured member of the faculty. The reality, in my eyes, having served my tour in these trenches, is the inverse. The teacher who can bravely stand and face thirty or more 9th-grade students and somehow lead them to a world of discovery of the written word is far more honourable than the teacher who can bully a class of college kids into submission in the face of the almighty data-driven, deficit model of teaching. It is easy to abuse the minds of students with the science of writing; it is insurmountably difficult to reach the minds of writers before they know they are writers on the wavelength that matters most to them. Teaching 'student-centred' is not just a catchy buzzword around pedagogy water coolers. It is a critical pillar of our entire craft. Writing is human, so to teach it, we must be human ourselves.

As writers, to be human is to be inhuman. Each of us has our cloaks of mystery, be they those of use presumed to be vampires, stealing away in the shadow of the night to draw the lifeblood out of our pages and ourselves, or those day walkers that, in their beauty and eccentricity, weave a cloak around them of unnervingly endearing curiosity. Writers are either seen and unknowable or known and unseen. In neither case does the writer compose their best writing when the idea of a box to fit in is even allowed to enter the brain? We are without boxes and without a science to our insanity. It is a theme I think worth exploring that the writer's spirit is one that does not fit into the boxes of the practices of teaching the craft. We have to fail our way into our own processes. Just recently I offered a similar remark that academic colleagues of mine will have heard before, I said to a colleague "I'm going to go lay on the floor now." And she asked, 'What is it about you and lying on the floor' to which I replied: "It's my process." We cannot be expected to know why we do what we do, only that the pursuit of the words to the page is paramount to the norms of the world around us. This is why my writing soul prefers the night, the silence of the darkness lurking in the windows and the absolute silence of responsibility. That is my process, I need to be free in the dark to be the inhuman beast that will hunch over the page until my muscles are sore and dare I say, until I bleed for my art.

How do you teach that to students? How do you stand at the front of a classroom and say to kids with a million responsibilities that you have to ignore them? You have to dedicate yourself to missed text messages, cancelled outings, sleepless nights, and the general reclusiveness that would land you somewhere in the realm of being a bad friend, partner, brother, etc. How do we tell our students that the practice of writing is something that consumes you entirely? Somewhere in the romanticism of the process, there is a real danger there. If you are to be a professional writer, you cannot be anything else at the moment. It is a full and total commitment to insanity and to the insanity you yourself brew for you alone. It is an isolation that becomes addicting as hell and one where we cannot hope to ever communicate outwardly why we do what we do.

This is why I have a great deal of respect for those who truly teach our craft with grace and humanity and the recognition of the student as a person and not a data point on the standard spectrum.

To do so requires a careful blend of the insanity of the writer, the discipline of the reader, and the empathy of humanity. If you remove all of these, you are left in the husk of writing as science, and that leaves the world dreary at best and in flames at worst. In my time teaching writing, however fleeting, I found there was a massive fear from one such teacher of the dangers of AI and 'make you smarter' programs. The idea that students would have the audacity to use a tool to make their writing sound more artificial and inhuman to fit the boxes defined for them was marketed as a cardinal sin of the writing student. I see this not as a major threat to academic integrity but as the culmination of all of the madness that has come down in the formality of teaching the science of writing. Students have no other choice than to resort to these impossible machines to meet impossible demands for a practice that is evolutionarily impossible. If writing is to be our intimate form of communication, the practice of reducing it to a formulaic reproduction of demands is the death of the intimacy of writing.

This said I recognize that genres of writing exist where humanity cannot exist. Having composed many 'professional' scholarly bits of nonsense in my time, I can see how the skill to fit in the box is important. However, the reality is that we learn the conventions of our chosen discipline by virtue of existing in it. I can write sociology and psychology because that is where I have roosted academically, I cannot write engineering papers, this is why I turn to my brother, an engineer, for such things. It is a skill to be able to write professionally, but the function of a composition class for college students is not to break them down to a voiceless automaton reproducing the teacher's skewed understanding of professional writing. A question that has plagued my mind the entirety of my time teaching composition and doing so under the intense requirements of my students' regular teacher is this: what have they written professionally? While it may seem rooted in ego, all I can offer is the notion echoed above that people who are engaged in the teaching of this craft must, in some regard, be actively practising it. Assigning grammar quizzes and short, meaningless daily tasks is not a mark of teaching proficiency, nor is it a way to teach the art of writing to college students. We cannot expect them to write scholarly articles from the onset, but to assume they cannot write a sentence is madness. In my experience, my students had the most stellar moments of artistic written creation when they were actually writing. I told them as much. The best soundtrack to a writing teacher's ears is the slow, methodical chorus of keyboard clacking and quiet, reserved conversation. This is what we ought to strive to compose in our students, a sense of collaborative companionship where they are surrounded by others striving for the same goal: to write something.

In a moment of poignant reality, halfway through my tenure here, I called my grandmother, who had also been an English teacher at the same school in 1960. She answered the phone by saying: "How was school today? Are they still making kids take grammar quizzes, or have they finally learned better?" The resulting conversation about having to give so many grammar quizzes that I could not keep track of them was echoed by her frustration that still today, the true craft of writing the written word was lost on teachers trying as hard as possible to meet the hallowed requirements.

This need not be the case. I do not have the space nor fortitude in this medium to cover the entire horrific history of College Board, nor do I have the stomach to write about the crimes against education set forth by Woodrow Wilson at the helm, but they exist even today as ghosts in the machine of higher education. I have and will always hold the position that Advanced Placement is a scam, one that duly robs high school students of their sanity and mental health, among other things, and that the equivalent in so-called advanced placement courses to real university work is absent at best and egregiously counter-productive at best. In such critically engaged disciplines as writing, literature, psychology, history, etc., there is no university equivalent that can be replicated in an AP classroom because, much to the shock perhaps of (some) AP teachers, we, in fact, are not just allowed but required to compose our own curricula. We do not 'teach to the test' as you do in "Advanced Placement". Therefore, our instruction is our own, wherein our expertise in a given discipline allows us the material and content to construct a unique and academically engaging environment for our students.

AP can, I concede, have its benefits for hard sciences, but I cannot pretend to care enough about such things to offer commentary at present. The barebones reality is that reducing the art of writing to the science of CollegeBoard's exam is a death knell for our students' creativity and humanity in the written medium. We bill AP not for academic excellence but to 'skip' required college courses typically, which, in the long run, may make sense. I skipped no college courses (I had to even backtrack into high school where mathematics was concerned), and the experience itself was mutually beneficial to some degree. I do not fault students for getting ahead, saving money, etc. That said, I must implore my fellow educators to cut the cord of AP being equal to university or college education; the simple fact of the matter is that it is not.

In a very cursory and brief review of the literature, several exploratory studies support the following points of discussion about Advanced Placement courses:

1. Their beneficence is questionable at best (students passing AP exams with 3's or 4's are being rejected credit at an increased amount of colleges and universities).

2. The expansive push to incorporate AP courses across all subjects and age levels in high school is devaluing the 'university equivalence' of the curricula.

3. AP Courses in Arts and Humanities (and some social sciences) offer little to no flexibility for course construction due to the standardized, postmodernist approach.

4. AP still represents a dividing line across socioeconomic, racial, ethnic and gender-based social identities.

Adapted From (Judson and Hobson 2015; Park, Caine, and Wimmer 2014; Rauh 2014; Warne et al. 2015)

Additionally, trends have shown that while enrolment in AP courses is increasing, success in AP exams has been trending down over the past two decades (Judson and Hobson 2015), and also that the age of students enrolling in AP courses is progressively trending lower (where historically 3rd or 4th-year secondary students would be the traditional target audience, 2nd or even 1st-year students are now undertaking AP courses). The question here must be that if we can have such a wide variety of students in our "advanced" courses, where in the curriculum are we able to make allowances for these varieties in experience? To further this point, how if the assessment is standardized based upon an arbitrary objective model set forth by a governing body, is there any chance at equity in the process of a deeply subjective endeavour such as writing? How can we expect a 2nd year high school student to be on par with a 4th year? And how can we trust that the outcome of their standardized AP exams will adequately reflect their 'ability'? This is not to disparage the talented 10th grader, nor to disparage the talented 12th grader, but rather to ask: where is the flexibility in a craft so individualized?

I am reminded now of a moment from middle school. In the state of Colorado, while I was a student in public education, we had to take a test called a "CSAP," something to the effect of the Colorado Student Assessment Program. Being that I attended a hippy school, we would pair testing season with a theatrical production and plenty of snacks. In effect, we would test in the mornings for some hours, then after lunch, jump into the arts of music, drama, dance, writing, painting and set design, to name a few. I still hold vivid memories of being suspended above a massive canvas mural on a forklift arm, painting trees into what would become a backdrop of one scene in our production while Green

Day's American Idiot album blasted from a boombox plastered in stickers. This, however, is not the memory that immediately shreds to mind. Instead, I remember a moment that is burned deeply into my psyche for two reasons: first, it taught me I couldn't trust my teachers, and second it taught me the most important maxim of my life: If People Do Not Like Your Writing, They Do Not Deserve to Read It. During the writing assessment portion of our test in fifth grade, we were responding to the prompt that asked us to compose an essay on someone who inspired us and to explain why. I, being a fifth grader with a crush, wrote what I still hope would be a passable essay about a classmate I had a crush on. Not my finest moment; extremely cringeworthy, but somehow honest in its naivety. Day one of the assessment had us compose a draft. Day two was to finalize and rewrite that draft as a final. Immediately after lunch, following our test section, our teacher, who was not supposed to have read our tests, held an impromptu lecture about hormones, crushes, love and romance and how it was somehow toxic to hold these feelings. I was mortified at this. No one knew I had written what I did, how this person had inspired me to be better for myself, etc., but I knew and that fucking hurt. Granted, penning a Victorian melodramatic essay about a crush in middle school was probably not the best move, but I was eleven years old. I sat through that painful lecture for what felt like hours, embarrassed, crushed, betrayed and very hurt. During the latter part of the test, where we were to finalize our draft, I erased my entire essay from the draft booklet and instead wrote my essay about some fucking stage monkey that had played the role of a monkey named 'Elmer' in the egregious 2000s reboot of The Little Rascals. I learned in that stark moment how to meet the box where it stood. And I have hated a small part of myself since that moment, halfway because I changed the essay, halfway because I wrote it in the first place. Why did I have to adapt to the box? Why did my teacher deliver this lecture? To the former, all I can say is that our school's funding was tied to our test scores. To the latter, this and many other moments led me to believe that she simply hated me as a student.

What this illustrates is a twofold reality: students remember what teachers say and do to them regarding their writing, and the feeling of having writing that you cared about torn to such public shreds for the sake of the almighty score distribution fucking hurts. Was that essay good? Chances are it was shit. Was it appropriate? God no. Do I regret that hormonal insanity? Absolutely. But. At the end of the day. It was something I wrote. Me. By myself. From my heart. It taught me in that painful, searing moment after the fact as my essay was dissected that I had a choice as a writer from then on to ignore the madness of teachers who themselves hated writing or to begin hating writing myself.

I hated writing for ten years after that day.

I reflect from time to time on the countless written moments I lost in that decade. While I hated writing, a friend in my class wrote a novel, a real, honest historical fiction novel complete with ephemera. She went on to win the Colorado Book Award and beat my first publication date by a year, which we have since laughed about. I hated writing because I couldn't freely be vulnerable in sharing it. I hated it because the reaction my words evoked was controversy, an invasion of privacy, and shame to an infinite degree. Remembering it now makes me relive the embarrassment and the stress even to this day. I learned then, although I would not know it until I began teaching, that I would not be the teacher to force students to share their writing in such a way. It would always be respected and consensual in my classrooms.

When we tack on the absurdity of an Advanced Placement logo to what we teach, especially if we are ill-equipped to actually teach our subject on the plane of empathy and humanity, we add only more layers of distance, artificiality, and monotony to the works of our students. By worshipping the box, we become the antithesis of a critically engaged writer. Thank God they can write an independent clause and praise the lord, for they may memorize rhetorical techniques, but God forbid they feel anything while doing so.

The most horrific element of the AP toxicity in that classroom is this: it is cross-blended with a real college credit course. Students earn both AP credit and accredited community college credit by completing the course. The one difference? The college credit comes without an objectified exam. I do not know the full justification for this except the vague myth that fewer colleges accept accredited hours from the community college than do accept AP credit. This said, for general education requirements such as writing composition, I cannot for the life of me imagine any but the most entrenched Ivy League schools not accepting a transfer. Instead, we offer both at the same time. Double the credit. Quadruple the stress. And, in the words of the instructor, "Only two or three will come out knowing how to play jazz." Imagine the madness of it all.

An Epilogue of a Tired Mind

I can continue. I can press beyond these pages into more condemnations. I can write *ad nauseam* about the subtle games, the playing with pedagogy for ego points, the micromanaging, the wild oversteps of boundaries into other teachers' daily teaching strategies, the condescension, the extreme lack of credentials and expertise, or the callous lack of human emotion as one teaches traumatic subject matter, or the general fear in the words of students when they talk about the writing teacher who doesn't write. But what would be the point of that exercise? Would it inspire change? Unlikely. Would it benefit anyone? Doubtful.

What it instead stands to represent is the simple truth that good teachers are hard to find, and great ones rarely stay because horrific ones somehow always get all the power. Teaching writing is not about power, ego, publications, teaching awards or any other nonsensical things. It is about working with your students to help them become better writers. It is sharing your process, your thoughts, your approaches, and for god's sake, it is about writing with them. The amount of pre-loaded, prewritten stuff being handed down their throats is worrisome. Instead of assigning a prompt from a bank and then providing the pre-selected 'correct' essay, maybe work through the prompt with your students. I did it in less than 10 minutes. It is not rocket surgery for someone who is actually marginally competent in the craft, and the wild reality is that such a small gesture of collaborative solidarity can mean the world to students. As I have said, I do not intend to stoop to the level of tit-for-tat gotcha moments, but when I told my writers that I had composed a sample essay that was from the same prompt as their assignment, three of the louder kids actually cheered. Imagine a world where in the pursuit of a craft so intimately artistic, you have a teacher willing to put their own written voice on the chopping block of the harshest critics we have to face: teenagers. I do not believe any teacher could submit their own work to their students, I do not feel particularly noteworthy for having done so, but rather I have just simply decided that my sense of self, of ability, of spirit is not tied to the level of control I can exert on a captive audience. I revelled too in the look of horror I received when I had remarked that while I told students they had to use the "hook" concept in their writing in this class, I also told them to abandon it as soon as they could because it is one of the dumbest conventions in modern English education for all but a very, very select handful of genres.

I told several colleagues that I do not like starting revolutions, and they all, in turn, told me that all I had done was step into one already brewing. It is sad to me that students are excited to write, to attend class, and to feel as though their work matters is a revolutionary concept. It is downright heartbreaking to be asked when I am coming back or to be told that even in my two weeks, I had made a difference. I did not want to be radically different, I wanted to be myself, and I was. It is sad to me that such a simple act, the literal bare minimum on my end, is something so meaningful to students the world over. I have said many times to colleagues ranging from tenured professors to teaching assistants working for me that the saddest thing about my job is that doing just this barest of minimum things (treating students like people with lives) is so meaningful. Being treated as someone with autonomy, agency, and personality should not be unexpected or surprising, especially in a writing class. Being told your voice matters but that you aren't compelled under threat to speak it out loud, that your experiences are valid, and that your history and memories are meaningful should be the base form of human connection, not radically new age teaching strategies.

I have learned in my time teaching that ego maniacs will always hate this approach. They hate it because it decentralizes power away from their voice, their podium, their PowerPoint, etc. They often are the ones too that either teach supposedly liberatory subjects or who have plastered their entire classrooms in meaningful quotes from civil rights leaders, revolutionaries and radicals. They hate the idea of losing that power. Imagine a room of twenty or thirty teenagers with the power of their own voices. To some, this is an uplifting and lofty goal.

To others, it is their worst nightmare. To them, to give even an inch of that power away is tantamount to blood sacrifice. It is sad to watch. These people tend to also have an overinflated sense of their own importance in their discipline, which amplifies the secondhand embarrassment felt when you see them impose their wills on a room of teenagers. For a time, I imagined I could fight the status quo openly by citing articles, theories, reviews, lecturers, books and so forth at conferences, in meetings, and whenever possible. I learned this is futile. The ego-centric educator will never understand what it means to put a student first, especially if they describe their pedagogy as "students first." They'll always have excuses, they'll almost always get angry, and they'll throw their hands up to their walls of awards and commendations, not knowing that so many of their students carry their hurtful words with them for decades after they are spoken.

How do we beat the egoist? We don't. They, unfortunately, rise up in the hierarchy too quickly and too effectively to be beaten. Once one steps over the edge, finally, instead of being fired or reprimanded, they're promoted to some steering position in the administration. The way we win is another story. For those of us who educate for the love of it without our egos tied to the front of the classroom, the way we beat our narcissistic colleagues is simple. We beat them by being better than them. Students are not stupid. They know good teachers. To borrow from Steve Martin: Be So Perfect They Can't Ignore You. Yes, it is stressful, and yes, it is exhausting, you will cry you will throw your hands up in anger, and you will have days where you want to give up. Don't let the darkness envelope you. Egotistical power-tripping teachers win by beating down competition and enforcing a web of conformity.

We must prevail. To do so, learn to revel in foiling their schemes and find joy in advocating for yourself and your students. I have found that if you rephrase their demands to them in a way that highlights their absurdity and places it comparatively to the correct approach, they'll fold because they do not want to be associated with disagreeing with something inherently good. If you back them into a rhetorical corner where their demand is shown in a negative light compared to your suggestion forward, especially in front of witnesses, they'll fold. Instead of arguing outright, we have to be diplomatically acute in our approach. If they demand X, reword it to them like this: "So what you're suggesting is [insert all of the flaws with X], instead of [all of the virtues of Y] is that correct?" "So, you are suggesting we enforce a grading scale that heavily favours conformity instead of critical thinking and exploration is that correct?" They can't say yes because it indemnifies them to the moral bad, and so they, in their defeat, either scramble to reframe their idea or flat-out agree to change their mind. Impose this strategy as long as it takes to preserve our students' sanity. It is effectively a pedagogical tapdancing trolley problem with all the inherent madness a name like that entails. Go wisely forward, comrades.

In closing, I doubt that I will have students reading this, but should there be some, what I will say to you is to never forget that your voice and your written words have power over them. You may feel they do not. You may feel enclosed, limited, and censored. Fight it. Fight like hell, and never, ever be afraid to ask your writing teacher what they are currently writing. The answers may shock you, and silence is the worst of all.

To the teachers who may read this: Those I have shared it with directly need not fret, as these condemnations are not for you, as you know. To those who have found it and are now wondering if it is about you...ask yourself why.

A closing thought:

I offered students in one of my classes a chance to include a final quote to this essay here. I said that if they wanted to, they could write an anonymous sentence on a notecard answering the question: "What Does Writing Mean to You" and I would include it here unattributed. Being they were all busy writing, only one had the time to do this for me, and I included their reflection here.

"Writing is a Form of Self-Guided Therapy"

Chapter 9

Dispatches from a City of Dreams

-Behind The Wire, We Learn Who We Are-

"Most people are other people. Their thoughts are someone else's opinions, their lives a mimicry, their passions a quotation."

-Oscar Wilde, De Profundis (11 February 1905)

The Calm Before the Drop; a Briefing:

There is a curious duality of landing upright in the dream world on your feet and the feeling of crashing out of it onto your back in bed. In each, we experience a new birth, a new breach into the world inhabited in our sleep or our waking experience. Each moment, in its own way, is a breathless gasp into being or nonbeing. Before us lies the unknowable tracts of our day or night of wandering through existence. In the dream world, what fantastical oddities await to present themselves to us is a mystery, and in waking, the very real nightmares that may lie just beyond the corners of the sunrise lurk ever closer to being real to us in our moments. Falling asleep and waking up are curious things. Falling implies an uncontrolled descent while waking somehow takes my mind to the feeling of being violently torn from a world asunder. I have written elsewhere of the pain of waking from good dreams and the power of reflection found in nightmares. Where we may now find ourselves wandering is in the ether between the two. The dreams that, while perhaps not regularly recurring, are ones that meet us with a sense of middling familiarity. The places we are known to that we know, that hold us not in an embrace but stand beside us as well-travelled sentries of our consciousness in these middle places. This is not the misty Dreamland of the writings on loss, instead it is something else entirely. It is a place that is mine, that I have always visted alone. There are shadowy illusions of other occupants, but I have yet to meet a face, a cloak, or a traveller on any of the doorsteps I have wandered so far. The city is not dead, though, not deserted; I just feel as though perhaps I am not permitted to know the residents; it is a feeling similar to finding yourself in a city where you do not speak the local language, there is life around, but it is a secret life that is not for you, the outsider. To be an outsider of your own dreamscapes is an odd feeling, being there on the periphery of what is and is not yours is so very, very strange. As such, I opt to approach this city of my dreams not as a local nor as one familiar with its history or future but as a correspondent dropped into the heat of it all, the madness of the busy lives of its residents, the beauty it holds in its secrets.

The following is presented in three dispatches from three districts of this city that I have explored. Each was accompanied by a snippet of text that I manically composed upon waking from an interrupted sleep several nights ago, having yet again visited this city for my fourth or fifth tour. I find that my dreams are more vivid when my sleep is not adequate (if what I consider sleep has ever been adequate per medical or biological standards). This particular rousing shock back into reality came as a combination of a sore throat impeding my slumber brought on by wildfire smoke and the intensely dry heat that happens to lay over my little mountain refuge in the later summer months.

Curiously, I have lied to myself about both of these hallmarks of climate change before, remarking often that the smell of wildfires is one of my favourites. I think this comes from growing up with a fire captain who, on many occasions, would strike out for days on end to fight such fires and the subsequent years of adulthood, where I found myself often in the truck officer seat next to my dad blasting off towards a myriad of infernos in the distance. I have also told myself I like the heat. Somehow I have lied to myself that I enjoy the 30 degree weather of blistering sun and 0% humidity like some phony facsimile of a modern day Lawrence of Arabia. Holden Caufield, I think, would dislike me for my meteorological hubris. But there, nestled neatly in bed less than a week ago, I found myself waking every two hours to my extreme frustration. Between the trips out into the sagebrush and smoke-scented early mornings to pee into the dawn light and the abject anger that fills one when one cannot find a comfortable place to sleep in bed, my mind opted for another trip to the city of dreams. Other visits have happened when I've been sick, battling a cold the 'old fashioned way' by lying in bed like a Victorian child awaiting their passing with calm resolve, where the fever and dehydration take me onward to the streets. Yet other times have come in the throes of near overdoses on caffeine (9 double shot espressos are the limit for productivity, comrades). I have not visited the city out of desperation, though. It comes as a destination of curiosity, not of pain. I cannot recall ever having had a bad trip through the streets, or up the road of the mountain, or at the inn (all to be revealed below). Instead, it seems a manifestation of a peaceful place in my mind. Curious too that it is a city of all things, being a lifelong rural dweller who only dabbles in the city life on occasion, I would expect, were I of the Freudian persuasion, that my 'peaceful respite' would be a solitary cabin alone in a sagebrush steppe somewhere, but alas, this is my daily being.

The city is not like one I have ever thoroughly explored or experienced. It is not the chaotic labyrinth of Denver (a place I would not send my worst enemy), it is not the madness of Portland (also terrible), nor is it the eccentricity of Victoria where the collision of British city planning meets the Canadian cognoscenti, nor does it carry the ancient grandeur of Vilnius or the seaside charm of Klaipeda. No. This is a whole other beast. The closest approximation I can theorize is, regrettably, a city described in fiction and, even more so, in a book I have referenced far too often in this space. The Hong Kong of LeCarre's Honourable Schoolboy, a character in the novel, existing just in the last gasp of British colonial control, simmers closely to what my mind creates for parts of this land. Similarly, the descriptions of late 1960s Phnom Penh and Vientiane add other grandiose imagery to the question of where we are. It is somewhere Eastern, somewhere existing in a time prior to modernity, somewhere on the peak of analog technology, but before the digital revolution, where communication is instant but quirky, where travel is quick but cumbersome, and where I, the foreigner who has no business whatsoever being there, finds myself stuck for sojourns aplenty in the weirdness of sleep. It is neither the residents, nor the architecture that tell me where this city of dreams is, it is not a matter of orientalism or of presumption, it is a feeling based purely on the life of the city itself. It is alive in ways even the most eastern of European cities cannot reproduce. The city is a collective space of individual lives living in concert, not a concrete jungle of strangers. There is a sense that the fishmongers, the sailors, the tradespeople, the customers in the market, the cooks in restaurants, the people in the newspaper offices, all of them know and respect each other's contributions to the world around them. They all give life to the city, and rely too on the knowledge that their gift of life is met tenfold in the passing strangers on the streets. It is St. Paul's Penney

Lane on the eve of the Chinese Communist takeover in the waning days of the American War in Vietnam. There's a sense that there is change coming, that massive wealth exists above us on the streets, and that there is a darkness somewhere beyond the cityscape. There is no direct evidence of any of this in the dreams themselves, but in my recollection of my routes through the streets, this is the sense I can ascribe to understanding it in my waking memory. Perhaps I am a victim too of what Michael Herr would have called a fabrication of my own swashbuckling experience in the country, but in sharp contrast to Herr's tours of duty, I've not left my bed, and I doubt very much that my words carry as much for the world as his. Maybe if one day I take the Sean Flynn route and drive off to the North of the city of dreams chasing a story to never be seen again, will my work be worth something. Something tells me that even in my wildest days, the courage to Sean Flynn myself would never rise. True character, that one, wild to the end. Hunter would be proud.

The following dispatches are part adventure story, part fairytale, part correspondence from the trenches of what is and isn't, and part nonsense, I'm sure. I cannot know fully what drives my hands to pen these words this morning, nor do I know if anyone will read them. At this point, I cannot even be sure if they exist vaguely in a way that conspires to convey something of a message either in the personal existentialism of my recent catalogue or in the sociological expectation of my pedigree. Either way, these three dispatches are presented to the reader from the frontlines of a wandering milieu of dreamy worlds far beyond ours. Imagine, if you may a bustling place of life, where steam rises off the sea in the mornings, rain blankets the streets in the evenings, and the mountains in the distance become awash in the mists of mystery that disguise the peerless places between here and there.

Dispatch 1: The Docks and The Street

Is it possible to dream of streets you've never walked yourself, to hear with regularity the familiarity of streets' ends that you cannot see the beginning of?

I land, as all others do, here at the docks on the fringe of the industrial quarter of the city. The smell of fish, of diesel, and of the sea fill my nostrils. I am not used to these, and they sting. There is a heat to the city that I cannot quite accommodate in my high-altitude foreigner's shell. This clearly is a reflection of my body overheating in dreamland, but to me, the lonely correspondent all by myself in this new place, it is as suffocating as the isolation itself. I never see the boat I arrive on, I cannot tell if it is because I wake to the dream following my disembarking or if the sprawling expanse in front of me is too awe-inspiring to allow my mind's dreaming eye to remember the state of the deck of the trawler or sailing junk I booked passage on. I know I never fly. In country, I never think about why, waking I cannot guess why. I think perhaps it is because my brain has no medium for reproducing late 60s air travel, as the times around me seem to reflect, but having spent time on boats, I can recreate the sense of arriving dockside. The means of my arrival are not important. I always come in the morning with a steady bustle of mania around the industrial docks. I step three steps forward and am met with a wall, one of the first splashes of familiarity in the city for me. The wall is nothing more than a floor-to-ceiling maze of stacked wire metal fishing trays, various traps, nets, supplies, etc. It is because the place where my faceless and unknown boat captain drops me off is a dock adjoining a massive wallless warehouse of fishing supplies that equip the fleets out into the sea each day. These, as one would imagine, have a distinct smell to them. Drying kelp and seaweed, salt, rust, decay. I walk from the boat forward towards an overlap in the wall that almost perfectly hides the reality that it is a narrow meter-wide passageway between the docks and the rest of the bustling industrial quarter. I feel often overlooked and intensely scrutinized here on the docks. The others working are both too busy to notice me, and I am too out of place to simultaneously not elicit some looks. They can probably tell by my steady disembarking that I am at least somewhat knowledgeable at sea, but also that in my awkwardness surrounding the patterns of the city's docks, they know, as well as I do, that I do not belong here and most likely never will. They are my customs agents, reminding me subtly and wordlessly that I am simply a visitor and one without much status at that. I never look behind me in these dreams; there is never a reason to. The tradecrafts that follow me in real life don't materialize here. Instead it is a linear path each time, boat to shore, shore to pavement, pavement to adventure. There is never a need to look back.

I wade through the massively tall maze of stacked trays and assorted fishing supplies until I am on a narrow street. I emerge out of a doorway, and suddenly, it is nighttime. It is always nighttime on this street. I do not know why. However, a new feeling of familiar comfort fills me this time. It is different than the wall of the docks; it is a place that I know my way home from. I know my place here, and I know how this street connects me to where I must go. The street is always light in varying neon colours, but most prominent is the pink glow of many of the neon signs above me. I look up and see blues and greens, dragons, beer mugs, nude bodies, foods of all assortments all carefully drawn in the glass tubes of gaslights high above the street. Despite the rainbow of colours, the pink glow hangs always over me and the street. It is the main arterial connection of the city; it is somehow industrial, commercial, perverse, alive, accessible and beautiful all at once. There are shops here that have found my feet on their floors; there are brothels aplenty that I have yet to patronize, knowable only through the explicit nature of their signage. Street vendors and restaurants are here, too. I never visit any of these, instead all of my meals on my times visting the city of dreams have come at a cozy corner table in the inn, but that is another dispatch itself.

The street connecting the always-morning docks to the perpetual night beyond is a place that is both chaos incarnate and calming infinitely. I no longer feel lost at the moment I make the corner out onto the street. In the past, I have walked here with various other dream companions. Siblings, partners, star-crossed cosmological crushes, and even once a cat that I could not even presume to have known anywhere but here. The street is where we always meet. We round our corners and fly off to that night's events. Once a quest to purchase a particular blue soft drink at the supermarket comprising three levels of escalators that in a wild turn of events played out on the ground floor as the childhood home my brother and I occupied before the arrival of our two younger siblings. In the breath between the ending of a relationship and the start of a new one, I walked arm-in-arm with a dreamt manifestation of what we sociologists call a hopelessly romantic crush between shops and alleyways on the way home to consummate the romance with a homecooked dinner we had shopped for. I have seen my dear desert dog Denali here on the street many times. He, unlike my other dream companions, always arrives with me, though. I meet the potential suitors, my partner, my siblings on the street, Denali rode in on the chartered boat with me. I will not offer any reason as to why other than that that is, in his words, "what good dogs do".

When he and I walk the street, there is more conversation than when I bring guests to my street. I think of it as my street even though there is nothing to suggest I even am allowed to be here. I talk to him much more than I do others in the street. Oddly, in all of my other dreamscapes where Comrade Denali appears, we do not talk very much; he is, instead, more my dog than my confidant in those spaces. But here, here, he is, my advisor, the receiver of my confessions, and somehow nonverbally the arbiter of all of the contradictory conundrums that bring me to pound the pavement in thought. All through our wanderings he keeps himself two steps ahead and always attached to my right leg. When we stop, he ever-so-gently presses his nose into my calf and makes a low 'oof' noise afterwards to remind me that he is still there. He guides me and I him; it is a symbiosis of visiting here. We are both at home, somehow. I know it is common to feel companionship in our canine comrades, but something about existing in a dreamscape on a compendium level of total intellectual and symbiotic equality is something else to be experienced. He does not 'talk' on the streets as he does in the voice my family and I affect for him in the waking hours. Instead he and I communicate through some unspeakable knowing of the other's intentions. We can exist this way in some instances in the waking world, where we can exchange winks (he winks back at me; it's curious), where at the sound of Wouldn't it Be Nice by the Beach Boys, he knows it is time to say good morning and proceeds to meet me at the edge of the bed, extend his hand to me and stretch before receiving his good morning hug. In the city of dreams, behind the wire, it is something altogether unworldly. I can think something to him and I do not hear an answer but I know that he knows and vice versa, intentionality drives me in certain directions and I always seem to be following him, rather than leading. I wonder as I write this now, while he sleeps on his bed, his head buried in a pillow, if he is there waiting for my return or to what extent his experiences are in the city of dreams in my absence. I've yet to read his columns on time spent in country.

With other companions, the walk is different. That is to be expected I think, there really is no human analog to the companionship of your dog by your side. I've yet to experience the carefree existence with another human being in the same way I do with my dogs, and there's something mystical about the nonverbal understanding of each other's thoughts that I fear can only be replicated in Tumblr shipping posts that are built on an idealized relational closeness that does not exist. This is not something to despair, though. We do not endeavour for our humanoid companions to be so in synch with us because then it is just a walk with ourselves in the mists, and I cannot imagine a worse travelling companion for me than myself. Our pairings require divergence in the idea of the self, that's what fuels the excitement, the adventure, the joy, the love. It is not in our synchronizing of thought, but it is in the wildly unpredictable differences in disposition that pull us closer.

My walks with my siblings reflect the state of our existence together as four adults with a shared childhood. We explore on the basis of knowing what each other wants to explore; we keenly look up and down the winding lane for what may catch the eye of the other. We strive to search for hidden, obscure treasures, to enlighten one another's aesthetics with unique places to discover. We share memories and contemporary experiences in a direct fashion with each footfall. With the older of my two brothers, we exchange a rapid-fire barrage of indecipherable film and popular culture references while comparing passport pages and exchanging tales of our other foreign postings. With my younger brother, we endeavour into the shops to find obscure sodas, odd treats, books of ancient magic or otherworldly horrors. With my sister, we stride through the artistic chaos of the street, synthesize the noise into a bantering musical score and envision the compositions of still life in the mire of the people beyond and those passing us.

Crushes are a particularly strange social experience. They can be simultaneously uplifting to the absolute infinite upper limit of human joy, and in their uncanny ability to clash in contrast to reality, can be some of the sources of our most intense pain. I have walked with two such crushes on this street on two varied occasions of visitations to the city. Each experience is different but ends the same, as all crushes do, with a crushing of reality at the break of dawn. In one instance, a venture into the marketplace, loud, overwhelming, the heat and humidity sweltering, we find various fresh vegetables and fruits, and we sample spices whose flavours I cannot remember. I know in this visit to the city my goal is to make dinner. Something I feel a strong degree of intimacy towards. I enjoy cooking for those I love, especially in the evenings, where in the crashing madness of culinary exploration, through burns and cuts and long hours standing over stoves, the joy of presenting a plate of homecooked food to your loved one at the crest of twilight is something unparalleled in its simple joys. It is not the same as making a sandwich on the trail or a simple lunch between meetings. It is not the same as breakfast in bed. Nor can any dining experience in a restaurant even match it. Dinner, a simple gathering of souls around a table as the sun dips behind the hills in the west and as the courses melt into coffee by the fire, has always been sacred to me. Perhaps also because it is the only socially real mealtime I am routinely conscious of. On our trek through the market I watch my crush select berries I cannot identify, we chat about our menu, revel in the exotic locale and the plethora of good memories to come. I wrote before that there was a desire to consummate this coupling in the city.

The city, as it may disappoint some readers, is not a place where the carnal aspects of loving crushes come to bear. There are other dreamscapes for such activities. Instead, the consummation of love of a crush (at least in the eyes of the hopelessly romantic sociologist and social philosopher) happens at the moment in time when the world falls away, and love is real and tangible there in that instant. The ever-elusive confirmation of the confirmation bias. We love to pretend we're right, we love to see evidence in the milieu around us, but good God do we love it when there's a tangible sign that just maybe our feelings are reciprocated. But always, as per an earlier sentence in a piece I wrote a lifetime ago, maybe it is murder to the mind. I think somewhere in my personal philosophy of being, a tear shed over a gift of food, over the creation of a memory, over the pure love communicated through simple symbolic actions is the true litmus test for the validity of a crush.

Varying wildly, the second excursion to the city with a crush is not built on some Lost Lenore-esque romanticism. I am no longer Poe in this case, nor Dante after his Beatrice. As in all cities, there is a carnal element, there is physicality, there is a perversion somewhere. To not sound as terrifically bleak as Alan Moore's Rorschach, but to still recognize that in the darkness and depravity of the human sexual soul, there is indeed a certain urbanity to the life in the city and flow of passion between the sparks of others. My second crush walk of the street was laced with an implicit inclination of something physical there in the ether, something in the absurdity of the coupling of human bodies that would, at some end of the tunnel, be something to share sparks between us. This foray into the city came at a moment shortly after I turned 27 when I decided I finally had enough of living in a perpetual state of psychological abuse and made the monumental decision to abandon a life of British Columbian academia and instead return my feet to the desert where they belonged. I was "single" again, and a single 27-year-old romantic loose in such a city, punch-drunk on the wanderlust of youth with the broken soul of someone whose midlife crisis has already been in full swing was a wild trip that I cannot recommend to anyone for their safety and serenity in the comfort of the mind. It is a madness of lust but not in the way that draws our fingers to Tinder, Grindr or the other plethora of orgasm-delivery services. Instead, my lust in this walk is different. It is lust paired with fear, with nerves, with the teenage awkwardness of first dates. We are both foreigners here and in our isolated status, we find an illusion of companionship that pulls us closer to an intimacy of comradery. We walk in stride down the street. We are not searching for anything specific, but there is a palpable hunger between us in the jokes exchanged the topics discussed, and the willingness to be vulnerable and honest in moments of levity. We are baring our souls to one another, and the street itself is not a setting but the hand moving the plot forward. We see the neon nudity and laugh at it; we casually intertwine innuendo into our speech on the most mundane of topics. Somewhere in a sitcom world this would potentially be called flirting, but I distance myself from that and instead chance that it was individually our own unique ways of experimenting with the temperature of receptivity of the waters between us. Much like how we dip our toes into the lake before jumping in to test its climate, we were doing the same with each other's defences. Testing the walls, seeing where the stones were firmly rooted, and where maybe a crack here and there may lead us to the inner workings of each other's hearts. I think of all of my walks on this street; this was the hardest to follow. It came at a point in the life of the writer that we try to keep out of the pages, despite it always clawing to come into the page in some way or another. I have not subscribed to the theory of hidden meanings in writing. I still flashback to a particularly acrid moment in my schooling where a 15-minute discussion on 'meaning' in the text was reduced to the colour of Holden Caufield's hat in The Catcher in the Rye, and I have yet to recover. There is not some grandiose plan in 99% of writers' minds when they include a descriptive adjective to have it be interpreted later as some depth of meaning that was intentional. Should meaning be found, wonderful, allow it to be, but in the words of author Brian Griffin: "That's for the scholars a hundred years from now..."

Wandering this foreign place, even before The Street with a crush is jarring to recall and more so to have experienced for the fact that it adds another fold of stress to the correspondent's plate. How now do we traverse two unknowns at once? Both are addled with high stakes, where, at the moment, they feel like life and death moments passing by in the foggy glass of the windows and the steam off the sea in the crisp morning sunshine. We may, in both cases, hope to meet either the city or the crush with the resolve of a seasoned traveller on these roads, but in reality, there is never a signpost of familiarity we may find in each case. Crushes are as treacherous as the city on the brink of something.

This is the sense contained in each of my wanderings thus far, where instead of leaning on the familiarity of the wall of plastic fishing trays stacked into the maze, nor the charming chaos of the street or the city at large, the sense that I am in a place at a time specifically before they become the wrong place and time. A sort of sixth sense that comes from being one of the Wonderkids who grew up too fast, too wild and perhaps too introverted for his own good. You get a sense there in the ways that pressures and tensions flow and stream across the common threads of shared experience. My sixth sense flashes red in this place each time I land. I know something is brewing, and it feels more like trouble than any revelry time and again. I almost have a sense that I am there on the eve of some terrible conflict, that bullets will soon be flying, fires raging, and people will evolve and devolve with the chaos to come to form that special subculture of our species in times of collective peril: the logical feral beast of apex predatory survival. This, as one may imagine, tinges the streets, the seaside, the docks, all of it with a tangible anxiety. To borrow a cliché, the tension of the band ready to snap is palpable here for some reason.

That gnawing anxiety is multiplied tenfold when the soul by my side is someone I was tangentially hopeful of allowing myself to love. Maybe, as it is, is murder to the mind. Exploring these feelings underlying your heart is difficult, to say the barest of minimums. Each move you make is somehow more hyperfocused in your mind, you become a master of watching yourself inside at out, am I presentable, am I making an impression, do they even LIKE me? In a moment, horrifically childish and immature, in another bleakly human. The mysteries we craft ourselves in these waves of time are so wildly damning to the spirit and its desires. I am broken here in my recollection with a memory of a text message conversation I had with a friend during the same period of flux in my life. Being the hopeless romantic I was attempting to deconstruct this feeling, this struggle with someone who was not my typical conversation partner in such things (sociologists who love a good deconstruction), and they blatantly said: "just say how you feel and see where it goes!" An introvert's death sentence. Why, pray, must we be combatted with such logic, such definitive paths to closure and results? In true fashion, all I could say was, "I don't think I can do that." Fear of rejection or a love of the mystery? That is for my eventual psychoanalyst to uncover in my twilight years on the couch.

When I landed in the city by the side of this person representing the object of my romantic attraction, I was in a period of time that I will no doubt someday refer to as my dark ages. I was 28 and had just followed through with finally ending a relationship that had lasted for a decade and that had left me scarred physically, psychologically, emotionally and metaphysically. In the vacuum of moving home to safety, away from constant stress and pain, and into the wildernesses of my childhood, I freewheeled into a period of abject confusion, I think. Work, teaching, writing, all of it became somewhat secondary and there was this sense of just trying to recover a semblance of humanity again. It is easy in those lulls in life to search for hope where we can; despite my best efforts to erase the word from my lexicon, hope was something that I was unintentionally manufacturing in my movements through life. It was not immediate, but as the dust settled around me from the fire that had been in existence prior, slowly out of the mists came a chance at hope and a chance at maybe, just maybe, feeling close to another human again. I will not disclose how this began, nor where it went, only to say that for a window of time, I walked beside an idealized future in someone else in my dreams, my fantasies, and whenever I landed in the city.

The visits here with that person who was my embodied hope of a warm future were the most stressful of each of my assignments here in the city. You feel simultaneously protective of them, wanting to ensure they make it out with you and terrified all the same that their time in the winding alleyways is as rich as yours. The temptation of the city is there tenfold as well in tandem with the sense of the pressure mounting towards calamity. Do I dare confess? Do I shatter the illusion or risk the infinitely small chance of it growing into something more wondrous than my imagination can produce? Where is the dividing line between believing in hope while acting on it and descending fully into total dismissal of it as a possibility? Retrospectively, the struggle here on those streets is simply Kierkegaard's leap of faith, taking the plunge into the unknown at the slight chance it may turn out to be better than the voices of angst in our minds predict. We may question regret in this case, do I regret my actions on the streets, my experiences there alongside someone who may have become more than just a friend? Metaphorically and realistically, I cannot say so far as I do not know the trajectory my life would have taken should that been the answer, but pragmatically considering where I have landed in the waking world today, I feel the choice made was as correct as such precarious things may be.

Therefore, the streets with this crush are the places I reflect on now as being some of the scariest, if not also some of the most exciting. In cities of dreams, we can fly if only we imagine it, and the flying highs of pure requited love with equal desire are ones that contribute even more movement and noise to the red-light haze of The Street in the din of its nightlife. They may never be a reality, but as breaks in the bleakness of material living and the regularity of movement through this city, they remain fond memories of the daring allure of correspondence work, a sort of romanticism all itself where the perceived danger, whirlwind loves and adventures from all corners of life come to produce a deeply addictive and dangerously enjoyable nectar of the mind still. Even better, the mystery remains to this day where a word, a motion, a nod, anything still stirs a wilderness of dreamscapes to explore. The mysteries are themselves quite addictive in their own rites.

Still yet, the streets stretch on, and while the thrill of wandering them astride a body you hope to one day fall asleep holding is nothing to the experience of doing so with the one you do wake up holding every morning. Stepping into the streets aside, your partner is wildly divergent from the strangeness of the crush wandering. There is security, regularity, safety, and sanity there. You become less concerned with the performance of your adventure and instead on the nature of what it is you stumble upon. Adventure then becomes adventure itself, it is not a curation of the self in the eyes of a potential partner, it is the freedom to wander as you would alone, not worrying to infinite degrees of concern on the subject of whether or not your comrade by your side would eventually become more than that. Travelling in companionship with those we are close to is wildly contrary to the experience of doing so on the wonders and wild desires of maybe. There is a synchronous nature to the footfalls in the night scene of the street, and there is no worry at the last turn of the labyrinth of the docks that you will befall some horrible need to self-heroize yourself in the face of protecting your potential partner, instead, you know you are both safe.

However, many more times than not, I travel the street alone. I know in this dreamscape that I do not dwell on or near the street, and so the alleyways and back streets are not markers of where I am going but instead show to see before making the trek. On each of my assignments in the city, I always begin here, but I do not linger for more than is needed. I do not stop for street food or for some Anthony Bourdain-adjacent monologue on forgotten or unfound places. I do not lavish in the exotic adventures culinary or social here. I feel instead, some call to report or to catalogue the experiences as a watcher, not as a participant, a lamplighter per Le Carre's circus. Someone prone to watching, listening, observing and more or less blending into the works of pavement artistry so as to appear as naturally placed as possible. This is, in my waking experience, reflective of my own actual travel proclivities. I prefer to see and be less than noticed, which never truly works out, but the romanticism of it is a fun notion to entertain all the same.

In each of my arrivals to the city, the street is the first place I visit, but in that regard, it is only a stop on the expansion of my assignments out into the environs and eventually above and beyond the city itself. It is a vivid place not because of the actions or stories that unfold there but because of the feelings it imparts to visitors each time. There is a living element to it, and it leaves an imprinted, lasting collection of thoughts and feelings in the hearts of those who come through it. I do not doubt that the lives lived there are ones filled with meaning and direction, but as is the unfortunate nature of the correspondent at times, we are to simply negate that livelihood for what our true focus is. I still do not know my assignments here in the city, but somewhere I am certain I am needed beyond the street itself. The faceless and nameless throngs of living moments that populate are familiar strangers to me, people I have yet to know or fear I will never truly know. Instead, I include this dispatch from their doorstep as a tribute to their stories I fear I will never follow or compose and as a memorial of to their existences in the wake of whatever tragedy it is I always feel is just around the corner of such a place.

-30-

Dispatch 2: Out of the City

Is it possible to create in the mind's eye a place outside space and memory to facilitate that which represents our exploration of the unknowns of our sociality?

If the streets represent an affective chaos of life, the Way Out is wholly contradictory. As I leave the street, through a maze of turning back alleys, I arrive instead on the side of a thoroughfare that leads into the innermost reaches of the city. I am walking in the opposite direction of traffic, and as I round the final gentle bend in the highway, I am met with another sight of familiarity: the outskirts of the city. It abuts rolling misty hills, where the skyscrapers hiding away The Others in their apartments and offices gradually fade into the sprawl of nature; the hills rise sharply, underscoring the present feeling that the city itself was hewn into a space in the valley that it does not belong. There are some cities that blend their natural environments into their zone of proximal existence; there are some that destroy it. The city lies somewhere in between the two. It looks simultaneously out of place and perfectly situated. It is part ancient monastic ruin settled neatly on the floor of the valley for centuries and part new gentrification of the greens and warmth of the natural countryside. The mist that is ever-present in the hills is thick and impenetrable when it circles the city; it lays low over the streets and clearly segregates the upper society high rises from the bustle of the street. I have never ventured above the mist line to the penthouses of the city, and I feel a visceral resistance to ever doing so. Something about existing in spaces of wealth, luxury, and unearned status always mars my soul, and in emerging from such times, I always remark to my dad, of all people, that I need a shower to wash the snob off of me. This is an odd reality to reconcile in both the circumstances of my childhood home (Aspen, the seat of useless wealth) and my profession (academia, the place of useless cultural capital and inherently toxic infighting). And for these collated reasons I do not climb the buildings, I do not escape the steam of the street levels to hide away in the creature comforts of urban living. I am unsure why this is entirely true. Somewhere buried deep inside me, there is a fantasy of the urban chic lifestyle. When I was in Victoria, taking a bus into the heart of the city, I would see the tall apartment buildings looking out over the bustle of the streets below and dream for an instant that I could be up there too. Elsewhere there is some romantic idea of a high-rise apartment somewhere in New York with a good view and a thriving bohemian culture of creative weirdos to blend into. But the voice in my mind that calls me to reality each time is the one tendered and nurtured outside of the boundaries of urbanity. I am a child of the wild and free parts of the country, where such overtones of urban life are, even if by a short distance, wholly removed from daily life if one so chooses. A 'good week' for me now is one where I do not need to venture into civilization at all until my weekly midnight radio program, and in that case, the sleeping town is one far more agreeable to my spirit than one that is awake.

This is what leads me out of the city, where beyond the din of neon in the dark embrace of night and past the chaos of loud lives being lived openly, I find that in my dreamscape wanderings, the morning always begins here at the transition point between the city and the mists of the wild unknowns beyond its zoning borders. Time in this city is odd, due to its composition as a dreamscape, it is perhaps understandable that the visitations to this locale are often done at various times, but this is not the case. It is always twilight when the boat lands, night always falls as I navigate the warehouse and spill out into the city's street, and morning always begins to seep into the surroundings as I emerge from the sidewalk of the underpass onto the last bend of the highway towards the mountains. The sun is regularly and with extreme beauty emerging from just over the hill to dance with the dewdrops suspended in the mists of morning. Contrary to what some who know me may infer, I do personally love the morning quite emphatically. There is an almost deafening stillness in the misty morning as day breaks across the mountainside. Mornings too, are places of great comfort and security, especially if we are fighting off the encroaching alarm clock's song. I have never felt more cozy, comfortable or peacefully asleep than I do if I awake 40 minutes before the scheduled alarm. In the autumn and the spring, the experience of sitting in a chair at the end of my porch facing the mountains and breathing in the first rays of sunlight ionizing on the cold air with a steaming cup of coffee is something that cannot be bested by any nocturnal behaviour. It is in this reflection of the morning that it is reinforced in my mind that I am not someone who craves the night for the peace it offers, but rather, I am one who exists in it spitefully as a creature not displaced to the regularity of real life in the morning. I cannot compose my work in the same hour that people begin to send emails or ask questions, instead I must do so in the cloak of darkness solely for the fact that it is the most agreeable to my being. If I had a choice, I would opt to experience sunrise upon waking from a restful sleep rather than seeing it drain in through the windows as my jaw clenches in the last death throes of a good night's writing. However, the correspondent never gets to choose how their stories break nor how they exist to capture them. I instead have surrendered to the reality of my temporality, and so I must strive to exist within its often-abusive tendrils.

The warmth of the morning sun is curious as it starts as a welcome relief from the night's chill navigating the street, but I know that soon it will become a fraught enemy for my ascent. I know my destination well, and I know too that while it holds many restful pleasures and delights, the trip to it is arduous. It is similar to the practice of backpacking hut trips, the goal is not the hike itself, but the memories you make in the cabin disconnected from everything. I am doing something similar, but I know too that I am not doing so recreationally, at least entirely. There is something...more there, something higher than a simple place to stay. It is, I think, some kind of manifestation of my imagined perfection. I have an innate migratory instinct to walk out of the city and on into the dawn towards the misty mountains. It is not a meditation or metaphor of my experience being from the mountains, but it is perhaps something rooted there, although not entirely grounded in its reality. I am somehow a traveller in this instance with some unknowable drive to wander, but in this sense, in this place, in this foreign land, there is something drawing me that is more than personal. Some kind of professional pull to the place in the mists. It is part refuge and part assignment desk. I am somewhere between Saigon and Hue City at the height of it or on some backstreet of East Berlin, ducking between steam vents and cinema entrances to dodge something out there. Every time I wander out of the city and its chaotic boundaries, I do so with an added degree of clandestine risk lurking just around the crest of sunrise. At this moment, I need to question if it's paranoid psychosis or something deeper, maybe a reflection of the version of myself I fear or that I've not yet had the displeasure of meeting. Some form of sinister horror out there in the mists after the city fades behind me is close by.

Can you hear its footsteps? It's coming. Danger close.

I cannot know even now if it is some KGB officer following me again (or maybe just a representation of the FSB ones that did in reality), if it is someone on the tree line with me in the crosshairs, or if the psyche of my own idiosyncratic understanding of myself that lurks there just beyond perception's gaze. One might assume it's a terrifying thing to be followed, to step into a space outside the boundaries of acceptable surveillance into the realm of supposed and assumed isolation only to know that just around any stone or tree trunk, there's a chance that the bullet, the horror, the shock of it all is just there out of reach. Yet, as I make my trek, I do so with a warm greeting for the horror. I do not dwell in it, nor do I enjoy its presence, instead I recognize it as a friend somehow. Something of a familiar face in a sea of blurs passing me by. Once, after a particularly cutting fight in another life where wounds were exchanged over verbal incursions across a variety of battlefields, I found myself in bed at some horrible hour isolated behind the wire, knowing at that moment that love was not real and that life was the cruellest of all realities. When love is tainted with the venom of humanity and reconciling the inconvenience of reality, it loses a great deal of the mystique it was supposed to once maybe hold. It is not dissimilar to the charred and scattered rubble remains of some mountain temple levelled by napalm in the eye of the morning sun. There's a beauty in the loss of innocence that itself breeds within us the pain that draws us to keep putting one foot ahead of the other. I think we need to let our idea of innocence die to reclaim a stable and sustainable sense of innocence itself. That is a need to let what holds us to the nostalgia of futures that will never come to pass die in the wind in order to allow for a rekindling of that which may pull us into the future we truly desire. Expectations are painful, maybe murder to the mind, and thought is what fucks us up, per Bob Dylan.

The city fades, the hills sprawl open in front, and into the mists, I go with wonder and a wild desire...

Dispatch 3: The Inn

How is it we can dream of places and know specifically where our home is despite never having heard our footfalls on their pavements?

The end of the road in this dreamscape, the place to which I always seem to arrive alone, the space of respite in the madness of the city and the hills, where the paranoia grows beyond fear of the horror into an awareness of the isolation lies nestled in the hills as a grand timber lodge. The windows from the floor to the ceiling lovingly frame the vista beneath us, the winding mountain paths up to the lodge, the misty foothills, and the city in its insanity in the distance. It is always warm here, always inviting, and it is always late morning when I arrive. I am never greeted by anyone, nor are there other travellers in these walls. Instead, there is a table in the back of the main lodge, through a threshold into the solarium where in the corner overlooking the sheer cliffs, I sit at a wooden table with ornamental tiles set into it where a clear glass of tea always seems to be waiting. There is a timeless reality to this setting, something from another century where I can perch myself and theoretically work on writings that need to be completed, or observe the people wandering through, or sample the scones or the day's soup on a rainy morning. None of these realities coalesce. It is always just the tea, the table, the corner of the glass sunroom, the view of the road behind me and the cliffs down and to my left.

There's a sense in this room that I am waiting for something, for someone to come and collect me, for something to unfold, something noteworthy of my investigation, but to date, it has yet to arrive. I am not sure the degree to which that reflects on actuality or reality, but the sense of waiting to wait and waiting for something is a real and tangible reality in this little charming sunroom. Is it some clandestine contact in some European café, something deeper? I cannot be sure. The sense, though, is something grander than a simple repose in a solarium, but it seems far more metaphysically critical than something so simple as a meeting. Meetings themselves are obnoxious human constructions, if I may add. Instead I think this reflects a larger sense of waiting that may be permeable out to those other satellite stations around us in the milieu of social life. There is a planetary sense of waiting now, I think. At times, with bated breath for the horrors to come, at others for the warmth of an embrace in loving passion. There is a humanity in waiting, where instead of expecting, we are there for the goal of receiving something or someone rather than guaranteeing in the factory of our minds that what we want will be there. The uncertainty of waiting is something that draws my sociological lens to it, where despite the setting of this bout of waiting, there is something so innately innocent to it. I am there unopposed to opportunity without the wherewithal to summon it agentically and this I think is where all of the greatest and most treasured momentary lapses in reality of life come from, in the unexpected, the uninhibited and the true return to innocence.

This table is where I am seated when I wake up—always, without exception. I still haven't found what I am looking for, and whatever I was waiting for has yet to reveal itself.

That which we may need is something in front of us invisible to the waiting eye.

Patience is the parent of innocence.

Wait.

Why worry when skies are gray

Why should we complain

Let's laugh at the cloudy day

Let's sing in the rain

Songwriters say the storm quickly passes

That's their philosophy

They see the world through rose-colored glasses

Why shouldn't we?

Just around the corner

There's a rainbow in the sky

So let's have another cup o' coffee

And let's have another piece o' pie

-Irving Berlin

Chapter 10

From the Skyward Side

"Sometimes you have to kind of die inside in order to rise from your own ashes and believe in yourself and love yourself to become a new person."

-Gerard Way; My Chemical Romance

As the season deepens, the air cools with a hint of mist, carrying the scent of damp earth and fallen leaves. The woods become a tapestry of amber and russet, where golden light filters through bare branches, casting shadows that stretch and twist like whispers from another time. Moss creeps over stone walls, soft and ancient, while the last wildflowers cling to the edges of winding paths, their petals fading into twilight hues. The world outside hums with a quiet life—crows perched in silence, distant owls calling through the dusk, as smoke curls from chimney tops, mingling with the scent of firewood. Indoors, there is a warmth that feels like an embrace—old books stacked beside candlelit windows, a pot simmering on the stove, the crackle of kindling in the hearth. It's a place where time slows, where every small detail—the rustle of dried herbs, the glow of a lantern—feels imbued with the weight of memory. Shadows and light dance together, drawing out a beauty that is both wild and soft, ancient yet deeply familiar, as though the very air holds the stories of those who have come before. Autumn here feels like a return to something quietly eternal, a brief pause where nature and stillness reign.

1. Death.

-It is the first autumn of my 30s.-

I began this book nearly three years ago now. Since then I have survived my long nights, my valleysongs, and a whole host of other absurdities and sparks of brilliance the world over. We are supposed to feel something as we crest thirty. Something dark, ominous, some encroaching of the twilight of life. I have friends who have gone through this. I myself cannot say that the crest of thirty was one that filled my heart with any emotion other than the promise of a resurgence. I have written before of a year during my undergraduate career that I lovingly remember as my 'soaring period,' and for some time, I had thought that such a peak of diligence, exploration, discovery and wonder would never again seep into my bones. I am happy now at the conclusion of this trek toward infinity that such shattered nostalgic notions are no longer ones I entertain. The road between 27 and now has been rocky, to say the very, very least. I have cried, I have experienced losses, I have bled, I have suffered, and yet somehow, here at this moment, I sit to pen the final composition for this project that has lingered so lovingly in my heart.

Since that pivotal moment at 27 I decided after weeks of languishing and after years of abuse to leave a tormented relationship, to leave the country I had adopted as my new home, to trek backwards to the mountains of my youth and to work to reclaim myself, I have felt pains deeper than I can fully ever hope to understand. Death, once a mystery to me and then a fascination through my career, has finally, I think, become an acquaintance to me. The third person I told about my plans to escape my relationship was a very dear childhood friend living just across the city from me in Victoria, BC. He told me in that conversation that he loved me. That ended up being the last words he ever spoke, being that he died within minutes of our call ending. It is a heavy weight I still carry to be the final voice that he spoke to. He was of a similar professional walk and our theoretical and philosophical conversations over cigarettes on the porch have I believe inspired my hand to write these words. Since that final call, I have thought of him often, and I feel somewhere in my writing now at this moment that perhaps a ghost of his is here telling me in his signature style that such a thing, a quarter-life memoir and one subtitled 'existentialist' at that, was and is the most pretentious fucking thing he had ever heard of. A year later, another friend died. I worked with her almost every single day during my PhD in Canada. She helped me bend rules to protect my students when they needed it. She always helped me make sure my paycheques came in on time. She also, in our countless hours of conversations, took care of me in ways I don't think either of us grasped in the moment. My colleagues in Canada did not know that, at the time, my family was fractured deeply, that I had essentially temporarily lost my mother as a positive force in my life, and she had no indication whatsoever that every time I left the office for those three years, that I was returning home to a psychological battleground that at many moments reduced me to a shell of a person. She was like a surrogate mother to me in the fleeting moments we shared. I learned she was terminally ill a week before she died on shaky cell service in the rain outside Glasgow, Scotland. I hastily composed a last letter to her after nearly on the brink of tears I confessed to my friend Adrian that I was tired of writing obituaries for people I loved. I sent her that letter via a mutual friend four days before the end. I have no idea if she ever had the chance or the strength to read it. I like to entertain the fantasy that she did. That she knew in her last moments that all of those afternoons and early mornings laughing together had not just healed wounds in my soul but had kept me alive in the most serious sense. I hope she knew the depth of the platonic love I held for her in those final moments, I hope she knew. People who make differences on the mortal plane rarely, if ever, know, and we, the living, rarely tell them in time.

During the summer following the height of the pandemic, I taught our department's first in-person course in over a year. Two sections of evening courses titled Death and Dying. Midway through the term, as I crossed the courtyard of my building on my way to class, I happened upon a small dead bird lying in the centre under a magnolia tree. I stopped for only a moment to acknowledge it before walking inside to perform my pre-lecture routine in my office three floors above. That night after our lecture, I walked home the same route and again was stopped by the bird. This time, I stayed with it for a time. The sun takes a long time to set in July on Vancouver Island. I sat with the bird until the darkness was nearly around us. I had many thoughts about this experience.

How did it die?

Why?

Did it hit a window?

It wouldn't have died if this stupid building wasn't here in its way.

This breeze on my face is a breeze that bird will never know existed, let alone glide along.

Should I be feeling this sad now?

After some time and two or three cigarettes and the last remnants of my coffee I stood up and operated somehow automatically. I turned back to the door, unlocked it, took the elevator upstairs, opened my office and left my bag on my chair. I walked home in the twilight and, upon returning, took a can of soda from my fridge and found a pair of nitrile exam gloves I kept in a first aid kit in our washroom. I was greeted by the happy howls of my dog, Denali who had not seen me for the past three-ish hours while I taught and sat with a dead bird. I talked to him often and did so then, too. I asked him if he would join me in an adventure (adventure being the word I used instead of 'walk' so as not to unleash the excitement in mundane conversation). I clipped the bag of homemade biscuits I baked for him to my belt loop and helped him into his walking gear, a purple full-body harness to protect his sensitive neck from his collar pulling and the 15-foot rainbow leash clipped in on top. I did not once see the partner I had moved to that house with, who I had adopted Denali with, who I had at one time loved, and I knew there was not a chance of this happening anyway; by that time, our house was only a storage facility for clothing and other possessions while he had functionally moved in with yet another hookup app disasters. At this moment, Denali and I were unphased by the absence; he was happy to go for his evening adventure, and I was being autopilot by the spirit of some bird in the courtyard.

Miraculously, it was still there when we arrived with only two or three flies having found it. No one had yet thrown it into a garbage can or stepped on it, and no feral creatures had yet taken it for supper. People have told me Denali is a gentle and sweet dog. This has been a source of pride for me as I had always hoped he would be the type of dog that people wouldn't be afraid of despite his large size and unplaceable breed makeup. I met that gentleness in his amber eyes that night in the courtyard. We approached the bird's resting place and stopped. He obviously smelled the bird, but I calmly told him no, this is not for Denali. He stopped sniffing and, seeing I was now crouching down near the bird, he sat beside me, his head cocked to one side in curiosity, and ever-so-slightly, he leaned his shoulder into mine as I crouched next to him. I would like to believe he did this out of knowing I needed the physical support and emotional care there, but in reality, I think he leans to offset his hip dysplasia. That said, after a perfectly delightful peanut butter oatmeal biscuit was crunched to pieces, he sat in stoic silence and watched me don my gloves. I reached down and gingerly took the bird into my hands. I had a thought then: "Their bones are hollow, you know". At this moment, I made the mistake of having no plan past this moment. Denali and I then walked over to the magnolia tree, and there, under its branches, I knew what I would do. I hastily dug a grave deep enough to protect the bird from future landscaping projects. I placed it in its new final resting place while my heart was thundering, and Denali, despite his calm demeanour, started to display the puppy shakes of anticipation for wanting to move on to the next part of our adventure. I hastily placed some picked flowers around the bird, as well as a small stone placed over its chest. I covered it with earth, and then, in a moment of sentimentality, I placed a larger stone over the grave of this little bird.

I was not ready for the profundity of this experience to hit me. In this moment, I felt that our task had been accomplished, and as we walked into the receding sunlight around campus and towards home, I believed that my time with the bird had ended.

I was wrong.

I returned home and couldn't shake the moment. I did what I always do in such moments, I fired up my computer (an Atari Video Computer System) and began to write. Being that I taught death, I knew the general idea of where I wanted to go, but I did not at that time know too much of the teachings of the philosophy of death. I went where I always do to begin a philosophical journey, Kierkegaard. I found, in my perusal of the results for a search string of "Kierkegaard, Death," an essay he wrote titled "At a Graveside". In essence, the essay teaches us five critical points, the latter two I opted to ignore:

1. Death is inevitable. It is our guaranteed fate outside of identity, class, status or history. It is the universal equalizer.

2. The importance of self-reflection on mortality. We are encouraged as we join Kierkegaard at this imaginary graveside to deeply question our own finite existence and the reality of the fact that the nature of being one of the living remaining after death is a powerful motivator for us to consider the nature of our life as it is, and the meaning of our existence in the context of that finite time we have to live.

3. Death is a teacher. There is an argument presented that death teaches us in some ways how to live, how to synthesize the elements of ourselves into a concrete understanding of ourselves and then to subsequently live outwardly in an authentic capacity. Despair, per Kierkegaard, comes from (among other places) the sad fact of not knowing ourselves or living in a way incongruent to our internal truth of self. Death paints that self explicitly and it allows us to see through the noise to establish a reality where our individuality is momentarily without the grey of being.

4. Death can lead to a spiritual awakening.

5. Death presents the role of faith.

In my work, I have tried in earnest to surgically excise Kierkegaard from faith and Christianity to varying degrees of frustration. I am not a religious person in the sense of Christianity, my faith is in humanity and their sociality, which is to say in some sense my faith is in sociology somehow. I do not, in my reading of Kierkegaard, dwell too long on the Christian aspects, either remapping it to a faith of knowledge (Gnosticism) or ignoring it entirely. In my office that July evening, with my dog happily snoozing nearby and The Pogues If I Should Fall from Grace With God appropriately chiming off the record player, I did not dwell on the Christianity of it all, and so the latter two points of this summation of the essay were thoroughly ignored. They are included in this book only for posterity. As such, the three initial points from this essay quite directly captured my sociological imagination in that compositional moment. The bird, its death mask, its limp and lifeless body, the delicacy of its skeletal structure, the intimacy of the moment between me, my dog, and this dead creature in front of us, all of it touched me in deeply profound ways. I knew full well that death was permanent and universal, but in the subtly of the breeze through my beard when I realized it was one the bird would not feel, that was where I fully came to know the reality of that finality and the inevitability. I will someday not feel the breeze down my mountainside as I so often do. I will miss moments, experiences, ideas, changes, and every minute interaction therein from the moment I leave the world.

I did not know it specifically at the time, nor did I in the entire composition of this book until this moment that that bird, with its wings no longer fluttering was what led me to compose an existentialist memoir between 27 and 30. I realized then that memoirs ought not to be relegated to the natural end of our lives, nor to the influential giants of life, but instead that memoirs can and should be something of a milepost we leave at certain turns in the path of life. I have opted here to pen this, a quarter-life (if all goes according to plan) memoir for the fact that coming to grips with such topics as explored here are the things that fully and most pressingly keep me grounded in trying to meet myself somewhere between here and there. I do not feel that I am in the twilight of my life, but then, neither did the bird when it crashed into the window of the Cornett Building at the University of Victoria in July of 2021.

The bird's story does not end in this reflection. The piece of writing I composed following our laying to-rest ceremony was one of the pieces of madness from my mid-pandemic, unmedicated, spiralling ADHD era. It is mostly finished, and I've not thought of it since. It sat, until recently, in a folder with a half dozen unfinished essays and articles on everything from abuse, sexuality, performative activism, pedagogy, and God knows what else. That article was titled I Saw a Bird. It is included, unfinished, in the appendix of this book.

The story does not end in this article either.

Being that I was teaching a class on death, it was only natural that my experience would be shared the next night in my class. In this stage of in-person instruction during the pandemic, we had a unique policy which, to my best recollection, was called 'COVID Angels'. These angels were volunteers from a variety of university support services (grounds, food service, custodial) who would meticulously sanitize our classrooms between each class to ensure we were minimizing transmission and 'flattening the curve'. The first night of this class I stopped to chat with our COVID Angels and I told them about the class and invited them to join us as it was three hours and they didn't need to sit alone in the hallway the entire time before cleaning the lecture hall. They usually took place in the upper balcony section of the room. The night after I saw the bird, I retold my story to my class and remarked that I had made this gravestone for my bird. I told them they could tag along after class to go and see the bird's grave with me as I walked home. After class, one of the ladies working with the COVID team came down to me and told me that what I had shared was beautiful. She asked me where the grave was and then asked me if I would be there about half an hour after class. I said I would. I did not know what to expect, but what happened next was the furthest I could imagine. She rounded up nearly 20 staffers from across campus to hold a makeshift vigil for our bird. Thinking back to it now, I cannot help but cry. What a beautiful moment. Twenty or so strangers connected in reverent silence around the grave of a tiny bird. No one really spoke.

The next day, as I walked back to my classroom again, I noticed that someone had scrawled 'RIP' on the bird's headstone in orange landscaping paint. Someone had pinned a card with a watercolour painting of a dove to the tree. Someone else had laid a wreath of fake flowers into the dirt around the grave. I was stunned. When I got to my classroom, the COVID Angels told me that the head of groundskeeping painted the rock, that my COVID Angel herself had pinned the painting and that a custodian volunteered at a pet cemetery and donated some flowers he used to decorate graves. It was a community in motion in the midst of global death and shared trauma, mourning not just for the bird but for our individuality, a collective mourning for our own losses. The next night, a beaded necklace had been left, a bouquet of flowers tied with feathers was placed at the grave, and yet another card had been left. For my contribution, I placed a card from my tarot deck in a branch above. The card was the death card, symbolizing the transformative nature of life and the universe. We talked constantly, my students, the staff, and I, about our shrine. I shared the saga with my friend, who would pass away some years later, and she felt drawn to it herself. I asked her if there were any rules about it being allowed, as I wanted it to stay. She said that as a building manager, she was perfectly fine with it. An email to my department chair confirmed that he, too, was in support of it.

Tragedy struck the next night.

As I approached our shrine, to my horror, it was destroyed. All of the tributes, the artifacts, and the pieces left in honour had been roughly and rudely decimated and were nowhere to be found. Angered and shocked I felt myself reeling and upon getting to class I said to the COVID Angels "Its gone. It's all gone." I called campus security and reported it as vandalism. The head of groundskeeping was called by the Angel, and he was livid. He stormed off into the night to find our shrine. He came back half an hour later with the headstone, having fished it out of a dumpster. He could not find anything else. He was shaking with anger and said if I wanted, he would go cut a metal memorial bench from anywhere on campus and pour it in concrete over the site. Together he and I carefully excavated the site and found that the bird had not been disturbed. We reburied it and together raged against the stupidity. The next day, our angel had made a discovery. Apparently, a vibrantly Christian and absurdly nosy day shift worker in the COVID detail had seen it and, upon seeing the tarot card, had assumed it was a satanic ritual site and demanded it removed by security as it was 'threatening'. I am told she was reamed by my Angel.

Over the weekend, an unknown number of staff made pilgrimages to that site and placed a massive boulder over the grave, redecorated and pledged to stand vigil. I opted instead to create official pieces of documentation to immortalize the bird in time, framing it as experiential education and, therefore, a piece of active learning that could not be removed by facilities. I wrote the following blurb and pinned 10 copies across the branches above the grave:

"To live in the hearts we leave behind is not to die"

-Thomas Campbell

Here Lies a Bird: An Experiential Educational Installation

INTERRED: WEDNESDAY JULY 28TH, 2021|CORNETT COURTYARD, UNIVERSITY OF VICTORIA|

Here Lies a Bird...

This spot commemorates a small bird that was found deceased in the courtyard of Cornett during the Summer Term of 2021, as COVID raged on, and weary students began to return from a year of isolation to campus. This space is dedicated to the memory of that bird, and to the freedom, flight, and uncaged spirit it held within its heart. It is a space where, in the waning hours of the dusk, as the sun retreats over the building, time flows slower, the cool wind whispers through, and we, the living, may take a moment to reflect on life itself. We may choose a silent memory to cherish the deceased, or a quiet reproach to the awesome power of the universe and the diversity of life within. We may live, if only for a moment in the memory of those that have passed both peacefully and not. We may share a word, or shed a tear for those no longer here, while always knowing that even if for just this moment in this space, that they will always live on within us. The symbolic weight of our time with those who have passed resonates on within us in our memories, both personal and collective, and in this space, let that resonance ring. It is the hope that this installation stands as a memorial to all beings that have passed that are remembered here, across time, cultures, histories, and species.

By the time I left Victoria a full year later, these pieces of paper still waved in the tree branches. I will share here, too, with permission, an anonymized account of a student who had ventured from my classroom to that shrine for an optional extra credit assignment:

When discussing the bird in class, I found it endearing and sweet, but ultimately, I saw it as a joke. I think I viewed the bird through humour because the symbolism for the bird could get dark. The bird faced the bureaucracy of death, represented human's disconnect from the natural world, was a reminder of mortality, and became connected to the turbulent times the world faced during the seven weeks of this course. So, viewing the bird's death and memorial as a wholesome joke was probably a way to avoid reflecting on these themes. Honestly, it was also a representation of my human self-importance and arrogance. I thought of myself as too important to engage with the bird or take the time to visit its final resting place because it was a bird, not a human. I wish that were not my initial response. Hopefully, I will grow away from my human superiority complex because that is also the complex that has assisted humans in destroying the only planet that can support us. So, I had not planned on visiting the bird, but eventually, I went.

As I approached the memorial, I was smiling beneath my mask as I saw a colourful paper hanging from the tree, and I was still thinking of the bird memorial as a wholesome joke. As I read the obituary, my arrogant smile was wiped from my face as the words were reflective and evoked introspection. The death of the bird became much bigger than the "natural circle of life." I started reflecting on the numerous events of death that have happened in this year of isolation, from COVID-19 to Israel and Palestine to the climate crisis to the finding of murdered Indigenous children and so much more. It felt as if the memorial allowed me to reflect and grieve over these events and connect them to mortality. When watching these headlines move through the news daily and society forgetting and moving on, I never felt like I was allowed to slow down and reflect on these deaths. At one moment, I felt a tear come to my eye and my throat tighten, during the last 11 years, I have had many experiences with death, and the narrative has always been to move on. I felt seen by the words on that page and allowed to endure the loss beyond the societal time limit after someone dies. After reading the obituary, I crouched down to be closer to the gravesite and acknowledged my sadness for the bird. Realistically my life is no more significant than the birds. It reminded me that all of us on this planet, every living and non-living thing, are playing a part, and it all falls apart when one of us does not play along (i.e., humans causing the climate crisis).

It becomes so easy to let societal expectations frame your life. Life is easier when you do not have to go against the current, but the bird reminded me that our societal expectations are why there is so much hurt and sadness. It is crucial to reflect on your grief and emotions, and it is necessary to slow down when you are overwhelmed. The bird reminded me of the sanctity of life and mortality, to remain humble about my position in the natural world, and to let societal expectations fall away when it comes to death and grief. Ultimately the memorial reminded me of the astronomically painful year everyone has experienced, especially regarding death and mortality, so it is crucially important to listen and be compassionate moving forward. Someone left a note at the site which stated they loved the bird, and I would have to agree. While I did not know the bird during its life, its death created an opportunity for the living to grapple with themes of death, loss and mortality and how our societal narratives about those themes are often harmful. So, while initially, the bird was a wholesome joke to me, it became a profoundly reflective experience and reminded me of my human arrogance regarding life and death.

I feel I cannot fully capture the experience better than this former student did. What started out as an impulse became an anchoring point of reality for me and for many others. I would later use this same installation to fulfill the requirements of a ludicrous teaching fellowship, and even then, it became not just a memorial for a bird but an unintentional memorial to those who had died during COVID. I do not think sentimentally about my teaching in Canada save for this singular contribution. I do not reflect often on the great moments with my students or the administrative battles I had to fight (one horrific instructor I worked for taught a Freudian justification for systemic racism, and I still have nightmares about those student essays...), but I instead think of the bird. The memorial. The community of grief we experienced in that first wake. If my legacy can be anything, I wish for it to be my bird. Aside from student papers on it, I saw something there that truly shook me to a point of pure positive emotion. While walking Denali the following summer, we crossed again through the courtyard, and as we did, a young family with a small child were stopped at the memorial standing by their bikes. I did not linger, but as I passed, I heard the child ask what it was, and the parents explained that it was a memorial for a dead bird. I did not hear the child's next question, but I did catch an inclination that the parents were, at that moment, having a conversation about death with their child for the first time. To think that somehow via a strange serendipitous moment, I could help to facilitate that conversation, the introduction of mortality, in this child's life is a thing I treasure. Not because I feel children ought to know about mortality or that I take pleasure in that crushing reality being brought to a child's ears, but rather in knowing that for one child, that conversation didn't come when a beloved pet died or when a loved one passed away.

It was there, in the sunset, in the evening warmth in a space of silence and solidarity and safety to question the nature of life itself. I never said a word to this family and instead smiled to myself for the entirety of my adventure with Denali.

The deaths that have come to me past 30 feel softer in the pain they bring because of this experience. After hearing a childhood friend's final words on the other end of a phone call and after sending a last letter to another friend, more death came into my life. First, the mentor who guided me in my journey growing up in our local community radio station passed away in February of 2023. This experience shocked me as we were not particularly close outside of a professional sense, and we had not spoken for a decade or more, but still, the loss of a mentor is a strong kind of death. It solidifies us in the knowledge of knowing that the knowledge we know because of the deceased is ours alone now. I think of him very often now. Every week, when I sit down to broadcast my radio show, I think of his wisdom and his words that took me to new heights of musical and social confidence.

Friends leave behind love; mentors leave behind wisdom.

At the time of composing this section, a fourth death has met me in my quarter-life. Very recently, my cousin passed away in a tragic car accident entirely out of nowhere. He was my age, and we grew up together, sharing many moments of childhood joy together, from video games to movies to collaborative work in the film and television industry as kids. We would play Nintendo64 games late into the night at his house and watch The Simpsons, South Park, and Austin Powers well past bedtime. Together, we saw Disney's Treasure Planet, the horrific Cat in the Hat film and The Da Vinci Code at Aspen's Isis Theatre with his dad. We held press passes to the Winter X Games in Aspen and shot video footage for ESPN together. As childhoods often go, we drifted apart in the interim time between then and now. I never fully knew him in a world where we were both adults.

His passing haunts me in ways I cannot yet articulate.

2. Pleasantries

"There is no pain so great as the memory of joy in present grief."

-Aeschylus

It remains a mystery to me, even here at the end, as to the nature of the title of this book. It came to me in a manic dreamlike state at the onset of my composition of a massive piece of writing that would grow into the genesis of this book and its two core chapters: The Long Nights and the Valleysong. At the time, this essay was solely existent for the purposes of processing experience, namely that of my survival of an abusive relationship in Canada and the winding road of madness therein. I scrawled in a note somewhere, "Pleasantries From the Skyward Side of Daydreaming". I had at the time envisioned it as a bookend to Valleysong, where I sacrifice the innocence of the art of daydreaming on the altar of reality. As I have grown from those long nights, the purpose has changed. What was a therapeutic movement became a project, and one that would push my sense of self into a state of near-continual observation of experience and an attempt here and there to weave vivid retellings of my youth and adolescence into a narrative patchwork of material that would itself fill some structural illusion.

The skyward side of daydreaming is what I think allures the reader, but before those secrets are revealed, I feel a compulsion to instead reduce the notion of the pleasantries themselves. What are they, and why do they come to us from the mystic vale of the skyward side?

They are not greetings, nor messages, they are scars. What we do not realize in our experience of self in the social, among many other things, is that we are not solely scarred by the passing of time between trauma and healing. We are scarred by the pleasantries we receive, the joy we undertake, and the moments of ecstasy that culminate in our being. Further, we are indeed also scarred by the mundane grey realities of our day-to-day existence, but the malady of mundanity is not what concerns us in this quest. I think these pleasantries are themselves something of a dream state of reconciliation of our innocence lost in the modern milieu of the inconvenience of growing up.

We lose something in the process of becoming older, and for so many of us, there is this sense of looking outside into the greener pastures of adulthood, only to find in the sanguine nostalgia of loss of innocence that what we had dreamt of was itself a waking nightmare.

This is the duality of life that intrigues me the most. Our ability to fabricate something in our waking daydreams that is so incredibly tantalizing to the spirit that upon its arrival, it is too good for us, or rather, what we compose in our mind's eye, that facsimile of our most hedonistic and treasured desires, is sometimes too much for our hearts to handle. It is in this duality of being that we are so drawn if a little innocently, to build a world for our imaginations out beyond the scope of what our rationality may permit as nascent tangible.

We are masters of our own destruction, and too often, that destruction hinges on our insanity for self-improvement. When we set our sights on a horizon beyond the scope of now, we find ourselves lost in the potentialities of what may come to be rather than learning the ability to fixate on what is in the moment. Somehow, this process creates more voids than pleasures in our experience of life. It is critical then to remember the now.

These pleasantries can be immediately gratifying to the spirit in the moment of their deliverance, but in the reality of their existence there is no reality to them, and this is what we must be careful of. The pleasantries of daydreaming, the sanguine thoughts that facilitate the masking of reality itself are the things we truly must meditate upon in life because they stand to structure our understanding of the situational reality of existence in ways that are warped to the mires of mistrust and allegorical positivity rather than a recentering of life as a momentary state of being from moment to moment.

This is not to encourage one to ignore the future or to exist specifically in the boundaries of now, nor is it a glorification of the struggles of now, but rather it is an observation that for us to be able to more calmly sail into adulthood and beyond we must do so with a symbiosis of temporality. We must embrace the historicity of our being, the malleability of the present and the abstraction of the future in equal agentic parts to fully and most completely reconcile our being in the moments between past and future.

The pleasantries come from somewhere deep inside as invitations to our minds from our hearts to be somehow more than what they are now, and while they are not altogether toxic, their potential for harm must be greatly considered in the experience of the now. We must be careful not to tread down the pathways of pleasantries by believing them but instead, reframe our intrusion of such invitations as a sign to reconsider the problem they offer a solution to rather than fixate solely on the sunshine of the solution.

Exist, but do so consciously of where you have been, where you are going, and where the end is.

3. From the Skyward Side...

If you want to tell me something new

I might stick around

If you want to say that I trust you

I might stick around

-Julian Lennon

In this text, together, we have walked through my life to this point in some varying degrees of eccentricity.

We have walked the streets of dreams, seen the front-lines of education, trauma, horror, hopeless romanticism and the lines between each.

This final part of this chapter is not long for this reason. I am here, you are here, we are all together, as the Beatles would have us know.

We made it, somehow.

We can raise a toast to those we've lost between there and here.

For those fellow 20th-century children, take this moment to congratulate yourself on being here to the now. It has not been easy.

I'll close now with this:

25 years and my life is still
Tryin' to get up that great big hill of hope
For a destination
I realized quickly when I knew I should
That the world was made up of this brotherhood of man
For whatever that means
And so I cry sometimes when I'm lying in bed
Just to get it all out what's in my head
And I, I am feeling a little peculiar
And so I wake in the morning and I step outside
And I take a deep breath and I get real high
And I scream from the top of my lungs
"What's going on?"
Linda Perry (1993)

-30-

Epilogue

In the closing of this book, I shall both embody the work of Kierkegaard here and negate a normative function of the written word and in my appropriation of his dedication, I do so also establish mine herein at the end; Where this essays bears the dedication to:

"That single individual whom I with joy and gratitude call my reader" (1849c:XI).

To close this meandering and far too self-indulgent mess of words, I turn to the effective philosophical point of this work and the inception of it in my mind as a piece of writing which necessitated a composition. In the quest to understand the nature of our existence and the struggles and triumphs situated within our unique temporalities, I call upon a reflection on the duality of existence as presented by Kierkegaard in T*he Lily in the Field and the Bird of the Air*, wherein lies a reflection on the duality of existence and the constant polarizing struggle between two polarized ends of the same spectrum of existence. That is the struggle as an active and agentic social actor to 'serve' two masters, and to reconcile this struggle in our everyday. Kierkegaard (1849a) classifies this as the struggle between God and mammon, that is, the divine and the covetous, the virtuous versus the inherent Simony of humanity. It is in the reframing of Kierkegaard along a line of Gnostic Existentialism (detailed methodologically elsewhere in my work), that we may instead reframe the Christian Orthodox allegorical framing of Kierkegaard's work in line with what may be more akin to an existentialism of the socioepistemological: That is the struggle of the divinity of reason, of *Gnosis* of the socioepistemological soul of the individual actor versus the inverse, the chagrining of *Gnosis* in light of the pitfalls of the human elements of both fantastical non-reasonable imaginative thinking, and the inauthenticity potentiality of the human performance and act of self in the social. It is in the esoteric magic of the Gnostics that we may draw a direct line from that teaching of the divine as knowledge and the knowledge as socially divine through the social facts of Durkheim into modern reflections and refutations the likes of Goffman, Blumer, and Bloch.

Rather than presenting a dualism of the soul in the agentic throes of the biblical skirmish of divinity and the corruptibility of the human spirit, we may, in a more modernistic stroke, establish a contemporary dualistic struggle of the soul between that which is divinely knowable, the *gnosis* of socioepistemological grounding in one's self and social identities and their proximal social structures, and the inauthentically unknowable conformity of the social identity to the patterns and waves of the pressing imaginative corruptibility. In a simpler word, That internalized struggle between the authentic and the inauthentic. The genuine presentation of self and the social as it reconciles the history and biography of the individual and the inverse anti-genuine aesthetic of the individual to occupy those spaces that flit into and out of existence as the images on the silver screen. It is within this struggle between that which is genuinely socially real and that which presents as socially real genuinely that we may establish a field of our concern and care for which we may opt to follow in our presentation of self in the social.

Kierkegaard (1849a) presents us the notion that aside from the existence of these polarized points of the horizon, there too lies the distinction in their spiritual nature that we cannot, nor should not be able to reconcile them both simultaneously, where summative there is no way to love and revere one over the other as a dedication to one presupposes a hatred and disregard of the latter. One, therefore, cannot rationally exist in tune with the rhythmic *Gnosis* of the social or *socioepistemology* while subletting a fall into the imaginatively eccentric. We cannot, therefore, proceed in our presentation of self authentically while clinging to the inauthentic, and subsequently, we cannot establish ourselves within the dreamscape of the imagined reality without dismissing into heresy the burdensome limitations of the rationally established. That is, social knowledge cannot remit itself to existence in the performance of the individual actor while their exigency of being stands within an imagined scenario or maladaptive state of lucidity-imagined. It is in this dualistic struggle, then, that the presentation of self becomes mired in querying the nature of either and both and their interactional interludes within and without one another.

This is to say that one cannot exist in a totalitarian vacuum of polarities on either end of the spectrum. In essence, this polarity is such that we are established transcendentally unable to exist in either or both as their positionality at the poles of this spectrum of social knowledge is such that we are unable to fully embody either due to their totality of spirit. That is to say, in the Christian sense that the divine is too perfectly above humanity to be attainable, and the inverse is such that it is so absurdly rooted in anti-humanism that we are only to perceive it as a foil to the unattainable divine rather than a descriptive state of being.

It is in this fact that dualism cannot encompass the spirit in total that we are then left to establish and recognize the placement of the human experience of the individual in some outstation point between the polarizing oblivions. In this regard, we are then more intimately tied to and intertwined with the facets and challenges of both the authenticity of divine social knowledge and the corruptibility of the facets of desire, lust, longing, debauchery and hedonism in light of the polar opposite stoic knowledgeability in rationality. We then appear awash in some murky middle-ground between hedonistic fantasy overtaking every facet of our being in the ultimate anti-*gnosis* of indulgences of the fantastical mind and the inverse total salvation divinity of the purely rational. It is within this duality spectrum that we, too, may further infer the existence of the struggle between two very ancient forces of nature: that which is materially real and that which possesses non-corporeal realness. It is then an age-old conflict between the physically real and rationally established and the ideally real within and beyond the confines of the human psychic experience of life. What we see is the firm establishment of distance and distinction between the human on the rock, the *Lily in the Field,* and the *Bird of the Air* as an allegorical manifestation of the struggle of that naturality of the world external to us and the richness of the internally apostolic of the self in apotheosis. In short, the psychic battle of nature versus the individual, wherein we may see a tangentially magnetic thread of connection: The Long Nights (Materiality) versus The Valleysong (Idealistic Imagined Perception). And here, we can, in some way, begin to unravel the conflicting tale of the two elements of the strife of the individual journeying home.

There is an innate dichotomy of being in the human experience wherein we are both tethered to and guided by our interactive ties to two worlds of being. The physical material world, wherein we are tied to the natural elements of our existence, and the immaterial world, which is so keenly divided into two distinctive planes:

the self and the social (Blumer 1969; Cooley 1902; Goffman 1956; Haraway 2016). It is in this duality of being that we do indeed find ourselves inherently embroiled in the conflict of spatial and temporal existence. It is, in this regard, the challenge of being human that we are *not* bound to the physical, the social, the spatial or the temporal, and instead, we occupy an in-between of all of these spaces. Wherein we are, by virtue of our social complexities and our innate internal realities, untethered to a singular space and time. Close your eyes for just a moment and imagine yourself in your first childhood bedroom. Are you truly there now physically? No. But spectrally, through your experiences of that past reality, you are able imaginatively to occupy that space at a specific point in time that is radically different than the one you exist in now. Now, imagine the bedroom you *want* to have in the future, let's say, ten years from now. Again, a different space and a different time. You have the unique ability as a social being with your own history and experience to reflect, to travel through time at will, and to reconcile these different temporalities into certain psychosocial sub-categories such as memory, recollection, nostalgia, past trauma, future hopes, dreams, goals, and eventualities. We are constantly awash in this inherently fluid internal temporality. But the material world is not innately tied to that fluidity. We are all, in a sense, intertwined with our own *Long Nights* and experiencing, in this very moment, our own *Valleysong*.

My Long Nights, as they have been reproduced here, represent two categorically important elements of our social being and the struggle for existence. It represents the lingering aspects of trauma, of memory, of experience in their totality and how they can reach socially beyond their immediacy of existence into the present and long into the abstract future. It is this point that is resonant in this work that that which is materially experienced *also* transcends the limitations of linear temporality to such a point that we are, in effect, non-temporal beings in our entire capacity, both materially and socially. The challenge lying within this, however, is the fact that we *exist* in a world that *is* temporally grounded to a sharp degree. That is, there is a need for linearity in temporal projections for the purpose of the continuation of fabrics of contemporary society that are dependent upon that linear progression for their survival. The very concept of history requires a linear progression; the Western conceptualization of reality itself and the means by which we tether our existentialism into any understandable reality to perceive ourselves is such that we must have some establishment of what has happened in the past, as a distinction between that which is happening and that which has not yet happened.

This distinction is critical to the continual operation and sustainment of two crucial contemporary systems of social order: late capitalism and neoliberalism, both of which draw upon both a careful colonization of historicity and a surgical monopoly on the state of being in the future. It is in these two divergent and complementary systems that we find the experience of the modern individual social actor pulled into categorical states of being that are both inauthentic in our understanding of the historicity of the reality of our existence and disingenuous towards our states of being towards what we may end up existing in following the progression into the future. There is a reliance within this regard on the a-temporality of uncertainty both to perpetuate a systemic capitalist mentality in the internal realities of the individual and to also propagate a fertile social space for the augmentation of autonomy and agency on the basis of subjugating the individual under a web of interlacing bureaucratic intricacies that lend to a sublimation of the autonomous human element to the degree of total subject-self.

This is evident in the converse of two points of earlier existentialism namely those from Kierkegaard (1846, 1849b), and Dostoyevsky (1864). Primarily of the former, there is the assertion that existence is inherently in conflict with the lack of existence of an autonomous human spirit, with the latter critiquing the radical determinism that reduces humanity to something inherently naturalistic and fixed in time and space. It is in both regards, then, that in the contemporary experience of the social actor amidst the neoliberal and capitalistic, the struggle between the spirit of the social and the reality of the material is such that it stands allegorically representative of the struggle between the social and internal machinations of self and the social construction of a reality beyond the individual and the continual dialectic of the material standing as something fluid and sedentary as a means of grounding the individual. In both cases, however, that which has been established in this text, both The Long Nights and the Valleysong represent deeper social elements in that they placate the divide of the social in the latter and the material in the former with the tempering modality of time as a means of reconciling affective historicity in the experience of the individual.

This is to say that both the experiential lingering of trauma and the dissonance of the loss of a sense of social grounding in the social spaces relied upon for safety from such trauma, that we exist in a place that is totally in its subjectivity and completely in its objective materiality over the realm of what is and is not effectively beneficial to the authentic experience of the individual in a social world. This is all to establish the criticality of the state of modern being such that we are drawn into a divide of uncertainty on the basis of linear time while experiencing the negation of active and agentic potentiality in our experience of reality while still being wholly dependent upon it for our experiencing of reality to be such that we are able to recognize it as socially or materially real. This is then the goal of this work, not to reconcile my own trauma nor the experience of coming home and recognizing the illusory reality of that experience, but rather to speak to the broader mystery of the social, temporal state of being. We are then, in effect, established in this experiential reality without a capacity to fully encapsulate it. It is then in this regard that existence in the contemporary sense is exigently impossible given the two governing stations of social order that actively negate the ability of the individual to exist naturalistically in our state of temporal flux.

In closing, then, it is a despairing reality that in the progression of social historicity as it currently stands we are not able to exist authentically. It haunts me to my core the degree to which we see the degradation and ruination of the experiential being for the benefit of the almighty dopamine hit. I am unsure that we are entirely able to dissociate from this reality entirely without radical social reform of the revolutionary form. Subsequent follow-ups to this might more closely examine the methodological elements of a neo-state construction that is established along the lines of the liberation from the despairing separation and internalized conflict between the natural and social and the artificial manipulation of social temporality for the benefit of the systems of oppression that cage our spirits. It is then entered here as a note of finality that what must be preserved always and entirely is the freedom to exist outside of the realm of the constructed fabric of time as we know it.

Эпиграф:

Two roads diverged in a yellow wood,

And sorry I could not travel both

And be one traveler, long I stood

And looked down one as far as I could

To where it bent in the undergrowth;

Then took the other, as just as fair,

And having perhaps the better claim,

Because it was grassy and wanted wear;

Though as for that the passing there

Had worn them really about the same,

And both that morning equally lay

In leaves no step had trodden black.

Oh, I kept the first for another day!

Yet knowing how way leads on to way,

I doubted if I should ever come back.

I shall be telling this with a sigh

Somewhere ages and ages hence:

Two roads diverged in a wood, and I—

I took the one less traveled by,

And that has made all the difference.

-Robert Frost, 1916

And so we arrive here in the end. What is to be done? Where do we find the intense authenticity needed to return to our internal naturalistic state of human experience?

The answer, at least for me where I now sit, is thus:

We go where we find our authenticity, and we find our genuine reality wherever it is we go, so go there. Go there without leaving your bed, your chair, your desk. But go there.

Do so with care. Go to where the sand is real, the mountains do indeed loom, the love is indeed warm and passionate, and the water is true and blue.

Seek reality in the real, approach the imagined with care and look for yourself inside yourself first.

And delete Instagram.

TF

Appendix I

I Saw A Bird...

An Essay Theorizing the Social Apotheosis

Or...

The Agentic Awareness of the Social Metaphysic in Death as an Interactional Reality

"The boundaries which divide Life from Death are at best shadowy and vague. Who shall say where the one ends, and the other begins?"

-Edgar Allan Poe, "The Premature Burial" (1844)

Introduction

Last night, in the courtyard of my office building, I saw a bird. It was dead. The feathers were pale and stark, contrasting white to the grey and cold concrete that comprised its deathbed. This is what first struck me. Where normally I would have shuffled beyond the corpse to my eventual destination-the obscure and covert corner wherein I take my secret cigarette breaks, tonight I did not. Instead, I found the gaze of the bird, and in that intimate eye contact, I saw beyond the bird. I saw the death of this creature and the contextual impact of its state of being, or rather, non-being. Something drew me to stay at the side of this above-ground grave and view the corpse of this bird as it lay in state as it were. The gaze, the unblinking, unmoving gaze, pierced straight through the depth of my existential conceptualization of my own state of being to touch well beyond the simple, desensitized means of thinking about death that typically inhabit my day-to-day routines. The eyes were simultaneously lifeless and full of life. The white feathers were mostly undisturbed. One leg was broken. There was no outward indication of the nature of the bird's means of dying. No blood. No noticeable trauma. It was, to an effect, peaceful. In this contemplation, as I knelt over the bird for what dragged on for a full motionless hour, I found that this is what disturbed me the most. This. The lack of trauma, of the evidence of some horrific end, of some kind of reason for the end of this flight. Was it so naïve a thought to be simply shocked that something beautiful could meet its end so peacefully? No. It was deeper than that. The bird itself is not entitled to existence, to life, and beauty has nothing to do with that reality. Rather, the horror of this scene was in the overwhelming sense of time lost. Of future loss.

In my nicotine alcove, I felt a breeze sweep easterly down the building. Rather than my thoughts marvelling at the cooling touch of the wind on my overheated skin, I had the singular thought: "This is a wind that the bird will never fly in." The finality of death and the curious ability it has to negate the sense of potentiality in our active and agentic futures was more staggering in that instant than it had been in over a year of a global pandemic. In my transfixion and further despondent state, the warm eyes of the ever-still bird led me to flashes of images of my own death that ranged from the mundane to the melancholic and finally to the spectacular. I saw not the social ramifications of my passing nor the sanguine images of an afterlife, but rather I saw the act. I saw suicides, homicides, euthanasia, execution, hospice, accident, tragedy, heroism. I saw the breadth of endings that may (and certainly shall) befall my corpse someday. There was no recoil nor fear in these flashes. And there was no peace either. All there was was the simple eyes of the bird. And the thought that their bones are hollow...

Towards Understanding the Social Metaphysic in the Construction, Preservation and Presentation of Self in the Individual Actor

In the theoretical spheres of the sociological sciences, there exists a point of convergence between the philosophical school of metaphysics and the sociological tradition of theoretically exploring (traditionally) the concepts of social order and organization. That barrier of material and ideal realities, wherein questions of existence (both psychic and bodily), the nature of reality, and the ontological positionality of the individual coincide with the broader exploration of social order and the means by which the social world is organized and (to a degree) how it 'functions' on a day-to-day or decade-to-decade basis. It is in this membranous junction between philosophy and the science of morality wherein the question of the social metaphysic emerges. That question is, in effect, to what degree does the social exist? The social metaphysic, which shall be defined within this paper, strives to present both a conceptualization of the social spaces wherein existence is felt tangibly and experienced with conscious action and individual agency. In order to explore the existence of the social metaphysic, two salient theoretical components must exist in order to fully facilitate the stage for this dialogue. First, there must be an instance of universality in a social experience, that is to say, a social event that will and has been experienced by any and all socially aware individual actors. The second, there must be and active and agentic conglomeration of the individual self as it is constructed, preserved and presented. It is at the intersection of these components that we may find a flashpoint for direct and immediate awareness of the social metaphysic, which shall be referred to as The Social Apotheosis, or rather that moment of pure clarity with respect to immediate social and metaphysical awareness of an actor's in/significance in the 'grander' scope of social reality.

The question may then arise: why are these the components to knowing the existence of the social metaphysic, or rather, how does a universal social experience and an active and agentic self unveil the existence of social reality? It may also come to the mind of some that this pretense is akin to some simplistic geometric proof, striving to unequivocally extol and validate the fact that a triangle has three angles. Rather, I posit that this methodological positionality itself is far from simplistic and within itself presents unique theoretical challenges beyond the concept being too simple. First, the notion of a universal social experience is directly counter to established tenants of social science in that we, by virtue of individual differences (the variety of social experience), cannot hold within our canon space for a social experience that is within itself wholly universal, which is not to say that we have not tried in our history to establish universality in social experience. To present such a fact may even run the risk of sounding reductionist in its approach. However, what we must consider is that in the variety of social experiences, there are two singular social events in life that are (barring the supernatural) entirely universal: birth and death. These events are also unique in that they are universal experiences that may even be had in a complete and total social vacuum. Birth, the inception of life for all consciously organic species, cannot be experienced alone in humans, as we are always uncannily present, as are the person who carried us to term in some capacity.

Death, however, is the penultimate social experience. It is that final moment that may be experienced socially, in isolation, in private or public, and in a great variety of ways. Both birth and death stand as social experiences we will all certainly engage with personally and (in a very likely degree) peripherally as well. Meaning we will experience births and deaths socially, in addition to our own typically. That is not to say we may necessarily be present at either, but in some social purview, they will present an interactional plane of reality for us to navigate, and these will surely happen following our births and preceding our deaths, should the laws of nature prevail as they have done so far. In their unique duality, birth and death are also both experienced socially at the moment of death, in that the reflective medium on the social interaction of death is the by-product of birth: Life.

The second component, that of the active and agentic self, must also be present within these social events should the Social Apotheosis aspire to take place. That is because this apotheosis, this transformative moment of socialized metacognition on the metaphysical existence of social reality, must be an interaction between the individual and the social world external to the body of the individual. Being active relates to the composite factors of the individual actor being aware of their innate tendency towards social interaction, as further elaborated by Blumer (1969), wherein the actor has a degree of active participation within the scope of their interactional stages. Further, Blumer presents that this is the mechanism by which the individual is continually involved in the construction of their social realities. Whereby the means by which reality is maintained and managed for the individual actor is linked directly to their active participation in that reality. From this, Blumer further posits a sense of individual autonomy in the preservation of this reality, wherein the secondary component of agentic social interaction comes into play. It is in this agency that we as social actors may break free from more deterministic social positioning (such as conflict and structural perspectives) and, in that agency, find both a degree of social investment and individual validation in the continuation of our social realities.

To more fully develop these notions, we may take, in addition, Goffman's (1956) dramaturgical perspective of social interaction, more specifically in the model of the stage. That being that actors are just that, actors upon a stage, festooned in costume and relying on both a script and backstage 'crew' to ensure the smooth operation of the presentation of self. The key insights of Goffman beyond this analogy are both the existence of an audience in the presentation of self and of the internal/external stagecraft that compose the social presentation of self. The latter is the existence of two 'stages' of social interactional reality: the front stage, being that which is presented to audiences for outward social approval (as per Cooley's (1902) Looking Glass Self). That is to say that the audience presents a positionality of interaction wherein the individual actor must implement both their performance (the front stage), that is, the presentation of self to be observed and the backstage wherein the actor (based on prior social experience and the experiential memory of social scripts/rituals (Goffman 1967)) interprets the active and agentic reactions of the audience to the aforementioned presentation of self. This reflection and interpretation (again built off of prior social experience and socialization) then contribute yet again to further the construction of social reality, creating a feedback loop of interaction/reaction/reflection/interaction. It is in this modality that the actor furthers their social reality on an everyday, minute-by-minute basis. This is the formative framework by which social reality comes to be created by the actor while simultaneously creating the actor.

It is in the interactional reality between the actor and audience that social scripts and rituals are constructed, socialized, reinforced, and internalized. Further, the internalization of such social interactions is additionally contingent upon the use, communication, and association of symbols with social interaction (Blumer 1969). Symbols are a varied 'language' of social interaction whereby meaning is ascribed to social objects (gestures, clothing, tone of voice, physical objects, etc.), which impart varying degrees of deeper nuance to the interactional stage. It is in these symbols and our interaction with them that the process of the construction of social reality comes to a complete sphere, wherein on top of our interactional performance, the added language of symbolic communication creates a deeply complex and highly individualized mode of social being and individual cosmology of self. The self and identity are key outcomes of this process. The self is that vessel by which we come to know our internal being as active and agentic (Elliott 2014), it is in effect that key component of social knowledge that sets the individual actor apart from the broader scope of other actors, whereby their conceptualization of individual metaphysical existence is distinguished in myriad intricacies of individual variety. Further, identity is a composite integration of proximate social structures (per Stets and Serpe (2016)) thereby being the culmination of the adjacent social structures and interactional ties that overall contribute to a sense of knowing one's self as separate from the social, while still inextricably tied to the swells of the social currents of interactional reality.

The complex construction, presentation and preservation of self, and the cyclical nature by which social reality is further constructed by and simultaneously constructing the self is critical to the presented theoretical moment of social apotheosis wherein one's individual cosmological positionality within the grander scheme of their social reality and their material and ideal realities is firmly cemented within the self, as per a cataclysmic social interaction. It is in the process of the social construction of reality and of the active and agentic nature of social interaction that the symbolic value of this penultimate social interaction constructs within itself a point of major convergence for the accumulation and precipitation of internal identity. This moment hinges entirely upon the capacity for the individual actor to interact (in symbolically significant ways), and to both offer components of self to this interaction, while taking on the symbolic weight of the experience within the folds of their interactional internal reality and conceptualization of self. That is, this moment, this social apotheosis, is that proximal social structure that supersedes others for supremacy in identity construction. It is the stage above all stages, the master scripts, and the final costume design. It is a period whereupon the individual actor, elevated on this high stage, is finally able (or forced) to confront their being and mortality, the fragility of their existence, and the impermanence of their experiential, conscious reality.

The key focal point of this essay is upon that moment whereupon the individual social actor comes to the metaphysical and social realization of their own mortality. This is not to say, however, that it explores the first experience or discourse on death itself in the life course of the individual, but rather it theorizes a moment in the social trajectory of life whereupon the individual experiences a profound internal moment of metaphysical significance which establishes within the understanding of their general insignificance in the overall scope of objective reality. It is in this moment, this intersection of the natural progression of life and the social conceptualization of the individual self, that we may observe at least two important congruencies. The first is that it is the moment wherein the individual comes to terms (so to say) with the linear passage of their lifetime and further their position in reality is to say, that it is a moment that forces the individual to reflect, in a metacognitive sense, both on their own collections of history and experience, but also on the social interactional ties they have to their own reality. Further, on a more meta scale for the sociological sciences, this represents the intersection of the age-old questions of metaphysics and the narratives on the social order that underlie and comprise the frameworks of our collective search for meaning and nuance in explaining the life of the individual in a social world.

However, in order to fully explore the social apotheosis, the notion of the social metaphysic must first be defined. Metaphysics itself, a complex school of philosophical thought tracing its Western roots to Aristotle, is classified by Collingwood (1948): "[Metaphysics]...is, therefore, the science of that which stands as an ultimate logical ground to everything that is studied by any other science" (pp. 10). To further expand this, it is that 'science' (in a classical sense of the word) is concerned with both pure being and the ultimate presuppositions underpinning all other pursuits of knowledge (Collingwood 1948). In essence, metaphysics plumbs the depths of that which grants being and essence to all spheres of existence. A challenge in this exploration, in direct competition with positivistic-oriented social science, is that by virtue of the varied experiences of individuals in a social world, we have collectively established within the social sciences that universal social experience, universal pure being as it were, cannot exist in a pure form in that due to the vast complexity and difference of experience in social order, there cannot be a social experience experienced the same way by two individuals. This is further explored by considering that social science, as a historical discipline with specific sociocultural contextual origins, struggles to present a universal understanding or 'story' of social life (Hiller 1979; Mukherji and Sengupta 2004). That is not to say that sociology or the social sciences specifically hinge upon universality, nor is it to say that other sciences have such luxuries, but it is rather critical to the point of this essay that we understand the limitations of social scientific exploration when it comes to asking and answering metaphysical questions.

A more classical approach to teaching metaphysics posits that it is the 'study of being' or rather the exploration of how we may come to know what is 'actually' real (Kenny 2007). That is to say, it is a philosophical school concerned with the question of the nature of being and the essence of existence with respect to questions of knowing the reality we experience. That is not to say it is wholly epistemological, but that systems of knowledge construction and formation are also key to knowing the state of reality and existence (Berger and Luckmann 1966; Durkheim 1972; Piaget 1955). From this, we may arrive at the question of the social metaphysic, that is to say, the metaphysical exploration of what we may come to judge as socially real. This may emerge as a somewhat facetious point of inquiry as it seems that it is a rather obvious realization that the social is, in fact, real, but the question of how we come to know what is real socially is a nuanced frontier of exploration that must be further expounded upon.

To begin, the social must be defined. The notion of the social is a somewhat nebulous instance of reality. However, it is absolutely crucial in constructing an understanding of the sociological and social metaphysical impacts of death and the overall theoretical moment of social apotheosis. Barring the longstanding debate of idealism vs. empiricism, what can be said of the social is that it is primarily 'real' because of the weights ascribed to it by those experiencing it. That is to say, the social is as much a construct of the actor as the actor is a construct of the social. Whereby the individual's actions and suppositions construct a sense of sociality within their social experience, so too does this social experience impart meaning and significance upon the overall state of being of the individual. That is to say, the social construction of reality is both cyclical and symbiotic between the 'thing' of the social and the experiential reality of the beings inhabiting it. More concisely, the social represents that membrane between the internal realities of the individual actor (such as the components of the self and identity), the externally shared empirical reality (the "real world"), and the internal realities of other social actors and agents. That is to say; it is the battlefield wherein individuals compose and present productions of self in an ever-evolving medium for the purpose of navigating empirical reality. The concept of the social may be something so minor as purchasing a coffee at a café or something so nuanced as navigating the early childhood agents of socialization and acquiring social and cultural normative values to safely navigate social life. It is the interconnectivity between social actors, both physically and psychologically. It is that which allows for the shared understanding of actions, speech, behaviour, emotion, and symbolic meaning of such realities.

Within this symbiotic and cyclical membrane, the individual actor, through their interactions between and within social actors, builds a system of coming to know themselves socially and to know the social as a physical and theoretical space wherein their being comes to be understood and validated in its abilities to interact socially. This social membrane is further nuanced through the many avenues of possible interactions and interactional rituals that exist across it (Goffman 1966). Culture, class, law, and language are aspects that are inherently a component of society and are things that both shape the individual actor while also simultaneously being constructions of the individuals themselves. That is not to say however, that each and every individual has the ability to construct a culture, a class, a language, but rather through collective collaboration, they may do so. This is the foundational basis of the sociological concept of social order or the means by which society is itself organized. This is also not to say that something such as 'language' requires an individual actor to be interactional, where the symbolic value of language may foster and complete interactions without necessarily having to be initiated by an individual in the beginning. This is the nature of the social, such that it may operate without the direct initiation by an actor, but that is still interactionally symbolic to the perceiving actor. Such an individual may interact with their culture without any actor enacting culture upon them. To a degree, the social is a conditioned reality in the individual actor, as much as it is a construction of that actor.

Given this, the social is, for the purpose of this paper and the discussions herein, the connection the individual actor has to the period of consciousness between birth and death: life. The social, that is to say, the world that is constructed and being constructed by the individual, is the vehicle through which they experience the daily, hourly, and yearly passage of time and then how they interpret and come to know the events between the instance of birth and the finality of death. That is to say that the passing of time becomes the mirror by which the social filters the exigent state of a physical being. Thereby examining this duality of the social as both filter and passage of time, we may come to recognize the moment of individual social apotheosis by which we transcend the period of metaphysical mortality and come to terms with this finality, this sense of an ending to borrow from Julian Barnes (2011).

References:

Barnes, Julian. 2011. *The Sense of an Ending*. Vintage International. New York: Vintage Books.

Berger, Peter, and Thomas Luckmann.1966. *The Social Construction of Reality*. New York: Anchor Books.

Blumer, Herbert. 1969. *Symbolic Interaction: Perspective and Method.*

Collingwood, R. G. 1948. *An Essay on Metaphysics*. Oxford, UK: Oxford University Press UK.

Cooley, Charles Horton. 1902. *Human Nature and the Social Order*. Transaction Publishers.

Dostoevsky, Fyodor. 1864. *Notes from the Underground*. Planet PDFs.

Durkheim, Emile. 1972. *Emile Durkheim: Selected Writings*. edited by A. Giddens. Cambridge, UK: CambridgeUniversity Press.

Elliott, Anthony. 2014. *Concepts of the Self*. 3rd ed. Cambridge, UK: Polity.

Goffman, Erving. 1956. *The Presentation of Self In Everyday Life*.

Haraway, Donna, J. 2016. *Staying with the Trouble: Making Kin in the Chthulucene*. Durham North Carolina: Duke University Press.

Judson, Eugene, and Angela Hobson. 2015. "Growth and Achievement Trends of Advanced Placement (AP) Exams in American High Schools." American Secondary Education 43(2):59–76.

Kierkegaard, Soren. 1846. *Two Ages: A Literary Review*. Vol. XIV. Princeton, NJ: Princeton University Press.

Kierkegaard, Soren. 1849a. "The Lily in the Field and the Bird of the Air: Three Devotional Discourses." Pp. 1–47 in *Without Authority, Kierkegaard's Writings*. Princeton, NJ: Princeton University Press.

Kierkegaard, Soren. 1849b. *The Sickness Unto Death: A Christian Psychological Exposition for Edification and Awakening*. Copenhagen.

Kierkegaard, Soren. 1849c. *Without Authority*. edited by H. V. Hong and E. H. Hong. Princeton, NJ: Princeton University Press.

Park, Kelly, Vera Caine, and Randolph Wimmer. 2014. "The Experiences of Advanced Placement and International Baccalaureate Diploma Program Participants: A Systematic Review of Qualitative Research." Journal of Advanced Academics 25(2):129–53. doi: 10.1177/1932202X14532258.

Rauh, John. 2014. "Advanced Placement English in a Solipsistic Era: How Structuralism Can Renew Meaning." Roeper Review 36(3):190–200. doi: 10.1080/02783193.2014.919624.

Tennov, Dorothy. 1979. *Love and Limerence: The Experience of Being in Love*. Lanham MD, USA: Scarborough House.

Warne, Russell T., Ross Larsen, Braydon Anderson, and Alyce J. Odasso. 2015. "The Impact of Participation in the Advanced Placement Program on Students' College Admissions Test Scores." Journal of Educational Research 108(5):400–416. doi: 10.1080/00220671.2014.917253.

Honour Roll:

With Love,

Mason Van Vleet

Adrian Howell

Lukah Shane Edward Roser

Brian Farris

Carol Farris

Doug & Dorothea Farris

Wyatt Farris

Grace Farris

Quentin Farris

From the Trenches:

Anna Stutsman

Kira Schlepp

Ondrea Vicklund

William H. Dodge

Odarley Morton

Nikole Roquebert Kieswetter

Samantha Hurley

Brooke Adams

Kelly Anne Dalton

Kristen Leigh

Priscilla Houliston

Pamela Schact

Basia Karpinska

Emily Lane

Cheyenne Faupel

Darian Zetterquist

Amanda Maier

Phlip Coggins

From Home:

Raleigh Burleigh

Amy Kimberley

Hunter S. Thompson

Dr. Slats Cabbage

Melissa Bowman

Rita Marsh

The Center for Human Flourishing

The Sopris Sun

KDNK Community Radio

Peppino's Pizza

Beijing Tokyo

Ming's Cafe

From the North:

Peyman Vahabzedeh

Martha McMahon

Emile De Rosnay

Sean Hier

Melissa Forsyth

Tyler Branston

Ali Morikawa

Finn Deschner

Aileen Chong

Zoe Lu

Ann Hamilton

Shailoo Bedi

Debra McIldoon

From the Past:

Rachel Cooper

Laura French

Mark Gray

Cliff Colia

Wendy Boland

From Nascent Academia:

Karen Yescavage

Susan Calhoun-Stuber

Chris & Sarah Messer

Ian Gomme

Iver Arnegard

Krista Bridgmon

Patricia Levy

W. Richard Walker

Jackie Stroud

Erin DeCuir

From the Pacific Northwest:

Allison Hurst

Steve Ortiz

Dwayne & Lauren Plaza

Amanda McDowell

From Beyond the Veil:

William G. Cockrell

Charles Wicker Moses III

Zoe Lu

Sammy Houston

Madame Bailey J. The Golden Retriever

The Four-Legged Assistants:

Her Grace Lady Wyndrose T. Farris, PhD Esq.

Comrade Professor Cosmonaut Denali

Mr. Bjort of Switzerland, Allegedly

About the Author

The Final Word

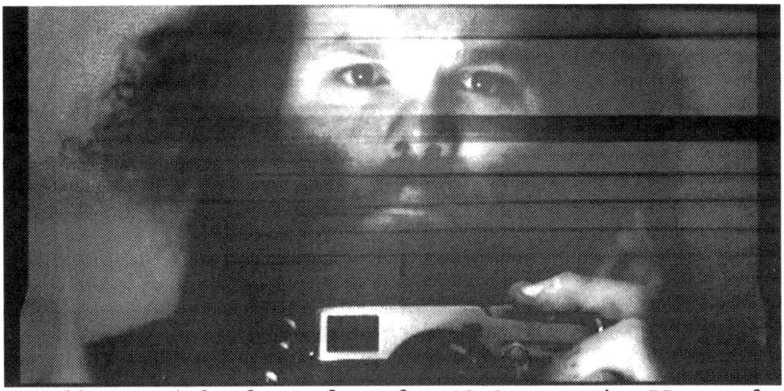

Self Portrait by the Author after 43 Consecutive Hours of Writing "The Long Nights and the Valleysong" (Nov. 25th, 2022)

Tucker D. Farris is a sociologist, philosopher and journalist originally from Woody Creek, Colorado. He grew up being tutored by Dr. Hunter S. Thompson while still an infant in his mother's jogger on daily treks up Woody Creek Road to Owl Farm. As a result of this early introduction to The Gonzo Way, his writing and academic pursuits have never followed a directed path and instead branch out along many winding thickets of the imagination.

He holds an honorary master's degree and PhD from Aspen State Teacher's College in social observational science and will eventually earn a dissertation-based doctorate in sociology from the University of Victoria in British Columbia with a specialization in social, cultural, and political thought when the spirit moves him to finish it.

He currently teaches upper-division sociology courses at Colorado State University-Pueblo and serves as a professor of sociology at Colorado Mountain College, while also contributing foreign correspondence dispatches and journalistic pieces to The Sopris Sun newspaper in Carbondale, Colorado.

His writings have appeared in The Progressive Magazine, Blood and Bourbon, and various conference proceedings, including Pedagogy and Theatre of the Oppressed, The Lithuanian Sociological Association, and the Southern Colorado Conference for the Arts, Humanities and Social Sciences.

His debut social theory text "*Institutional Interactionism: The Theory of the Institutional Self*" is available worldwide from Amazon, Barnes and Noble and many other fine booksellers.

Following this text, his next book titled "*Two Prayers for the Lost Souls in the Endless Night: Antemortem Meditations on Being Lost*" is a collection of seven serialized essays exploring the concept of being lost after cresting the hill of 25 years of age. It is currently being released in an irregular serialized form and will be published in full upon the end of the serial's run with a foreword by Lukah Roser.

Made in United States
Troutdale, OR
01/06/2025

27337019R00265